The Historical Bible

THE FOUNDERS AND RULERS

OF

UNITED ISRAEL

FROM THE DEATH OF MOSES TO THE DIVISION
OF THE HEBREW KINGDOM

BY

CHARLES FOSTER KENT, Ph.D.

WOOLSEY PROFESSOR OF BIBLICAL LITERATURE IN YALE UNIVERSITY

WITH MAPS AND PLANS

NEW YORK
CHARLES SCRIBNER'S SONS
1909

COPYRIGHT, 1908, BY
CHARLES SCRIBNER'S SONS

PREFACE

Israel's history is divided into four distinct periods. The first, which ends with the crossing of the Jordan, represents the childhood of the race. It was then that the memory of the nation was weak; but its imagination was strong, as the character of the earliest traditions testifies. The second, which extended to the division of the kingdom at the death of Solomon, was Israel's adolescent period. The third, to the fall of Jerusalem in 586 B.C., brought to the nation grave social, political and religious problems, which rapidly developed the ethical and spiritual consciousness of the race. During the fourth period, from the beginning of the exile to the first Christian century, Judaism, in the trying school of affliction, attained its full maturity and crystallized into a closely knit racial and religious unit.

The second period of Hebrew history, with which this volume deals, was Israel's heroic age, when physical strength, courage and patriotism were the prominent virtues, and the deeper spiritual and ethical qualities were only partially developed. It was during this period that the Hebrews most resembled their neighbors in character and faith. Their dominant ambitions were to acquire territory and to extend their authority; and these ambitions were fully realized. Within two short centuries, the tribes from the wilderness became a strong nation, and then grew into a powerful empire.

Written records now for the first time began to take the place of popular tradition. As a result, the miraculous element, so prominent in the early tradition, almost completely disappears. The greater part of the material in Samuel and Kings is evidently taken from two early, independent histories. The one told of the call of Saul by Samuel, and of the reign of Israel's first king; the other, which begins with the latter part of the sixteenth chapter of I Samuel, tells of the rise of David and of the glories and sins of the Judean shepherd who made Israel one of the powerful nations of southwestern Asia. These quotations from the Saul and David histories are remarkably picturesque and full of detail.

v

PREFACE

Although probably not written until after the division of the Hebrew kingdom, the stories which they contain were doubtless told in the days of Saul and David, and therefore shed almost contemporary light upon the chief characters and events of the period.

Their language, point of view and ideas are those of the golden era, when Israel was rapidly attaining its full material growth and splendor. They are full of dramatic action and simple, strong emotion. The reader is made to behold with his own eyes the more important scenes in this stirring epoch of Israel's history. Through the vivid dialogues he is admitted to the councils of kings, prophets and warriors. His attention is constantly fixed on the fortunes and deeds of certain heroes, and through their personal experiences the significant facts and forces of the history are clearly revealed. In these oldest records there is no attempt to idealize the history or to conceal the faults of its heroes. Life and human nature are presented with a simple realism which makes these narratives invaluable guides to all who would know the soul of man and the eternal laws which govern human life.

The selection of material and the prominence given to the personal element also reveal the noble religious and ethical purpose which actuated the later prophetic authors of Joshua, Judges, Samuel and Kings. They aim not merely to write a history of their nation, but also through its most significant characters to interpret that history, so that the vital spiritual truths which it illustrates shall stand out in clear relief.

Fortunately, the Greek translation has preserved many clauses and even verses, which have been lost in the Hebrew text. Restoring these, the result is a remarkably complete and well-rounded narrative. The language in these stories, which come from the lips of the ancient story-tellers, is often exceedingly idiomatic and even colloquial; and an attempt has been made in the present translation to reproduce these picturesque qualities. The evidence which has determined the analysis of the sources, and detailed textual notes, will be found in the corresponding volumes of the author's *Student's Old Testament*, to which references are made in the table of contents.

C. F. K.

YALE UNIVERSITY,
  May, 1908.

CONTENTS

THE SETTLEMENT AND CONQUEST OF CANAAN

vii

CONTENTS

THE FOUNDING OF THE HEBREW KINGDOM

CONTENTS

THE DECLINE OF SAUL AND THE RISE OF DAVID

CONTENTS

CONTENTS

xi

CONTENTS

LIST OF MAPS

THE SETTLEMENT AND CONQUEST OF CANAAN

§ XXXI. THE CROSSING OF THE JORDAN

Now it was told the king of Jericho, saying, There came hither to-night men from the Israelites to explore the land. And the king of Jericho sent to Rahab saying, Bring forth the men who have come to you, for they have come to explore all the land. And she said, It is true, certain men came to me, but I did not know whence they came, nor do I know whither they have gone. She had, however, brought them up to the roof and hid them with the stalks of flax which she had laid in order upon the roof.

But before they had lain down, she came up to them on the roof, and said to the men, I know that Jehovah hath given you the land. Now therefore swear to me by Jehovah, since I have dealt kindly with you, that you will also deal kindly with my father's house, and give me a true token. And the men said to her, It shall be, when Jehovah giveth us the land, that we will deal kindly and truly with you. Behold, when we come into the land, you shall bind this cord of scarlet thread in the window; and you shall gather to yourself into the house, your father and your mother and your brothers, and all your father's household. And it shall be, if any one goes out of the doors of your house into the street, his blood shall be upon his head, and we shall be guiltless; but if any one stays with you in the house, his blood shall be on our heads, if an injury befalls him. And she said, Let it be as you say. So she sent them away, and they departed, and she bound the scarlet cord in the window.

Then Joshua rose up early in the morning, and he and all the Israelites came to the Jordan and spent the night there before they passed over. And Joshua said to the people, Sanctify yourselves, for to-morrow Jehovah will do wonders among you. Joshua also said to the Israelites, Come hither and hear the words of Jehovah your God.

1

By this you shall know that a living God is among you. Behold, the ark is about to pass over before you into the Jordan. And it shall come to pass when the soles of the feet of the priests that bear the ark of Jehovah shall rest in the waters of Jordan, that the waters of Jordan shall be cut off; and the waters that come down from above shall rise in a heap.

4. The damming of the waters

And so when those who were carrying the ark came to the Jordan—the Jordan overflows its banks all the time of harvest—its waters rose up in a heap, a great way off at Adam, the city that is beside Zarethan, and those that went down toward the sea of the Arabah, the Salt Sea, were wholly cut off. And the people stood opposite Jericho.

5. Command to set up twelve memorial stones

Then Jehovah said to Joshua, Command them saying, 'Take hence from the midst of the Jordan twelve stones, and carry them over with you and lay them down in the camping-place, where you shall pass the night, that this may be a sign among you, that, when your children ask in time to come, saying, "What do you mean by these stones?" then you shall say to them, "Because the waters of the Jordan were cut off before the ark of Jehovah; when it passed over the Jordan, the waters of the Jordan were cut off."' So they took up twelve stones out of the midst of the Jordan, and they carried them over with them to the place where they camped, and laid them down there.

6. Crossing of the people

Then the people passed over quickly. And when all the people had passed over, the ark of Jehovah passed over, and the priests, in the presence of the people. And when the priests who were carrying the ark of Jehovah came up from the midst of the Jordan, and the soles of the priests' feet were lifted up on the dry ground, the waters of the Jordan returned to their place and went over all its banks as before.

I. **The Records of the Settlement and Conquest.** The crossing of the Jordan (about 1150 B.C.) marks a new era in biblical history. Up to this time Israel's traditions record simply the experiences of nomadic or semi-nomadic tribes. Henceforth they deal with definite events in the life of a people with a fixed place of abode and with a growing body of customs and institutions. At this point, therefore, the history of the Hebrew people properly begins.

RECORDS OF THE SETTLEMENT AND CONQUEST

The first century, popularly known as the *Period of the Judges*, is marked by the settlement of the Hebrew tribes in Canaan and by gradual movements toward tribal and national consolidation. The events of this period are recorded in the books of Joshua and Judges. The book of Joshua falls naturally into three distinct divisions: The first division, chapters 1–12, consists, for the most part, of extracts from the early prophetic histories, and records the first stages in the conquest of Canaan. The second division, 13–22, contains the very late priestly tradition regarding the allotment of the territory of Canaan among the different tribes. It reflects the later traditional view that the conquest was accomplished in about seven years, and that the distribution of the land was decided by lot rather than by the fortunes of the sword. The third division, 23 and 24, includes the two versions of Joshua's farewell address.

The book of Judges also falls naturally into three divisions: Chapters 1^1–2^5 contain a brief epitome of the early Judean account of the settlement in Canaan. They emphasize the fact that, long after the Hebrews had gained a foothold in the west-Jordan land, the Canaanites and older inhabitants continued to hold most of the important cities and points of vantage. This oldest narrative is not the sequel, but is parallel to the traditions found in the book of Joshua. The second division of Judges, 2^6–16^{31}, tells of the achievements of the different Hebrew leaders, who delivered their tribes from foreign invaders and laid the foundations for the future empire. The stories are taken from the early prophetic histories and are prefaced by stereotyped introductions, which give the later prophetic interpretation of the religious significance of the history. The third division, 17–21, is an appendix. It contains an account of the conquests of the Danites, and of the crime of the Gibeathites and of their punishment at the hands of the neighboring Hebrew tribes. These narratives of Judges are not continuous, but rather present vivid and true pictures of the more important characters and events throughout this stirring pioneer period.

II. Political Conditions in Canaan. In the light of the patriarchal stories, the Egyptian inscriptions and the el-Amarna letters, it is possible to determine very definitely the conditions prevailing in Canaan at the beginning of the period of Hebrew settlement. Beside each important spring had grown up a Canaanite city or village. The larger towns, like Jericho, Hebron and Jebus, and those in central and northern Palestine, were encircled by stone or mud walls, which rendered them practically immune from Bedouin attack. Each of these cities

3

had its independent king and controlled the immediately adjacent territory. When free from foreign rule these petty city-states were almost constantly at war with each other.

The strong hand of Egypt for a long period held them in partial check; but Egyptian rule had drained the resources of Palestine. It contributed little in return; for the policy of Egypt had been simply to extract heavy tribute and then to leave the subject peoples to their own devices. The result was that after Egypt finally lost control of Palestine, as it had by the middle of the twelfth century B.C., the old suicidal rivalry between the petty city-states reasserted itself. The Canaanite civilization was still largely a reflection of the Babylonian culture, which for centuries had permeated and dominated southwestern Asia. The Canaanites also appear to have absorbed the worst elements in the effete civilizations of the East and the West. Their degeneracy had long since destroyed their military efficiency and left them ripe for conquest by the ruder but more virile peoples from the wilderness.

As in the days of Thotmose III, the rocky uplands and the outlying districts of Canaan were still open to the peoples from the desert, who were thus able without opposition to gain a foothold in Palestine. As these Arab tribes increased in numbers, they were able gradually by intermarriage, with the native population, by alliances, and by the sword, to conquer additional territory and in time to become masters even of the Canaanite cities.

III. **Strategic Importance of Jericho.** The older traditions indicate that a few cities of eastern Canaan proved the exception to the general rule. Chief among these was the town of Jericho, which commanded the fertile plain of the lower Jordan and the great highways which led south-westward into the territory later occupied by the tribe of Judah and north-westward into central Canaan. Jericho was so apart from the other Canaanite cities, that it could anticipate no help from the petty kingdoms of central Palestine. The possession of this city and its rich surrounding territory, therefore, gave to the Hebrews a base from which they could advance gradually to the occupation and ultimate conquest of Canaan.

IV. **Significance of the Visit of the Spies.** The early Judean prophetic version of the story of the experiences of the spies in Jericho reveals the designs of the Hebrews. The story is also significant, because it indicates that in the family of Rahab the nomadic invaders had allies within the walls of Jericho itself. Possibly Rahab repre-

4

sented one of those Kenite clans which about this time entered southern Canaan, and which according to the record in Judges (§ XXXIII⁶) went up with the Judahites from this city of palms to the conquest of the South Country. The promise that all the members of Rahab's clan, together with their possessions, should be preserved was perhaps the price paid not only for delivering the spies, but also for betraying the city at the time of the Hebrew attack.

V. Triple Tradition of the Crossing of the Jordan. Three distinct accounts are found in Joshua of the crossing of the Jordan. ¹The river itself after the late spring freshets have subsided, is readily fordable at several points. The Northern Israelite version suggests that the Hebrews crossed the river when Jehovah had thus dried up its waters. As in the story of the exodus, the late priestly writers give a highly miraculous account of this important event: contrary to all natural laws, the waters are piled up on either side and the Hebrews pass in solemn array between the walls of water. The early Judean narrative, however, is undoubtedly the more historical and gives a very different picture.

VI. The Method of the Crossing According to the Oldest Narrative. The time of the year is that of harvest, when the Jordan overflows its banks. When the Hebrews approach the river they find that the water has disappeared, leaving the bed of the stream dry. The cause of this remarkable phenomenon is definitely stated. Far up the Jordan, at the village of Adam, whose name probably means *Red Earth*, the waters had been temporarily held back, while those in the lower part of the stream flowed on to the Dead Sea. Interpreted into scientific language, it would appear that the high waters had undermined the clay banks at a point up the river where they came close together, causing a great landslide. This mass of earth had blocked up the river until the increasing waters were sufficient to brush away the obstruction and resume their usual course.

The incident, therefore, was in many ways parallel to that recounted in the history of Sultan Bibars. In 1257 A.D. it was suddenly found necessary to repair the foundation of the bridge Jisr Damieh in order to save the retreating Moslem army. On arriving at the bridge the workmen found the river bed empty. This continued for a few hours, until the work of repairing was nearly completed, when the waters again came rushing down. The historian states that the cause was a landslide higher up the river, but he regards the deliverance as a remarkable evidence of Allah's favor.

VII. **Significance of the Event in Hebrew History.** To the Hebrews this remarkable provision for their crossing of the Jordan seemed a direct act of divine interposition. In many ways it was strikingly similar to the deliverance from Egypt. As at many another great crisis in their history, they received, not through supernatural but through natural means, the clear evidence of Jehovah's care and guidance.

When the Hebrews crossed the Jordan they carried with them the traditions and customs of the wilderness, but many of these were destined gradually to disappear before the highly developed agricultural civilization, already firmly established in the land of Canaan. With the crossing of the Jordan began that great conflict between the simple faith of the desert and the alluring but degenerate cults of the land of Canaan. It was a conflict which continued for over five hundred years, until, amidst the trying experiences of the Babylonian exile, the religion of Moses and of the later prophets at last emerged completely triumphant.

§ XXXII.   CAPTURE OF JERICHO AND AI

1. Jehovah's directions regarding the attack

Now when Joshua was near Jericho, he lifted up his eyes and looked, and, behold, there stood a man over against him with his drawn sword in his hand. And Joshua went to him, and said to him, Art thou for us or for our adversaries? And he said, Nay, but as Prince of the host of Jehovah have I now come. Then Joshua fell on his face to the earth, and worshipped, and said to him, What has my lord to say to his servant? And the Prince of Jehovah's host said to Joshua, Take off thy sandals from thy feet; for the place on which thou art standing is holy. Then Jehovah said to Joshua, See, I have given into thy power Jericho, and its king, with the mighty men of valor. And ye shall march around the city, all the warriors going about the city once. Thus shall ye do six days. And the seventh day the people shall go up every man straight before him.

2. Joshua's commands to the people

Then Joshua called the priests and said to them, Take up the ark; and to the people he said, March around the city, and let the armed men pass on before the ark of Jehovah. Joshua also commanded the people saying, You shall not shout the battle-cry, nor let your voice be heard, neither shall a word go out of your mouth, until the day I say to you, 'Shout the battle-cry'; then you shall shout.

6

So he caused the ark of Jehovah to march around the city, going about it once. Then they came into the camp, and lodged in the camp. And Joshua rose early in the morning, and the second day they marched around the city once, and returned to the camp. Thus they did six days. And it came to pass on the seventh day that they rose early at the dawning of the day; and when they had made the circuit of the city after the same manner, Joshua said to the people, Shout the battle-cry; for Jehovah hath given you the city. And the city shall be completely devoted to Jehovah, together with all that is in it; only Rahab the harlot shall live, both she and those who are with her in the house, because she hid the messengers whom we sent. So the people shouted the battle-cry, and went up into the city, every man straight before him, and they took the city.

3. March around the city

4. Capture of the city

Then they completely destroyed by the sword all that was in the city, both man and woman, both young and old, and ox, and sheep, and ass. But Rahab the harlot and her father's household and all that she had, Joshua saved; and they have dwelt in the midst of Israel even until this day, because she hid the messengers whom Joshua sent to spy out Jericho. At that time Joshua made them subscribe to this oath:

5. Fate of its inhabitants

Cursed be that man before Jehovah
   Who undertakes to rebuild this city;
With the loss of his first-born shall he lay its foundation,
And with the loss of his youngest son shall he set up its
    gates.

So Jehovah was with Joshua, and his fame was in all the land.

And Joshua sent men from Jericho to Ai, which is on the east side of Bethel, and commanded them saying, Go up and spy out the land. So the men went and spied out Ai. And when they returned to Joshua, they said to him, Do not let all the people go up, but let two or three thousand men go up and smite Ai; do not make all the people toil up there; for they are few. So there went up thither of the people about three thousand men; but they fled before the

6. Defeat of the three hundred

7

men of Ai. And the men of Ai smote of them, about thirty-six men, and pursued them from before the gate even to Shebarim, and smote them at the descent; and the people lost heart to resist and became as weak as water.

7. Joshua's complaint to Jehovah

Then Joshua rent his clothes, and fell to the earth upon his face before Jehovah until the evening, together with the elders of Israel; and they put dust upon their heads. And Joshua said, Alas, O Lord Jehovah, why hast thou at all brought this people over the Jordan. Would that we had been contented and stayed beyond the Jordan! O Lord, what shall I say, after Israel hath turned his back before his enemies! For the Canaanites and all the inhabitants of the land will hear of it, and will surround us, and cut off our name from the earth; and what wilt thou do for thy great name?

8. Cause of the defeat

Then Jehovah said to Joshua, Arise ! why art thou lying prostrate thus? Israel hath sinned; indeed they have even taken of the accursed thing and so have been guilty of theft and deception; and they have even put it among their own things. That is why the Israelites cannot stand before their enemies, because they are accursed. I will not be with you any more, unless ye destroy from among you that which is accursed. Arise, sanctify the people, and say, ' Sanctify yourselves for to-morrow; for thus saith Jehovah, the God of Israel, " There is in the midst of thee, O Israel, that which is accursed, thou canst not stand before thine enemies until ye take away the accursed thing from among you." In the morning therefore ye shall be brought near by your tribes; and it shall be that the tribe which Jehovah shall take, shall come near by families; and the family which Jehovah shall take, shall come near by households; and the household which Jehovah shall take, shall come near man by man. And it shall be that he who is taken with the accursed thing shall be burnt with fire, together with all that he hath, because he hath committed a shameful crime in Israel.'

9. Discovery of the culprit

So Joshua rose up early in the morning, and brought Israel near by their tribes, and the tribe of Judah was taken. Then he brought near the family of Judah; and he took the family of the Zerahites, and he brought near the family of the Zerahites, man by man; and Zabdi was taken. Then he brought near his household, man by man; and Achan was taken. Then Joshua said to Achan, Tell me now what you have done: do not conceal it from me. And Achan answered Joshua and said, Truly, I have sinned against Jehovah the God of Israel, and thus and thus have I done: when I saw among the spoil a beautiful Babylonian mantle, and two hundred shekels of silver, and a bar of gold of fifty shekels' weight, I coveted them and took them, and now they are hidden in the earth in the middle of my tent, with the money underneath.

So Joshua sent messengers, and they ran to the tent, and there it was hidden in his tent, with the money underneath. And they took them from the midst of the tent, and brought them to Joshua and all the Israelites, and laid them down before Jehovah. Then Joshua took Achan the son of Zerah and all that he had and brought them to the valley of Achor. And Joshua said, Why have you brought trouble upon us? Jehovah shall bring trouble upon you to-day. And they burned them with fire, and they raised over him a great heap of stones. Then Jehovah turned from the fierceness of his anger. Hence the name of the place has been called the valley of Achor [Trouble] to this day. *10. Achan's punishment*

Then Jehovah said to Joshua, Do not fear, neither be dismayed; take all the warriors with thee; set an ambush for the city behind it. So Joshua arose with all the warriors to go up to Ai, and Joshua selected thirty thousand mighty men of valor, and sent them forth by night. And he commanded them saying, Behold, you are to lie in ambush against the city, behind the city; do not go very far from the city, but be ready all of you; and I and all the people who are with me will approach the city. And it shall come to pass, when they come out against us as at the first, that we will flee before them; and they will come out after us, until we have drawn them away from the city; for they will say, 'They flee before us as at the first'; and then you shall rise up from the ambush, and take possession of the city; for Jehovah your God will give it into your power. And when you have seized the city, set it on fire; see, I have commanded you. *11. Arrangements for the ambush*

12. The ambush

So Joshua sent them forth, and they went to the place of the ambush, and stationed themselves between Bethel and Ai, on the west side of Ai; but Joshua spent that night among the people.

13. Capture and destruction of Ai and its inhabitants

Then Joshua rose early in the morning and mustered the people, and went up together with the elders of Israel, before the people of Ai. And the warriors who were with him went up, and came before the city. And it came to pass when the king of Ai saw it, both he and all his people hastened to a certain place in the direction of the Arabah, but he did not know that there was an ambush against him behind the city. Then Israel fled by way of the wilderness, and all the people that were in the city were called together to pursue them. And they left the city unguarded and pursued Israel. Thereupon the men in ambush arose quickly out of their place, and hastened to set the city on fire. And when the men of Ai looked behind them, they saw the smoke of the city ascending to heaven, and they had no chance to flee this way or that, for the people who had been fleeing to the wilderness turned back upon the pursuers. When the smoke of the city ascended, the others came forth out of the city against them; so they were in the midst of Israel, some on this side, and some on that; and they smote them, so that they let none of them remain or escape.

14. Fate of the king of Ai

And they captured the king of Ai alive, and brought him to Joshua. And the king of Ai he hanged on a tree until eventide; and at sunset Joshua gave command, and they took his body down from the tree, and threw it down at the entrance of the gate of the city, and raised over it a great heap of stones, which is there to this day.

15. Deception of the Gibeonites

Now when the inhabitants of Gibeon heard what Joshua had done to Jericho and Ai, they practised deception; they proceeded to take provisions and old sacks upon their asses, and wine-skins, old and torn and bound up, and old, patched shoes on their feet, and old garments upon their backs; and all the bread with which they provided themselves was dry and crumbled. And they went to Joshua at the camp in Gilgal, and they said to the men of Israel, We have come from a far country; now therefore make a treaty with us. And the men of Israel said to the villagers [Hivites], Perhaps you live among us; then how can we make a treaty with you? And they said to Joshua, We are your servants. And Joshua said to them, Who are you? and whence do you come? And they said to him, From a very far country your servants have come. And our elders and all the inhabitants of our country said to us, 'Take provision in your hand for the journey, and go to meet them and say to them, "We are your servants."' This bread of ours we took hot for our provision out of our houses on the day we set out to come to you; but now see, it has become dry and crumbled; and these wine-skins, which we filled, were new; now see, they are torn; and these garments and shoes of ours have become old because of the very long journey. Therefore, now make a treaty with us. So the men of Israel took of their provisions, and did not ask counsel at the mouth of Jehovah, but made a treaty with them, to let them live.

But after they had made a treaty with them, the men of Israel heard that they dwelt among them. And the Israelites journeyed and came to their cities on the third day. Then Joshua called for them and said to them, Why have you deceived us? saying, ' We are very far from you,' when you dwell among us? Now therefore you are under a curse, and there shall never cease to be of you bondmen, both hewers of wood and drawers of water for the house of my God. And they answered Joshua, Behold we are in your power; do as it seems good and right to you to do to us. And so he did to them, and saved them from the hand of the Israelites, so that they did not slay them. And Joshua made them that day hewers of wood and drawers of water.

16. Their fate

I. The Situation and Character of Jericho.

The ruins of the ancient town of Jericho rise directly to the west of the famous spring, which now bears the name *Ain es Sultan*. The mound is about twelve hundred feet long and at many points about fifty feet in height. The Roman Jericho of Herod's time was built further down the valley where the Wady Kelt breaks through the western bluffs. The modern Jericho is a squalid little hamlet lying further out on the plain.

The presence of Canaanite pottery on the surface of the imposing mound, which rises above Ain es Sultan, has long been accepted as conclusive evidence that it represents the ancient city conquered by the

Hebrews. From the size of this mound it is clear that it represents fully a thousand years of Canaanite history. Excavations begun in April, 1907, by the Germans, under the direction of Professor Sellin, have confirmed this conclusion beyond all doubt. The remains of the old Canaanite civilization were discovered only a foot or two beneath the surface of the mound. Much of the original wall has already been uncovered. It rests upon a stone foundation about two feet in height, and is constructed of bricks of burned clay. It is about ten feet high, and from ten to thirty feet thick. At one point a stone staircase with nineteen steps leads up from the plain to the top of the wall.

The most interesting ruin thus far uncovered is on the northern side of the mound. It proves to be a massive tower, three stories high, of unburned brick. It has four apartments on the first floor, seven on the second and six on the third. Many of the partition walls of these rooms still remain intact. Sixteen steps of the stone staircase which ran up through the three stories to the flat roof have been discovered. The blackened walls of the tower show that it had been destroyed by fire. The remnants of pottery, the stone knives, the twenty-two small, unburned clay tablets intended for writing, but unfortunately not inscribed, which have been found inside it, and the general character of its architecture indicate that the structure comes from the Canaanite period. It is also the best preserved example of Canaanite architecture thus far discovered.

The total area of ancient Jericho was not much more than that occupied by four modern city blocks. From its slight elevation the city commanded a beautiful view of the fertile plain of the Jordan, which at this point is fourteen miles wide and is watered by a crystal brook which runs from the spring at the foot of the mound. To the west the hills rise abruptly and are pierced by the valley which leads up into central Canaan, past Ai toward Bethel.

II. **The Two Accounts of the Capture of Jericho.** A short march across the level plain of the lower Jordan brought the Hebrews to the Canaanite city of Jericho. Two variant accounts have been handed down of the manner in which this walled city was captured. One, the Northern Israelite version, represents the Hebrews as marching seven times around the walls, with the ark at their head and with seven priests blowing seven trumpets. On the seventh time at the final blast, the people shouted loudly and the walls fell down. In the mind of the later Israelites, the capture of this strong, fortified town seemed indeed a miracle, but the early Judean version gives a much simpler and more natural account of the event.

III. The Judean Account of the Capture. According to the oldest version, Jericho was captured not by miracle but by strategy. Once each day for seven days, fully armed, with the ark at their head, the Hebrews marched silently around the city. It requires little imagination to picture the scene. On the first day the inhabitants of Jericho were on the defensive with guarded gates and warriors alert to repulse any attack. On the following days their alarm yielded to wonder, ridicule and scorn. The seventh day apparently found them entirely off their guard and offered an excellent opportunity for a sudden and successful attack. The members of the family of Rahab within the city had been promised by the Hebrews a reward for their treachery. It is not improbable that at the signal they unbolted the city gates, so that, when at last the lips of the Israelite warriors were unsealed and they raised their war cry and "rushed up into the city every man straight before him," they found the way open before them.

IV. The Fate of the Inhabitants of Jericho. There is little doubt that the account of the destruction of Jericho is historical. All living things found in the city were devoted to Jehovah (that is, given as a bloody offering), and therefore destroyed. The spoil likewise was consecrated to Israel's god. Even the ruins were guarded by a curse which was to descend upon any one who attempted to rebuild them. In I Kings 16³⁴ it is stated that "in the days of Ahab, Hiel, the Bethelite, built Jericho. He laid the foundations with the loss of Abiram, his first-born, and set up its gates with the loss of his youngest son, Segub, as Jehovah had spoken by Joshua the son of Nun." The same fanatical zeal in destroying their foes is revealed in the inscription of Mesha, who ruled over Moab in the days of Omri and Ahab. In his inscription he states that he captured the city Ataroth from Israel and slew all the people and made the city a ruin. In a subsequent passage he relates that "Chemosh said to me, 'Go and take Nebo against Israel.' Then I went by night and fought against it from the break of dawn until noon and I took it and slew them all—seven thousand men, women and slaves—for I had devoted it to Ashtar-Chemosh."

Although the cruelty of the Hebrews in treating their foes was condemned by their later and more enlightened prophets, these early narratives reveal the devotion and fanatical zeal with which Israel went out to fight the wars of Jehovah. So completely did the Hebrews and their kinsmen, the Moabites and Edomites, identify their national interest

13

with that of their tribal gods that they regarded wholesale slaughter of their foes as a virtue which would win the divine approval. In times of great crises, these same peoples, who still retained much of the fierce fanatical zeal of the desert, did not hesitate to sacrifice even their own sons to win the favor of their tribal god. Their religious conceptions were crude and in many respects wrong, but their devotion lacked neither in intensity nor in forcible expression.

V. The Sin of Achan. Before the author of the book of Job combated the popular dogma, misfortune and calamity were universally interpreted as signs of divine displeasure. When, therefore, the attack upon Ai proved unsuccessful, the only question raised by the Israelites was, "Who has sinned?" Appeal was accordingly made to the sacred lot, which was probably in the charge of a priest or seer. Achan, who was thus singled out as the guilty man, confessed his guilt. His crime was stealing from Jehovah that which had been solemnly consecrated to him. Even the Code of Hammurabi (§ 6) eight or ten centuries before had provided, "If a man has stolen goods from a temple or house he shall be put to death." According to early Hebrew usage, the penalty was death, not only for the culprit but also for his family. Accordingly Achan and all his household were burned to death by the outraged community.

VI. The Capture of Ai. The strategy employed by the Hebrews in capturing the town of Ai was one often used by nomadic invaders against the inhabitants of walled cities. Secreting a band of warriors in a secluded valley, the Hebrews advanced against the city. When the inhabitants sallied forth for the attack, the main body of the Hebrews turned in flight. The pursuers left their gates open behind them, and the men in ambush rushed into the town and set it on fire. Soon the rising smoke revealed to the pursuers the trap into which they had fallen. Upon the people of Ai was visited the same pitiless fate that had overtaken the inhabitants of Jericho.

VII. The Treaty with the Villagers. Far down through the period of the judges, even to the days of the united kingdom, a group of Canaanite towns including Jebus, Shaalbim, Gibeon and Gezer, remained in the possession of the Canaanites. The traditional reason why these cities were allowed to retain their independence is found in the story of the treaty made with them when the Hebrews first crossed the Jordan. With patched shoes and tattered garments on their backs, dry and mouldy bread in their wallets, representatives of these upland villages appeared in the camp of the Israelites. Their appearance gave weight to their assurance that they came from a distant country to make terms with the new invaders. Accordingly, without consulting Jehovah, a treaty was made, and the peoples, whom these messengers represented, were promised immunity from Hebrew attack. Their deception, however, was in time made an excuse for enslaving the Gibeonites. Later, Saul for some reason put certain of them to death. This act, however, was repudiated by the Israelites in the days of David; and Saul's seven sons were publicly hanged in order to win Jehovah's forgiveness for breaking the solemn treaty (§ L).

VIII. **The Character of Joshua.** The name of Joshua does not appear to have been found in the earliest prophetic history. This surprising omission is perhaps due to the fact that the brief Judean account of the settlement in Judges 1 (§ XXXIII), deals with the experiences of the individual tribes rather than with the achievements of the leaders. Joshua seems to have been the leader of the northern tribes in their advance toward Canaan. His character and work were adapted to the needs of his age. He figures in the Northern Israelite history as an ideal military commander, wise in council, fertile in strategy, quick to strike and courageous in action. Trained in the school of Moses and the wilderness, he is the first of those tribal leaders and deliverers who appear in this stirring period of settlement and conquest. The same spirit of devotion to Jehovah and of dependence upon his guidance are characteristic of Joshua as of Israel's earlier leaders. Although later tradition has clearly extended the sphere of his activity and idealized his work, he appears to have made a deep impression upon this formative period of Israel's history.

§ XXXIII. CONDITIONS AND CONQUESTS IN CANAAN

Then it came to pass that the Israelites inquired of Jehovah, Which of us shall first go up to fight against the Canaanites? And Jehovah said, Judah shall go; behold I will give the land into his hand. Then Judah said to Simeon his brother, Come up with me into the territory allotted to me, that we may fight against the Canaanites; then I will also go with you into the territory allotted to you. So Simeon went with him. _1. The advance of Judah and Simeon_

And they found Adoni-bezek in Bezek, and they fought against him and smote the Canaanites and the Perizzites. _2. Battle of Bezek_

15

And Adoni-bezek fled, but they pursued and caught him, and cut off his thumbs and his great toes. And Adoni-bezek said, Seventy kings, with their thumbs and their great toes cut off, pick up crumbs under my table; as I have done, so God hath requited me! And they brought him to Jerusalem, and there he died. But the Judahites could not dispossess the Jebusites, the inhabitants of Jerusalem; but the Jebusites dwell to this day with the Judahites at Jerusalem.

3. Wars in the south

And afterward the Judahites went to fight against the Canaanites who dwelt in the hills and in the South Country and in the lowlands.

4. Capture and fate of Hebron

And Judah went against the Canaanites who dwelt in Hebron (the earlier name of Hebron was Kiriath-arba); and they slew Sheshai, and Ahiman, and Talmai. And they gave Hebron to Caleb, as Moses had commanded; and he drove out from there the three sons of Anak.

5. Of Debir

And from there Judah went against the inhabitants of Debir (the older name of Debir was Kiriath-sepher). And Caleb said, To the man who attacks Kiriath-sepher and takes it, I will give Achsah my daughter in marriage. And Caleb's younger brother, Othniel the son of Kenaz, took it; and Caleb gave Achsah his daughter to him in marriage. And when she came to him she moved her to ask of her father a field; and she alighted from her ass; and when Caleb said to her, What is it? she answered, Give me a present; since you have assigned me to the South Country, give me now springs of water. So Caleb gave her the upper and lower springs.

6. Conquests in the South Country

And the children of the Kenite, Moses's father-in-law, went up out of the city of palm trees [Jericho] with the Judahites into the wilderness of Judah, which is south of Arad; and they went and dwelt with their people. Then Judah went with Simeon his brother, and they smote the Canaanites who inhabited Zephath and completely destroyed it. Therefore the name of the city was called Hormah [Devoted to destruction]. And Jehovah was with Judah, so that he gained possession of the hill-country; but he could not drive out the inhabitants of the plain, because they had chariots of iron.

And the house of Joseph also went up against Bethel; and Jehovah was with them. And the house of Joseph went to spy out Bethel (the earlier name of the city was Luz). And the spies saw a man coming out of the city and they said to him, Show us, we pray you, the way to enter the city, and we will treat you kindly. So he showed them the way to enter the city; and they put the inhabitants of the city to the sword; but they let the man go with all his family. And the man went to the land of the Hittites, and built a city, and called its name Luz, which is its name to this day. *7. Capture of Bethel by the house of Joseph*

But Manasseh did not drive out the inhabitants of Beth-shean and its towns, nor of Taanach and its towns, nor the inhabitants of Dor and its towns, nor the inhabitants of Ibleam and its towns, nor the inhabitants of Megiddo and its towns; but the Canaanites maintained their hold in that region. However when Israel became strong they put the Canaanites to taskwork, but did not completely drive them out. And Ephraim did not drive out the Canaanites who dwelt in Gezer; but the Canaanites remained in Gezer among them. Zebulun did not drive out the inhabitants of Kitron, nor the inhabitants of Nahalol; but the Canaanites remained among them and became subject to taskwork. Asher did not drive out the inhabitants of Acco, nor the inhabitants of Sidon, nor of Ahlab, nor of Achzib, nor of Helbah, nor of Aphik nor of Rehob; but the Asherites dwelt among the Canaanite inhabitants of the land; for they could not drive them out. Naphtali did not drive out the inhabitants of Beth-shemesh, nor the inhabitants of Beth-anath; but he dwelt among the Canaanite inhabitants of the land; nevertheless the inhabitants of Beth-shemesh and of Beth-anath became subject to taskwork. And the Amorites forced the Danites into the hill-country; for they would not allow them to come down into the plain; but the Amorites maintained their hold in Mount Heres, in Aijalon, and in Shaalbim; yet when the house of Joseph grew stronger they became subject to taskwork. *8. The Canaanites who retained their territory*

So Jehovah left those nations, not driving them out at once; merely that the successive generations of the Israelites might become familiar with war. And the Israelites dwelt among the Canaanites, and they took their daughters as wives, and gave their own daughters to their sons, and served their gods. *9. Effect upon the Hebrews*

17

10. Assassination of the king of Moab by Ehud

Then the Israelites became subject to Eglon the king of Moab. And they cried to Jehovah, and Jehovah raised them up a deliverer, Ehud the son of Gera, the Benjamite, a left-handed man. Now the Israelites sent tribute by him to Eglon the king of Moab. And Ehud made him a two-edged dagger about a foot in length, and hung it under his clothing upon his right thigh. And he offered the tribute to Eglon king of Moab. Now Eglon was a very fat man. And when Ehud had finished offering the tribute, he sent away the people who had carried the tribute. But he himself turned back from the sculptured stones near Gilgal, and said, I have a private message for you, O king, And the king said, Silence! And all who stood by him went out from his presence. Then Ehud went in to him, as he was sitting alone in the cool upper apartment. And Ehud said, I have a message from God for you. And as he arose from his seat, Ehud reached out his left hand, and took the dagger from his right thigh, and plunged it into his body, so that the hilt also went in after the blade, and the fat closed over the blade, for he did not draw the dagger out of his body; and the filth came out.

11. His escape

Then Ehud went out into the porch, and shut the doors of the upper apartment upon him and locked them. Now when he had gone out, the king's servants came; and they looked, and, behold, the doors of the upper apartment were locked; and they said, Surely he must be covering his feet in the private room in the cool apartment. So they waited till they were perplexed by his strange failure to open the doors of the upper room; therefore they took the key and opened them, and there was their lord lying prostrate on the earth, dead. But Ehud had slipped away, while they were waiting, and had passed beyond the sculptured stones, and was making good his escape to Seirah.

12. His rally of the Ephraimites and repulse of the Moabites

And when he arrived, he blew a trumpet in the hill-country of Ephraim; and the Israelites went down with him from the hill-country and he at their head. For he said to them, Follow me, because Jehovah hath delivered your enemies, the Moabites, into your hand. So they followed him and seized the fords of the Jordan against the Moabites, and did not allow a man to pass over.

18

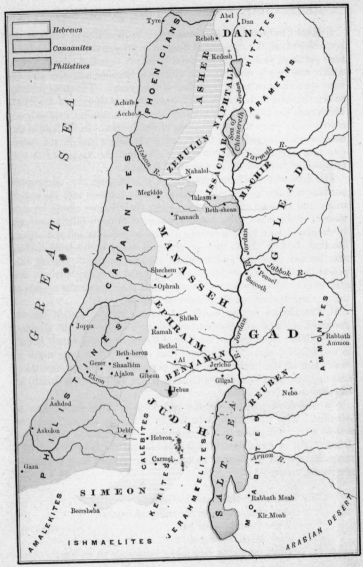

TERRITORIAL DIVISION OF CANAAN AFTER THE CONQUEST.

REAL CHARACTER OF THE CONQUEST

I. Real Character of the Conquest. In the different strata of the book of Joshua, the conquest of Canaan is presented from several distinct points of view. The late priestly writers regarded it as complete within less than a decade. The Northern Israelite narrative also assigns later victories to the beginning of this period. The great decisive battle, recorded in the fourth and fifth chapters of Judges (§ XXXVI), which gave the Hebrews the mastery over the Canaanites, evidently occurred many years after the crossing of the Jordan. In the light of the oldest records found in the first chapters of Judges and in the corresponding early sections of Joshua, it is clear that the conquest followed rather than preceded the settlement of Canaan.

The conquest itself was gradual. By colonizing the unoccupied portions of Palestine, by intermarriage and by alliance with the native tribes, and in some cases by open attack, the Hebrews slowly became masters of the land. The process continued through fully a century. It was the pioneer stage in Israel's history—a period of toil and almost constant conflict. Each tribe or group of tribes under local leaders won its own victories and defended its own borders. During this period the Hebrews were intent not only upon acquiring territory but also upon building houses and learning from their Canaanite neighbors the arts and institutions of agricultural life.

II. Conditions in the South. According to the earliest record, the tribes of Judah and Simeon, accompanied by clans of the Kenites, went up alone from Jericho, the City of Palms, to conquer their homes in southern Canaan. The order of their conquests was from north to south, and all the implications of the narrative support the conclusion that they entered Canaan from the east rather than from the south, as has sometimes been urged.

But one decisive battle for the possession of southern Canaan is recorded. The Canaanites were led by a certain Adoni-Bezek (or Zedek) who, in the later Judean narrative, is described as the king of Jebus. It is in connection with this battle that the later Judean historian has quoted the famous stanza from the ancient song commemorating the victory:

> Thou sun stand still in Gibeon,
> And thou, moon, in the valley of Aijalon.
> Then the sun stood still,
> And the moon stayed
> Until the nation had taken vengeance on its foes.

19

The later historian has interpreted these highly poetical words literally. In their original setting they emphasize the extent of the victory. So great was this victory that to those who contemplated it the day seemed to have been supernaturally lengthened. Upon the vanquished king was visited the same cruel fate as had overtaken the other conquered foes who fell into the hands of the Israelites. Jebus, the citadel of ancient Urusalamu (*i. e.* Jerusalem), remained, however, in the possession of the Canaanites until the days of David.

Still further south, the Calebites had apparently already secured a foothold upon the borders of Canaan (*cf.* § XXVIII), and the Judahites joined with them in vanquishing the older inhabitants. The city of Hebron lay within the territory of Caleb, while the neighboring city of Debir was held by the kindred tribe of Othniel. In time the conquest of the southern tribes extended out into the South Country. This territory was the home of the Simeonites, who largely retained their nomadic habits and never played a very important part in Israel's history. Instead, the powerful tribe of Judah gradually assimilated such kindred Arab tribes as the Calebites, the Othnielites and the Jerahmeelites, until it gained complete possession of the uplands of southern Canaan.

In this region the influence of the desert life and customs was strongest, and the traditions and beliefs of Moses and of the wilderness were retained with the greatest tenacity. The older Canaanite population appears to have been largely extirpated, so that the blood of the Judahites was not so much diluted by intermarriage with neighboring peoples as that of their kinsmen in the north. A zone of Canaanite cities, beginning with Gezer on the borders of the Philistine plain, and including Shaalbim, Jebus and Gideon, shut off the Israelites of the North from those of the South so completely that, in the great rally of the Israelite tribes against the Canaanites in the days of Deborah, no mention is made of Judah or of Simeon.

III. **Conditions in the North.** The oldest records tell of but one Northern city captured by the Hebrews in the initial period of settlement. That was the famous town of Bethel, a few miles from Ai, which probably became from the first, as its name, *House of God*, suggests, one of the favorite sanctuaries of the Northern Israelites. Other smaller villages on the borders of the upland pastures doubtless soon fell into the possession of the Hebrew immigrants. The earliest Judean narrative, however, states very definitely that all the important towns of northern Canaan at first remained in the possession of the Canaanites.

These included the important zone of cities which extended across the plain of Esdraelon, beginning with Bethshean on the east, and including Taanach, Ibleam and Megiddo, and extending to Dor on the coast of the Mediterranean. This group of Canaanite cities in turn separated the northern tribes of Ephraim and Manasseh on the south from the tribes, which were struggling for homes in the rich lands further north.

The later account (found in a secondary group of Judean narratives, Josh. 11¹⁻¹⁵), which represents the Israelites under the leadership of Joshua as achieving a great victory over the Canaanite kings of the north, is either a popular version of the sweeping victory recorded in the fourth and fifth chapters of Judges, or else the record is of a subsequent victory over the Canaanites in the far north.

IV. **The Conflict with the Moabites.** Occupied, as they were, with the task of conquering the soil and of building homes, and separated from each other by strong Canaanite cities, the Israelites were ill-prepared to resist foreign invasions. Local interests and the old nomadic aversion for any central authority prevented a general union of the Hebrew tribes. The result was that they fell an easy prey to the attacks of their hostile and well organized neighbors.

It is difficult to determine the order of events recorded in the book of Judges, but it is probable that the different incidents in this warlike period have been arranged in approximately their chronological order. If so, one of the earliest attacks came from the Edomites in the south, and was repulsed by the tribe of Othniel, whose territory lay immediately to the south of Canaan.

Across the Jordan the Moabites, under the leadership of their king, Eglon, soon succeeded in levying a tribute upon the tribes immediately west of Jericho. The Israelites in time found a bloody deliverer in Ehud, the Benjamite who, gaining admission to the palace as an ambassador, assassinated the Moabite king. Under the leadership of Ehud, the Ephraimites seized the fords of the Jordan, and thus delivered themselves from the aggressions of the Moabites.

During the remainder of the so-called period of the Judges, the southern tribes appear to have been free from outside attack, except from the west. How early the Philistines began their forays up through the rocky gorges, which led from the maritime plain to central Canaan, cannot be determined. Their united and aggressive advance marks the close of the period and inaugurates the era of the united monarchy. Meantime the stories of the book of Judges focus attention on events in the north, where the great problems in Israel's early history were gradually being worked out. There was fought the great battle which gave the Hebrews possession of Canaan, and there were laid the foundations for the future Hebrew empire.

§ XXXIV. THE ESTABLISHMENT OF THE DANITE TRIBE AND SANCTUARY

1. Origin of Micah's sanctuary

Now there was a man of the hill-country of Ephraim, whose name was Micah. And he said to his mother, The eleven hundred shekels of silver which were taken from you, about which you took an oath, saying it aloud in my hearing, behold, the silver is with me; it was I who took it. Now therefore I restore it to you. And his mother said, Blessed of Jehovah is my son. Then he restored the eleven hundred shekels of silver to his mother and his mother said, I solemnly consecrate the silver to Jehovah from my hand through my son, to make a carved and a molten image. So, when he restored the money to his mother, his mother took two hundred shekels of silver, and gave them to the founder, who made with it a carved and a molten image; and it was in the house of Micah. And the man Micah had a shrine, and he made an ephod and household gods, and installed one of his sons who became his priest. In those days there was no king in Israel; every one did as he thought was right.

2. Appointment of a young Levite as his priest

Now there was a young man of Bethlehem in Judah of the family of Judah, who was a Levite; and he was dwelling there. And the man departed from the city, from Bethlehem in Judah, to make his home in whatever place he could find. And as he journeyed, he came to the hill-country of Ephraim to the house of Micah. And Micah said to him, Whence do you come? And he said to him, I am a Levite from Bethlehem in Judah, and I am travelling to find a home, wherever I may. And Micah said to him, Stay with me, and be a father and a priest to me, and I will give you ten shekels of silver by the year, and a suit of clothes, and your living. So the Levite entered into an agreement to dwell with the man; and the young man was to him as one of his sons. Thus Micah consecrated the Levite, and the young man became his priest, and was in the house of

Micah. Then said Micah, Now I know that Jehovah will prosper me, since I have a Levite as my priest.

Now in those days the tribe of the Danites sought them an inheritance in which to dwell. And the Danites sent five men of their clan from their whole number, valiant men from Zorah and from Eshtaol, to explore the land, and to examine it; and they said to them, Go, examine the land. And they came to the hill-country of Ephraim, to the house of Micah and passed the night there. And when they were near the house of Micah they recognized the voice of the young man, the Levite; so they turned aside there, and said to him, Who brought you here? and what are you doing in this place? and what have you here? And he said to them, Thus and so Micah has done for me, and he has hired me and I have become his priest. And they said to him, Inquire of God, will you, that we may know whether or not our undertaking shall be successful. And the priest said to them, Go in peace: your undertaking is under the care of Jehovah.

Then the five men went on and came to Laish and found the people, who were there, dwelling in security, as do the Sidonians, quiet and not suspicious of danger; for there was no one in the land possessing authority to restrain them from anything, and they were far from the Sidonians and had nothing to do with any one else. Then they came to their kinsmen at Zorah and Eshtaol, and their kinsmen said to them, What is your report? And they said, Arise, and let us go up against them; we have seen the land, and, behold, it is very good, and you are sitting idle. Do not delay to go and to enter in to take possession of the land. When you go, you will come to a people who suspect no danger, and the land is large; for God hath given it into your hand, a place where there is no want of anything that is on the earth.

So there set forth from thence of the clan of the Danites, from Zorah and Eshtaol, six hundred men girded with weapons of war. And they went up and encamped near Kiriath-jearim in Judah; hence they call that place Mahaneh-dan [Camp of Dan] to this day; it is west of Kiriath-jearim. And they passed on from there to the hill-country of Ephraim, and came to the house of Micah.

3. The Danite spies at Micah's sanctuary

4. Favorable report of the spies

5. Departure of the Danites

6. Their seizure of Micah's images and priest

Then the five men, who went to explore the country of Laish, spoke up and said to their kinsmen, Do you know that there is in these houses an ephod, and household gods, and a carved and a molten image? Now therefore decide what you will do. And they turned aside there and came to the house of the young man, the Levite, even the house of Micah, and greeted him. Meanwhile the six hundred men, who were of the Danites, girded with their weapons of war, stood by the entrance of the gate. But the five men who had gone to explore the land went up, entered in there, and took the carved image, and the ephod, and the household gods, and the molten image, while the priest stood by the entrance of the gate with the six hundred men who were girded with weapons of war. And when these went into Micah's house, and took the carved image, the ephod, and the household gods, and the molten image, the priest said to them, What are you doing? And they said to him, Be still! lay your hand upon your mouth, and go with us, and be a father and a priest to us. Is it better for you to be priest to one man's household, or to be priest to a tribe and a clan in Israel? And the priest was glad, and he took the ephod, and the household gods, and the carved image and went along with the people. Then they turned and departed, when they had put the little ones and the cattle and the goods before them.

7. Their reply to Micah's protest

After they had gone some distance from the house of Micah, the men who were in the houses near Micah's house gathered together and overtook the Danites. And when they shouted to the Danites, they turned about and said to Micah, What is the matter with you that you are out with such a crowd? And he said, You have taken away my gods which I made, and the priest, and are gone away, and what have I left? What do you mean by asking, 'What is the matter with you?' And the Danites said to him, Do not let your voice be heard among us, lest some fierce fellows fall upon you and you lose your life, with the lives of your household. Then the Danites went on their way; and, since Micah saw that they were too strong for him, he turned and went back to his house.

Thus they took that which Micah had made, and the priest whom he had, and came to Laish, to a people living in unsuspecting quiet, and put them to the sword, and burnt the city with fire. And there was no one to give any succor, because it was far from Sidon, and they had no dealings with any one else; and it was in the valley which belongs to Beth-rehob. And they built the city and dwelt in it, and called the name of the city Dan. But the earlier name of the city was Laish.

8. Capture of Laish

And the Danites set up for themselves the carved image; and Jonathan, the son of Gershom the son of Moses, and his descendants were priests to the tribe of the Danites. So they set up Micah's graven image which he made, as long as the house of God was in Shiloh.

9. Establishment of the Danite sanctuary

I. **Character of the Story.** The clearest information regarding the experiences of the tribes in seeking homes in Canaan comes from this ancient story found in the appendix to the book of Judges. Its object is to give the history of the founding of the famous sanctuary at Dan. Its thought and point of view are those of the earliest period of Israel's history, and the section may be regarded as an almost contemporary picture of the events which it records.

II. **The Sanctuary of Micah the Ephraimite.** The origin of the sanctuary of Micah the Ephraimite was simple but not altogether glorious. The occasion appears to have been the restoration of certain money stolen by Micah from his mother. This money she consecrated to the deity. It was given to a founder, who made a carved and molten image. Ephod in these early narratives is clearly the designation of some form of idol (*cf.* also § XXXVII[11]). Jehovah was the God worshipped at this shrine, but the old heathen symbolism was retained without protest or without any suggestion that it was regarded as illegal. Also the religious head of each tribe or clan was the tribal sheik or the father of the household. It was his privilege, however, to delegate his authority to whomsoever he might select. In this case one of Micah's sons was at first appointed priest.

Later a young Levite from Bethlehem in Judah made a journey through the hill-country of Ephraim and visited the house of Micah. He was forthwith engaged for a stipulated sum to remain in the household of Micah and take charge of the family shrine. The story implies that already the Levites were regarded as especially eligible for this office (*cf.* further § XXXV^{IV}). The subsequent narrative indicates that his primary duty was to give a divine decision or oracle, whenever a question was presented. It is also probable that he acted as guardian of the sanctuary and attended to the details of the sacrifices at the annual feasts, although this function may still have been performed by Micah as head of the household.

III. **Report of the Danite Spies.** Originally the Danites appear to have settled to the southwest of Ephraim. Their territory was therefore constricted by the powerful tribe of Ephraim, pressing them from the east and north, and by the zone of Canaanite cities on the south and by the aggressive Philistines on the plain to the west. Always a comparatively small tribe, they were apparently unable to maintain their position and much less to win the new territory which their increasing numbers required. Accordingly they sent spies to discover a more favorable site. In passing by the sanctuary of Micah, these spies consulted the oracle, and proceeded on their journey assured of Jehovah's approval. Far in the North, at the foot of Mount Hermon, they found the Canaanite city of Laish. This city had been originally settled by Phœnician colonists, but was so far removed that it received no protection from the parent state. It, therefore, in every way satisfied the requirements of the Danites, and this fact was so reported by their spies.

IV. **The Plunder of Micah's Sanctuary.** As the Danite warriors set out to conquer the Canaanite city of Laish, one of the spies, without thought of gratitude, suggested that they plunder the sanctuary of Micah, where they had so recently consulted the oracle. The law of might was evidently the only standard recognized by these early warriors, even in dealing with their Israelite kinsmen. The images and the priest were carried away to the North in the face of the unavailing protest of Micah. Arriving at Laish, the city was suddenly attacked, its inhabitants put to death and the town itself burned. On the ruined site they built the famous city of Dan. There, under the shadow of Mount Hermon, amidst the rushing waters which come bubbling up from the roots of the mountain, surrounded by fertile fields and almost tropical vegetation, was reared the famous shrine, which Jeroboam I, after the division of the Hebrew empire, selected as one of his two royal sanctuaries. There were set up the images of Micah the Ephraimite. Jonathan the Levite, the grandson of Moses, was placed in charge, and there his descendants long continued to preside over this northern temple.

V. **Prevailing Ethical Standards and Religious Ideals.** The ethical standards in force during this transitional period of settlement may be inferred from these ancient stories. The murder of a heathen foe was evidently regarded as a virtue rather than a crime. Stealing, even from a member of another Hebrew tribe, was not condemned. The law of might still made right. The sanctity of the marriage relation, however, was carefully guarded. The story of the crime of the Gibeathites, found in the concluding chapters of the book of Judges, shows with what zeal the Hebrews punished the crimes of inhospitality and shameless adultery. A covenant, even with an alien people like the Gibeonites, was sacredly kept. A vow, which was a solemn agreement between an individual and Jehovah, was faithfully discharged even though, as in the story of Jephthah's daughter, it involved the crime of murder. The old primitive rites, the graven images and the crude paraphernalia of worship still survived; but Jehovah commanded the unquestioning loyalty of every true Israelite. Even though Micah the Ephraimite did not hesitate to steal silver from his own mother, he gladly reared a family shrine for Jehovah, and faithfully provided for the performance of the religious rites connected with it. Thus it is clear that the essence of Israel's religion during this period was loyalty to Jehovah—a loyalty which chiefly found expression, in accordance with the ancient decalogue, in forms and in ceremonies. The religion of life, and the duties of justice, mercy and love were to be first clearly proclaimed by the prophets of a later age.

§ XXXV. EXPERIENCES OF THE DIFFERENT TRIBES

Assemble and hear, O sons of Jacob,
And listen to Israel your father.

1. Exordium

Reuben thou art my first-born,
My strength and the first fruit of my manhood,
Pre-eminent in dignity and strength
Boiling over like water, thou shalt not be pre-eminent,
For thou wentest up to the bed of thy father,
Then thou defiledst my couch in going upon it.

2. Reuben, ruled by ungovernable passions

Simeon and Levi are akin,
Weapons of violence are their swords,
Into their council, O my soul, do not enter,
In their assembly, O my heart, do not join.
For men in their anger they slew,

3. Simeon and Levi, violent and treacherous

27

And oxen in their wantonness they hocked.
Accursed is their anger, that it is so fierce,
And their wrath because it is so cruel;
    I will divide them in Jacob
    And scatter them in Israel.

4. Judah, the ruling tribe, victorious and prosperous

Judah, thy brothers praise thee!
Thy hand is on the neck of thy enemies,
Before thee thy father's sons bow down.
Judah is a lion's whelp,
From the prey, my son, thou hast gone up.
He has crouched, he has lain down as a lion,
As an old lion, who will disturb him?
The sceptre shall not pass from Judah,
Nor the royal staff from between his feet,
Until that one comes to whom it belongs,
And him the people obey.
Binding his foal to the vine,
And his ass' colt to the choice vine,
He hath washed his garments in wine,
And his clothing in the blood of grapes;
His eyes are red with wine,
And his teeth are white with milk.

5. Benjamin, famous in war

Benjamin is a ravening wolf,
In the morning he devoureth prey,
And at evening divideth spoil.

6. Zebulon's favored situation

Zebulon, by the sea-shore he dwells:
He is by a shore that is lined with ships,
And his border extends to Sidon.

7. Issachar's ignominious submission

Issachar, he is a strong-limbed ass,
Crouching down between the sheepfolds;
And when he saw the resting-place was good,
That the land also was pleasant,
He bowed his shoulder to bear,
And became a slave under a taskmaster.

Dan is a serpent by the way,
A horned-adder beside the path,
That biteth the horse's heel,
So that his rider falleth backward.
I have waited for thy deliverance, O Jehovah!

8. Dan, inde-pen-dent, small, but quick to avenge

Gad, robber-bands press upon him,
But he also shall press upon their heel.

9. Gad, ex-posed but warlike

Asher, his bread is fatness,
And he yields royal dainties.

10. Ash-er, rich

Naphtali, he is a flourishing terebinth
That sends forth beautiful branches.

11. Naph-tali, flour-ishing

Joseph, he is a fruitful branch,
A fruitful branch by a spring,
His tendrils run over the wall.
They bitterly attack, they shoot at him,
The archers hatefully assail him,
But his bow remains ever bent,
His forearms also are supple,
Through the power of the mighty one of Jacob,
In the name of the Shepherd of Israel,
Even by the God of thy fathers, who ever helpeth thee,
And El-Shaddai [God Almighty], who blesseth thee,
With blessings of heaven above,
And of the great deep that coucheth beneath,
With blessings of the breast and womb,
With blessings of father and mother,
With blessings of the everlasting mountains,
With the gifts of the ancient hills!
They shall be on the head of Joseph,
On the head of the one consecrated among his brothers.

12. Jo-seph, valiant and pre-emi-nently pros-perous

I. The So=called Blessing of Jacob. The oldest surviving records of the experiences of the individual tribes during the period of settlement are found in the forty-ninth chapter of Genesis. These consist of ancient tribal songs, loosely joined together. They are appropriately put into the mouth of Jacob-Israel, the traditional father of the twelve tribes of Israel. The aged patriarch is represented as gathering his sons about his death-bed to warn them against their peculiar faults, to reprimand or commend them for their past acts and to predict the future which lay before them.

The literary form of these songs is crude, but the figures are strong and rugged. Their spirit is that of the primitive age from which they come. The Judah oracle contains detail references to the rise and victories of the house of David, and therefore in its final form comes from the days of the united Hebrew kingdom. Probably, like the oracles of Balaam, these ancient songs were collected and sung by some court poet in the reign of David or Solomon.

II. **The Tribe of Reuben.** As in the traditions of the North, Reuben is here regarded as the oldest child. This probably reflects the fact that Reuben was the first of the Hebrew tribes to gain a foothold in Palestine, east of the lower Jordan. Reference is made in the poem to the obscure event recorded in Genesis 35²². The allusion, which may be to an ignominious alliance with some native tribe, is intended to explain why the tribe of Reuben never played an important role among the other tribes of Israel. Apparently from the first its numbers were limited, and its position, with the Moabites on the south, the Ammonites on the east and the aggressive tribe of Gad on the north, gave it little opportunity for expansion. Peace could only be purchased by alliance, which appears in time to have meant practical absorption among the local peoples, so that Reuben early disappears from Hebrew history.

III. **History of the Tribes of Levi and Simeon.** The ancient song of Genesis 49 contributes additional information regarding the mysterious tribe of Levi. This song alludes to the early story of Dinah and Shechem found in Genesis 34. Obviously, that ancient tradition deals with experiences of tribes rather than with those of individuals. Shechem continued to be a strong Canaanite city almost to the close of the period of settlement. The fact that the tribes of Simeon and Levi are classified as the sons of Jacob's first wife, Leah, perhaps suggests that they penetrated into central Canaan before the other tribes. The narrative in Genesis 34 clearly indicates that at a very early period these tribes made a close alliance with the Canaanites at Shechem. In time, however, perhaps because of the religious zeal of the Levites, they repudiated this covenant and slew many of the people of Shechem. This act is regarded with horror both in the ancient song of Genesis 49 and in the prose narrative of Genesis 34. An overwhelming judgment was visited upon them by the outraged Canaanites. This early incident furnishes the most satisfactory explanation of the fact that these tribes were scattered and in later history have no definite place of abode.

IV. **The Peculiar Position of the Levites.** In time the sons of Levi appear as the guardians of the different sanctuaries throughout the land of Israel. Even down in the days of Josiah the terms *priest* and *son of Levi* are synonymous.

In the later Northern Israelite account of the making of the golden calf is found another comparatively early reference to the Levites. When Moses returned from the mount of revelation, and in the name of Jehovah condemned the idolatry of the people, the Levites alone of all the Israelites, ignoring the bonds of kinship, rose and slew their guilty fellow Israelites.

These different traditions present great difficulties, and yet suggest the early history of the Levites. The statement in the story of the Danites, that Jonathan, the Levite, was a descendant of Moses, confirms the testimony of the later traditions that Moses belonged to the tribe of Levi. Already in the days of Micah the Ephraimite, the Levites evidently enjoyed a certain prestige and were looked upon as the divinely chosen guardians of even the local family sanctuaries. The most natural explanation of this fact is that they were of the same clan as Israel's great prophetic leader. Their close connection with Moses best explains the fierce zeal which they showed in combatting apostasy and the alliances with the heathen Canaanites.

If the testimony of Genesis 34 has been rightly interpreted, this fierce religious zeal further explains, not only why they were scattered, but also why they were regarded from the first as especially fitted to take charge of Jehovah's oracles and sanctuaries.

In later times all priests in charge of local shrines were designated as sons of Levi. In many cases they were probably lineal descendants of the ancient tribe. In other cases the term *son of Levi* may have simply become a designation of a class, and therefore similar to such titles as *sons of the prophets* or *sons of the goldsmiths*. When in the days of Josiah the high places outside of Jerusalem were declared illegal and all religion was centralized at the temple of Solomon, the descendants of those who had ministered at the Jerusalem sanctuary were known as priests, and the ancient designation *sons of Levi* was limited to those connected with the older local shrines.

V. **The Tribes of the South.** In the ancient poem, Judah is recognized as the leading tribe of the South. The rise of the house of David and its victorious conquests are clearly portrayed. This oracle and those attributed to Balaam (§ XXIX) represent the beginning of that series of predictions which were intended to exalt the glories and achievements of Judah's reigning house. The type of agricultural prosperity peculiar to vine-clad Judah is also pictured in a variety of striking figures: wine and milk are so plentiful that they are used as freely as water.

The warlike clan of Benjamin is likened to a ravening wolf growling over its prey. The poet probably had in mind the valiant deeds of the Israelites under the leadership of the Benjamite Saul.

VI. The Northern Tribes. Originally the tribe of Zebulun appears to have dwelt west of the plain of Esdraelon, along the shore of the modern Bay of Haifa. Issachar, on the northeastern side of the plain of Esdraelon, along the valley of the Jordan, occupied one of the garden spots of Palestine. The ancient song states that, although the tribe was strong in numbers and resources, in order to retain its place during the earlier part of the period of the Judges it was obliged to submit to Canaanite bondage.

Little Dan, far to the north, away from the other tribes, open to attack, especially from the east, simply by its courage and warlike skill maintained its position against all intruders. The tribe of Gad, likewise on the borderland of Israel, was constantly exposed to the attack of wandering Arabs, as well as to encroachments of its Moabite foes immediately to the south.

The tribe of Asher, long intrenched in the land and probably containing a very large Canaanite element, enjoyed quiet and prosperity in its home to the northwest on the uplands east of Phœnicia. Naphtali, in its fertile territory west of the Jordan, is likened to one of the flourishing, sturdy terebinths, or oaks, which in ancient times imparted greenness and beauty to the Palestinian landscape.

VII. The Tribe of Joseph. The poem culminates in a description of the tribe of Joseph. No mention is made by name of the sub-tribes of Ephraim and Manasseh which Joseph represents. The fertility of their territory, bounded on the north by the plain of Esdraelon, on the east by the Jordan, and extending westward to the maritime plain, is described in luxuriant figures. (The strong tribe of Joseph is likened to a fruitful vine, whose roots are supplied with never-failing water, and whose tendrils run in every direction in rich profusion.) Attacks from Philistine foes on the west and Ammonite and other desert foes on the east are suggested; but, like a mighty warrior, this powerful tribe of central Israel, conscious of Jehovah's strength and guidance, is represented as defeating and repelling them all.) Upon the head of Joseph descends in superlative measure the richest gifts that Nature can bestow—indubitable evidences to the ancient mind of Jehovah's favor.)

§ XXXVI. THE GREAT VICTORY OVER THE CANAANITES

Now Deborah, a prophetess, the wife of Lappidoth, sent and summoned Barak the son of Abinoam from Kadesh Naphtali, and said to him, Doth not Jehovah, the God of Israel, command, 'Go and proceed to Mount Tabor, and take with thee ten thousand men of the Naphtalites and of the Zebulunites? And I will entice out to thee at the river Kishon, Sisera, with his chariots and his troops, and will deliver him into thy hand'. And Barak said to her, If you will go with me, I will go; but if you will not go with me, I will not go. And she said, I will certainly go with you; only you will not have the glory in this enterprise on which you are embarking; for Jehovah will sell Sisera into the power of a woman. So Deborah arose, and went with Barak to Kadesh. And Barak called Zebulun and Naphtali together at Kadesh; and ten thousand men followed after him.

1. Deborah's message to Barak

Now Heber the Kenite had separated himself from the Kenites, from the children of Hobab the father-in-law of Moses, and had pitched his tent as far away as the oak of Bezaananaim, which is by Kadesh.

2. Heber the Kenite

And they told Sisera that Barak the son of Abinoam had gone up to Mount Tabor. Then Sisera gathered together all his chariots, nine hundred chariots of iron, and all the people he had from Harosheth of the Gentiles, to the river Kishon. Thereupon Deborah said to Barak, Arise! for this is the day in which Jehovah hath delivered Sisera into your hand. Hath not Jehovah gone out before you? So Barak went down from Mount Tabor, with ten thousand men following him. Then Jehovah threw Sisera and all his chariots, and all his host into confusion at the onslaught of Barak's swordsmen, and Sisera dismounted from his chariot, and fled on foot. But Barak pursued the chariots and the host to Harosheth of the Gentiles; and all the host of Sisera was put to the sword; not a single man was left.

3. The battle and defeat of the Canaanites

4. Death of Sisera at the hands of Jael

But Sisera fled on foot to the tent of Jael the wife of Heber the Kenite; for there was peace between him and the house of Heber the Kenite. And Jael went out to meet Sisera, and said to him, Turn in, my lord, turn in to me; do not be afraid. So he turned aside to her and went into the tent, and she covered him with a rug. And he said to her, Give me, I pray, a little water to drink, for I am thirsty. So, opening the milk-skin, she gave him a drink, and covered him. Then he said to her, Stand in the door of the tent, and if any one comes and inquires of you, 'Is there any one here?' say, 'No.' But Jael, Heber's wife, took a tent-pin and took a hammer in her hand, and went stealthily to him and drove the pin into his temples, so that it went through into the ground; for he was fast asleep and weary; so he died. And just then Barak appeared in pursuit of Sisera. And Jael went out to meet him and said to him, Come, I will show you the man whom you are seeking. And he went in with her; and there Sisera lay dead, with the tent-pin in his temples.

5. Introduction to the triumphal ode

Then they sang this song on that day:

That the leaders took the lead in Israel,
That the people volunteered readily,
    Bless Jehovah!
    Hear, O kings,
    Give ear, O rulers.
I myself, yea, I will sing to Jehovah,
I will sing praise to Jehovah the God of Israel.

6. Jehovah's advent

Jehovah, when thou wentest forth from Seir,
When thou marchedst from the land of Edom,
The earth trembled violently;
The heavens also dripped,
Yea, the clouds dropped water;
The mountains quaked before Jehovah,
Yon Sinai, before Jehovah the God of Israel.

7. Conditions before the war

In the days of Shamgar, the son of Anath,
In the days of Jael, the highways were unused,
And travellers walked by round-about paths.

THE GREAT VICTORY OVER THE CANAANITES

The rulers ceased in Israel, they ceased,
    Until thou, Deborah, didst arise,
    Until thou didst arise a mother in Israel.
A shield was not seen in five cities,
Nor a spear among forty thousand.

My heart is with the commanders of Israel, 8. Present causes for thanksgiving
Who volunteered readily among the people;
    Bless Jehovah!
You who ride on tawny asses,
Who sit on rich saddle-cloths,
And you who walk by the way, proclaim it.
Far from the sound of the division of spoil,
In the places where water is drawn,
There let them rehearse the righteous acts of
    Jehovah,
Even the righteous acts of his rule in Israel.

Then the people of Jehovah went down to the gates 9. The rally about Deborah and Barak
[crying],
    'Arise, arise, Deborah,
    Arise, arise, strike up the song!
    Arise, Barak, be strong,
    Take thy captives, son of Abinoam!'
So a remnant went down against the powerful,
The people of Jehovah against the mighty:
From Ephraim they rushed into the valley,
Thy brother Benjamin among thy peoples;
From Machir went down commanders,
And from Zebulun those who carry the marshal's
    staff.
And the princes of Issachar were with Deborah;
And Naphtali was even so with Barak,
Into the valley they rushed forth at his back.

By the brooks of Reuben great were the resolves! 10. The cowards who remained at home
    Why didst thou sit amongst the sheepfolds,
    Listening to the pipings of the flocks?
By the brooks of Reuben there were great questionings!
    Gilead remained beyond Jordan;

And Dan, why does he stay by the ships as an alien?
Asher sits still by the shore of the sea,
    And remains by its landing places.

11. The battle by the Kishon

Zebulun was a people who exposed themselves to deadly peril,
And Naphtali on the heights of the open field.
    Kings came, they fought;
    They fought, the kings of Canaan,
    At Taanach by the waters of Megiddo;
    They took no booty of silver.
    From heaven fought the stars,
    From their courses fought against Sisera.
    The river Kishon swept them away,
    The ancient river, the river Kishon.
    O my soul, march on with strength!
    Then did the horse-hoofs resound
    With the galloping, galloping of their steeds.

12. The cowardly people of Meroz

    Curse Meroz, said the Messenger of Jehovah,
    Curse bitterly its inhabitants;
    For they came not to the help of Jehovah,
    To the help of Jehovah against the mighty.

13. Jael's brave act

    Blessed above women shall Jael be,
    That wife of Heber the Kenite,
    Blessed above all nomad women!
    Water he asked, milk she gave;
Curdled milk she brought him in a bowl fit for lords.
    She put her hand to the tent-pin,
    Even her right hand to the workman's hammer;
And she struck Sisera, she crushed his head,
    She shattered, she pierced his temple.
At her feet he bowed, he fell, he lay still,
    At her feet he bowed, he fell;
Where he bowed, there he fell a victim slain.

14. The anxiety in Sisera's palace

Through the window peered and loudly cried
The mother of Sisera, through the lattice;
' Why is his chariot so long in coming?

Why tarry the hoof-beats of his chariotry?'
The wisest of her ladies answered her,
Yea, she herself answered her question,
'Are they not indeed finding, dividing the spoil?
A woman or two for each of the warriors;
For Sisera a spoil of dyed stuffs,
A spoil of dyed stuffs embroidered,
A piece or two of embroidery for his neck?'

So shall all thine enemies perish, O Jehovah;   15.Epi-
But they who love him shall be as the sun, rising in   logue
its invincible splendor.

I. The Prose and Poetic Versions of the Story. The importance
of the event has led the early compiler of Judges to preserve not only the
prose account but also the ancient poem which commemorates the great
victory over the Canaanites. Instead of blending the two accounts he
has introduced them, the one after the other. The prose version evidently comes from the Northern Israelite history. With this version
has been combined another tradition of a great victory over the Canaanites led by Jabin, king of Hazor (*cf.* for a fuller version Josh. 11¹⁻¹⁵).

In certain details, the two accounts of the victory over Sisera differ,
as for example, concerning the tribes from which Deborah and Barak
came; but in general the prose story and the poem are in close agreement, and supplement each other at many points.

The poetic version is one of the oldest and noblest examples of early
Hebrew poetry. In vigor and vividness it is unsurpassed. Some of
its language is archaic, and the poem has suffered greatly in transmission;
but with the aid of later texts it can for the most part be restored. In a
series of vivid pictures it presents the different scenes in the great conflict. The reader is made at once an interested spectator of the succeeding events. He feels the importance of the great crisis; he sees the clans
rally about the tribal chieftains; he hears the shock of battle and the
pounding of the hoofs of the Canaanite chariot horses; with exultation
he follows the flight of the terror-stricken Canaanites. He burns with
indignation at the cowardice of the people of Meroz, and exults over the
bloody deed of Jael, the wife of Heber the Kenite. With mingled pity
and thanksgiving, he listens to the pathetic questions of Sisera's mother,
as she waits for the return of the Canaanite leader.

The later tradition embodied in the superscription attributed the poem to Deborah and Barak. The way in which they are addressed in the poem and the prominence given to their achievements imply that it was composed not by Deborah and Barak themselves but by some gifted contemporary. The emphasis given to the achievements of Deborah and Jael, and the interest in the feelings of the mother of Sisera, as she sits surrounded by her maidens, strongly suggest the feminine point of view. It is exceedingly probable that a song like this was sung by the women of Israel, as they went out to greet the conquering heroes. It is similar in general theme, spirit and setting to the song which the women of Israel sang at a later time, when Saul and David returned from a memorable victory over the Philistines (*cf.* § XLIII).

II. **The Historical Situation.** The song gives a glimpse of conditions in Canaan before the battle. In point of numbers and material strength the Canaanites surpassed the Hebrews. They were also in possession of the strategic points. The broad zone of Canaanite cities, which began with Bethshean on the east, and extended across the plain of Esdraelon to Megiddo and Dor on the west, completely separated the Hebrews of central Canaan from those in the north. All the important cities in the north still remained in the hands of the Canaanites. Only the intervening territory was held by the Israelites, who probably still followed their flocks and lived in tents or rude huts. Each family or clan lived apart by itself, meeting single-handed its peculiar dangers and problems. A few tribal sheiks, like Gideon, doubtless enjoyed a reputation which extended beyond the limits of their tribe. The Hebrews were weak, not so much because they were lacking in courage or skill in warfare, but because there was no strong leader or bond to unite them.

In the presence of a coalition of Canaanite cities, which had apparently been formed by Sisera because of the fear inspired by the rapidly increasing numbers and strength of the Hebrews, the latter seemed helpless. This was another of those great crises which characterize Israel's history. If these scattered Hebrew tribes had been subdued and assimilated by the Canaanites, the work of Moses would have been in vain. Even when the Hebrews conquered the Canaanites, they were able to resist only in part the seductive influences of the Canaanite civilization and religion. As serfs of the Canaanites, without unity or leadership, it is difficult to conceive how they could have maintained their loyalty to Jehovah.

III. **Deborah, the Prophetess.** The situation called for a leader with prophetic insight to rally the Hebrews and inspire them to united action. That leader the Hebrews found in Deborah, who is rightly called, in the later tradition, a prophetess. This tradition suggests that she already enjoyed a wide reputation. Like Samuel, the seer of Ramah, she appears to have been often consulted, as Jehovah's representative, on questions of personal and private import. Her title, *prophetess*, rests, however, on higher grounds. Like the prophets of earlier and later times, she appreciated the significance of the great crisis and saw clearly what the needs of the situation required. More than that, she knew how to act. Like Samuel at a later time, she did not herself take the sword, but found a man who already enjoyed the confidence of his people, and was fitted to lead them to victory. Together Barak, the northern chieftain, and Deborah, the prophetess, rallied the tribes of central Israel.

IV. **The Rally of the Tribes.** In certain ways the conditions that confronted Deborah were similar to those which the earlier prophet, Moses, found in the land of Egypt. The danger of being reduced to serfdom and the common need of deliverance were powerful bonds with which to bind the Hebrews together. Deborah, however, like Moses, appealed to a higher motive. The war cry which she sent forth by messengers throughout the land of Canaan, appears to have been, "Come up to the help of Jehovah against the mighty." This appeal suggested the great need. At the same time it appealed to the courage and warlike spirit of the bravest in Israel. It recalled the achievements of the past. Above all, it challenged them to prove by deed their loyalty to the God of their race. Before Canaan could become Jehovah's land, it must be conquered by his chosen people. Thus they were called to fight, not merely for their freedom and their homes, but for the glory of their God. With this challenge came the assurance that Jehovah would not fail them in this great crisis in their history, for the voice that called them was the voice of his prophetess, Deborah.

In response to this call, all the important tribes of central Canaan rallied about their tribal leaders. From the north came Barak, followed by the clansmen of Naphtali and Zebulun. With Deborah came the chieftains of Issachar. From the south came the tribesmen of Ephraim and Benjamin, and from across the Jordan, warriors from the powerful clan of Machir. Certain outlying tribes, like those of Reuben and Gilead, felt the call of duty, but preferred to remain beside their flocks. In the northwest the tribes of Dan and Asher, closely affiliated with their Phœnician neighbors, were intent only on their own selfish interests. It is also significant that the tribes of Judah, Simeon and Levi are not even mentioned. Apparently they were so far separated from the tribes of the north by the wall of Canaanite cities and by diversity of interests that they were not reckoned as a part of Israel.

V. The Battle. The Hebrews appear to have rallied near Mount Tabor. Thence they marched southward along the broad valley which leads to the plain of Esdraelon. The Canaanites evidently chose this wide, level plain as the battle-field, for there their chariots could readily manœuvre. Although they had all the advantages of superior military equipment and resources, they lacked what the Hebrews alone possessed: courage, faith and religious enthusiasm.

The description at the beginning of the poem of Jehovah's advent, riding on the storm clouds and heralded by the reverberating thunder, and the statement that the stars fought from heaven against Sisera indicate that, while the battle was in progress, a heavy storm swept across the plain. Ordinarily the Kishon is an insignificant, slow-flowing creek, but as the poem distinctly states, it suddenly became a raging torrent. A heavy fall of rain would quickly transform the alluvial soil of the plain into a muddy marsh making the manœuvres of the chariot practically impossible. With marvellous skill, the poet has brought out in the Hebrew the sound of the plunging of the horses' hoofs in the miry soil. To the minds of the Hebrews such a storm was clearest evidence that Jehovah was present and fighting for his people. In the hearts of the cowardly Canaanites it evidently struck dismay and terror. In mad flight they rushed into the muddy Kishon and were swept down toward the sea. The few who did escape would have been cut off, had the inhabitants of the Meroz been responsive to their opportunity and "come up to the help of Jehovah against the mighty."

VI. The Fate of Sisera. Sisera, the commander of the Canaanites, fled northward alone, and finally sought food and refuge in the tent of a certain Heber. This Heber belonged to a clan of the wandering Kenites from whence came Moses'· wife. These Kenite clans frequently figured in the history of the Hebrews during the wilderness and settlement periods. They appear to have moved northward with the Israelites, and were evidently in sympathy with them. With a courage which is rare, even among women brought up amidst the hardships of nomadic life, Jael, the wife of Heber, actively espoused the cause of the Hebrews. According to the ancient poem she brought, in response to Sisera's request for water, a bowl of curdled milk, and apparently when he was about to drink, she dealt him a fatal blow with the hammer which she held in her right hand. Thus was visited upon Sisera the most ignominious fate known to the ancient East—death at the hand of a woman.

The magnitude of the disaster is brought out in bold relief by the monologue on the lips of Sisera's mother. Instead of the victor laden with spoils, there came to her in time the knowledge of the overwhelming defeat that had overtaken her son, and the shame and ignominy of the conquered.

VII. **The Significance of the Victory.** Evidently the victory on the plain of Esdraelon gave to the Hebrews for the first time undisputed possession of central Canaan. It was the great decisive battle of Hebrew history. Henceforth the Canaanites ceased to be a barrier to the growth of the Hebrew nation. From this time on in the north the process of assimilating the older Canaanite population went on rapidly. From the Canaanites the Hebrews learned the arts of agriculture and civilization, and soon left far behind the rude habits of the wilderness. They also adopted the Canaanite sanctuaries and many of the rites and religious institutions which had grown up about these sacred places.

The victory over the Canaanites also demonstrated to the Hebrews the necessity and advantages of united action. In a later period of adversity they could not fail to recall that, when they had laid aside their tribal jealousies and fought shoulder to shoulder, they had proved invincible. The experience, therefore, pointed clearly to that united Hebrew kingdom, which later rose out of the midst of cruel foreign oppression. Above all, the Hebrews learned again the great lesson that in the time of their supreme need the God, who had led them forth from the land of Egypt, was still present to deliver. Thus it was that in the school of actual experience Israel's faith was developed.

§ XXXVII. REIGNS OF GIDEON AND HIS SON ABIMELECH

In time it came to pass that, when Israel had sown, the Midianites would come up, and leave no sustenance in Israel, neither sheep nor ox nor ass. For they would come up with their cattle and their tents. And Israel was greatly impoverished because of Midian.

1. The Midianite oppression

Then the Messenger of Jehovah came and sat down under the oak which was in Ophrah, that belonged to Joash the Abiezrite; and his son Gideon was beating out wheat in the wine-press, to hide it from the Midianites. And the Messenger of Jehovah appeared to him, and said to him, Jehovah

2. Gideon's call to repel the Midianites

is with you, valiant warrior! And Gideon said to him, O, my Lord, if Jehovah is with us, why then has all this befallen us? But now Jehovah hath cast us off and delivered us into the hand of Midian. Then Jehovah turned to him and said, Go in this might of thine and save Israel from the power of Midian; have I not sent thee? But he said to him, O, Lord, how shall I save Israel? Behold, my family is the poorest in Manasseh, and I am the most insignificant in my father's house. And Jehovah said to him, Surely I will be with thee, and thou shalt smite the Midianites as one man.

3. The divine sign Then he said to him, If now I have found favor in thy sight, then show me a sign that it is thou who art talking with me. Do not go from here, I pray, until I come to thee, and bring forth my present and lay it before thee. And he said, I will wait until thou comest back. So Gideon went in and prepared a kid, and unleavened cakes of about a bushel of flour; he put the flesh in a basket, and the broth in a pot, and brought out to him under the oak, and presented it. And the Messenger of God said to him, Take the flesh and the unleavened cakes, and lay them upon this rock, and pour out the broth. And he did so. Then the Messenger of Jehovah reached out the end of the staff which was in his hand, and touched the flesh and the unleavened cakes, and fire went up out of the rock and consumed the flesh and the unleavened cakes. Then the Messenger of Jehovah vanished from his sight. So Gideon saw that it had been the Messenger of Jehovah; and Gideon said, Alas, O Lord Jehovah! for I have seen the Messenger of Jehovah face to face! But Jehovah said to him, Peace be to thee; do not be afraid; thou shalt not die. Then Gideon built an altar there to Jehovah, and called it Jehovah-shalom [Jehovah is well-disposed]. Even to the present day it is still in Ophrah of the Abiezrites.

4. The rally And the Spirit of Jehovah came upon Gideon and he blew a trumpet, and Abiezer assembled under his leadership.

5. The refusal of Succoth and Penuel to furnish food And Gideon came to the Jordan, and passed over, he and the three hundred men who were with him, faint, yet pursuing. And he said to the men of Succoth, Give, I pray you, loaves of bread to the people who follow me; for they are faint and I am pursuing after Zebah and Zalmunna, the kings of Midian. But the princes of Succoth said, Are Zebah and Zalmunna already in your hand that we should give bread to your army? Then Gideon said, Therefore, when Jehovah hath delivered Zebah and Zalmunna into my hand, I will thresh your flesh with thorns of the wilderness and with briers. And he went up from there to Penuel, and made the same request of them; and the men of Penuel gave the same answer as the men of Succoth. Then he said also to the men of Penuel, When I come back victorious, I will break down this tower.

Now Zebah and Zalmunna were in Karkor, and their hosts with them, about fifteen thousand men. And Gideon went up by the caravan road east of Nobah and Jogbehah, and attacked the host, as it lay without fear of attack. And he divided the three hundred men into three companies and gave them empty jars with torches within the jars. And he said, Look at me and do as I do, and say, ' For Jehovah and Gideon.' So Gideon and the hundred men with him came to the camp in the beginning of the middle watch, when it had just been set, and broke in pieces the jars in their hands. And the three companies broke their jars, and took the torches in their left hands and their swords in their right and cried, For Jehovah and Gideon. And the entire host awakened and they sounded the alarm and fled.

Zebah and Zalmunna also fled; but he pursued them and captured the two kings of Midian, Zebah and Zalmunna, and threw all the host into a panic.

Then Gideon the son of Joash returned from the battle from the ascent of Heres. And he captured a young man of the men of Succoth, and inquired of him, and the young man gave him a list of the princes of Succoth, and its elders, seventy-seven men. And when he came to the men of Succoth, he said, Behold Zebah and Zalmunna concerning whom you taunted me, saying, 'Are Zebah and Zalmunna already in your power that we should give bread to your men who are weary?' Then he took the elders of the city, and thorns of the wilderness and briers, and he threshed the men of Succoth upon them. He also broke down the tower of Penuel, and slew the men of the city.

6 Gideon's strategy

7. His capture of the chiefs

8. His punishment of Succoth and Penuel

**9.
Blood-
ven-
geance
upon
the
Midian-
ite
chiefs**

Then said he to Zebah and Zalmunna, What kind of men were they whom you slew at Tabor? And they answered, As you are, so were they; each one resembled the children of a king. And he said, They were my brothers, the sons of my mother. As Jehovah liveth, if you had saved them alive, I would not slay you now. Then he said to Jether his first-born, Up and slay them. But the youth did not draw his sword, because he was afraid, since he was yet a youth. Then Zebah and Zalmunna said, Rise yourself and fall upon us; for a man has a man's strength. So Gideon arose and slew Zebah and Zalmunna, and took the crescents that were on their camels' necks.

**10.
Offer of
the
king-
ship to
Gideon**

Then the men of Israel said to Gideon, Rule over us, both you and your son, and your son's son also; for you have saved us from the hand of Midian. But Gideon said to them, I will not rule over you, neither shall my son rule over you; Jehovah shall rule over you.

**11.Ori-
gin of
the idol
in Gid-
eon's
capital,
Ophrah**

And Gideon said to [the Abiezrites], I will make a request of you, that you give me every man the ear-rings from his spoil. (For they had golden ear-rings because they were Ishmaelites). And they answered, We will willingly give them. So they spread a garment, and each man cast into it the ear-rings from his spoil. And the weight of the golden ear-rings for which he had asked was seventeen hundred shekels of gold; besides the crescents, and the pendants, and the purple raiment that was on the kings of Midian, and besides the chains which were about their camels' necks. And Gideon made it into an ephod, and put it in his city Ophrah.

**12.
Reign
and
family
of
Gideon**

And Gideon had seventy sons, for he had many wives. And his concubine, who was in Shechem, also bore him a son, and he called his name Abimelech. And Gideon, the son of Joash, died in a good old age, and was buried in the sepulchre of Joash, his father, in Ophrah of the Abiezrites.

**13.
Abim-
elech's
as-
sump-
tion of
the
king-
ship**

And Abimelech the son of Jerubbaal went to Shechem to his mother's kinsmen, and spoke to them, and to all the clan of the house of his mother's father, saying, Put this question to all the citizens of Shechem, 'Which is better for you, that seventy persons should rule over you—all sons of Jerubbaal—or that one should rule over you?'

Remember too that I am your bone and flesh. So his mother's kinsmen spoke all these words concerning him in the hearing of all the men of Shechem; and they were inclined to follow Abimelech; for they said, He is our kinsman. And they gave him seventy shekels of silver from the house of Baal-berith, with which Abimelech hired worthless and reckless fellows, who followed him. And he went to his father's house at Ophrah, and slew his brothers, the sons of Jerubbaal, seventy men on one stone; but Jotham the youngest son of Jerubbaal was left; for he hid himself....

And Gaal the son of Ebed came with his kinsmen and went over to Shechem; and the men of Shechem put confidence in him. They then held festival, and went into the house of their god, and ate and drank, and cursed Abimelech. And Gaal the son of Ebed said, Who is Abimelech, and who are the Shechemites that we should serve him? Is not he the son of Jerubbaal? and is not Zebul his officer? Be subject to the people of Hamor, the father of Shechem; for why should we be subject to him? Would that this people were under my authority! then would I remove Abimelech. And he said to Abimelech, Increase your army and come out. **14. Rebellion of the Shechemites**

And when Zebul the governor of the city heard the words of Gaal the son of Ebed, his anger was aroused. And he sent messengers to Abimelech at Arumah, saying, Behold, Gaal the son of Ebed and his kinsmen have come to Shechem, and now they are stirring the city to revolt against you. Now therefore, arise by night, you and the people who are with you, and lie in wait in the fields; and in the morning as soon as the sun is up, rise early and rush upon the city; and, behold, when he and the people who are with him come out against you, you can do to him as opportunity offers. **15 Zebul's warning and advice to Abimelech**

So they laid wait against Shechem in four companies. And when Gaal the son of Ebed went out and stood in the entrance of the gate of the city, Abimelech rose up with the people who were with him, from the place of ambush. Then, when Gaal saw the people, he said to Zebul, Behold, people are coming down from the tops of the mountains. But Zebul said to him, It is the shadow of the mountains that you see as if they were men. But Gaal said again, **16. Abimelech's attack and defeat of the rebels**

See there are people coming down from beside the hill, and one company is coming by the way of the Diviner's Tree. Then Zebul said to him, Where is now the boast which you made, 'Who is Abimelech that we should serve him?' is not this the people whom you despised? Go out now, I pray, and fight with them. Then Gaal went out before the men of Shechem, and fought with Abimelech. And Abimelech pursued him, and he fled before him, and there fell many wounded, even to the entrance of the gate. But Abimelech continued to live at Arumah, while Zebul drove out Gaal and his kinsmen, that they should not dwell in Shechem.

17. Abimelech's ignominious death

Then Abimelech went to Thebez, and encamped against Thebez and captured it. But there was a strong tower within the city, and thither all the men and women fled, and all the people of the city, and shut themselves in and went up to the roof of the tower. And Abimelech came to the tower, and fought against it, and was drawing near to the door of the tower to burn it with fire, when a certain woman threw an upper mill-stone on Abimelech's head, and crushed his skull. Then he called quickly to the young man, his armorbearer, and said to him, Draw your sword and kill me, that men may not say of me, A woman killed him. So his young man ran him through and he died. And when the men of Israel saw that Abimelech was dead, they departed every man to his home.

18. Moral of the story

Thus God brought home to Abimelech the crime which he committed against his father, in slaying his seventy brothers.

I. The Two Accounts. The evidence that there are two parallel accounts of the founding of Gideon's kingdom has long been recognized by biblical scholars. In the one version Gideon is a religious reformer rather than a warrior. He is represented as first destroying the altar of Baal and then as rallying several of the tribes against the Midianites. The three hundred men who ultimately follow him are the eager warriors, who in their zeal stop only to lap up the water with their hands, as they rush out in pursuit of the enemy.

In what is evidently the older version, the immediate cause of the pursuit was the slaying of Gideon's brothers by the Midianites. The motive which impelled him, therefore, was the most sacred obligation in early

46

Semitic life, the law of blood-revenge. Already he was a famous warrior, and the three hundred who followed him were the members of his own clan of Abiezer.

Two distinct and yet complete accounts of the reign of Abimelech are also found in the ninth chapter of Judges. In general these two versions are in agreement, but in details there are wide variations. The one clearly comes from Northern Israel and the other from Southern Israel. Of these two, the Judean as usual, is evidently the older and more historical, although together they give a very definite and reliable account of these important events of the reign.

II. **The Historical Situation.** Evidently the Hebrews are already masters of central Canaan. Deborah and Barak, however, have passed away, and there is no organized government binding the different tribes together. The result is that the Hebrews are an easy prey to the attacks of different marauding tribes that come in from the desert. Like the inhabitants of the outlying districts of Palestine to-day, the different villages and clans submit to robbery, and doubtless pay tribute rather than resort to the sword in protecting their rights. Above all, they lack a determined leader to take the initiative in repelling the robber attacks.

The Midianites figure in early Hebrew history as wandering tribes, living to the southeast and east of Palestine. Possibly the attacking tribe had followed in the wake of the Hebrew advance from the east-Jordan. They approached from the point where the plain of Jezreel runs down to the Jordan, and closely connects central Canaan with the headlands of Moab and the desert beyond. Their systematic attack had continued for some years; but there would have been no effective resistance had not a certain Midianite band killed the brothers of Gideon.

III. **Gideon's Call.** The solemn obligation of blood-revenge was clearly the chief motive which influenced Gideon to rally his clansmen and attack the Midianites. The early Judean narrative adds, what is doubtless true, that he was also inspired by patriotic and religious zeal. The earliest account of his call is exceedingly graphic. As in the stories of Abraham, a divine Messenger, subsequently identified with Jehovah himself, commands him as a valiant warrior to go forth and save Israel from the power of Midian. Like Abraham of old, he also prepares a meal for the divine guest. The Messenger, however, does not taste the food but touches it with the end of his staff so that it is consumed by fire. The incident is exceedingly instructive, for it vividly illustrates the primitive idea of sacrifice. The food which Gideon provides is that which he would set before any guest, whether human or divine. Even so in later times, the Hebrews brought the best products of the field and flock, and at the annual festivals set them before Jehovah as a sacred meal. Part they ate themselves, and the part intended especially for Jehovah they burned with fire. Thus, according to their thought, they renewed their covenant, as they ate the sacrificial meal, sharing it with their divine guest. The older belief that at times the god or gods came down in bodily form and ate the food which was set before them, was crude and childlike; but the deeper conviction that Jehovah was ever present in the joyful, as well as the solemn experiences of life, anticipates the profoundest doctrine of modern philosophy. Later Judaism lost sight of this belief in the immediate presence of God. Jesus, standing on the high vantage ground attained by the earlier prophets, restored it to the race.

Back of the early story of Gideon's call lies the fact that, like all the great leaders of Israel's history, he was raised up not by chance but in accordance with the divine purpose to do a great work for his people. Again the need found the man, and under the influence of the divine spirit he undertook the important task intrusted to him.

IV. The Pursuit of the Midianites. Gideon's native city, Ophrah, appears to have been situated eight or ten miles northeast of Shechem, at the head of the modern Wadi Farah, the chief western confluent of the Jordan. Along this valley, which leads directly to the Jordan, Gideon led his three hundred clansmen. Across the Jordan the two Israelite towns of Succoth and Penuel, beside the Jabbok, refused to give bread to Gideon and his followers. The reason for their refusal was evidently because they feared the Midianites, to whom they doubtless paid an annual tribute that they might enjoy immunity from attack. Vowing vengeance, Gideon pressed on in hot pursuit and overtook the Midianites, encamped at night beside the caravan route, out on the borders of the desert.

V. Gideon's Vengeance Upon His Foes. Two accounts of the method of attack have evidently been closely blended. In the older account Gideon employed a very effective strategy. The attack was made at midnight when the Midianites, after their long journey, were wrapped in deep sleep. Doubtless the fear of blood-revenge had hastened their flight and increased their weariness. Dividing his followers into three companies, he provided all his men with empty jars in which were placed lighted torches. In their right hands they carried swords ready for the attack. At the given signal the war cry, "For Jehovah and Gideon," was raised, and the jars were suddenly broken, revealing to the awakening Midianites what seemed to them to be a vast host. Terror seized these cowardly desert robbers, and they were soon in flight, pursued by the Hebrew warriors. The two Midianite chieftains were brought back captive by Gideon. He first executed his threat of vengeance upon the inhospitable towns of Succoth and Penuel, and then discharged the obligation imposed by the law of blood-revenge, slaying with his own hand these robber foes who had killed his brothers.

VI. Gideon's Sanctuary and Rule. Gideon's valiant act revealed a strong and able deliverer. His rigorous treatment of his foes demonstrated his ability to rule in an age when might largely made right. Accordingly he was asked by his own tribesmen, not only to rule over them, but also to transmit his authority to his descendants. This simple request and Gideon's compliance mark the all important transition from the ephemeral rule of local tribesmen and deliverers to the kingship and a permanent central authority.

To establish his rule, Gideon caused an ephod to be made from the spoils of gold and silver captured from the Midianites. This image was set up in his capital Ophrah. Like the later temple of Solomon at Jerusalem, the royal shrine thus established undoubtedly strengthened the authority of the new dynasty. Gideon also made many marriages with the daughters of the neighboring sheiks. Among these was a certain Canaanite woman from the town of Shechem. Thus it would seem that by the prestige of his sword and by intermarriage he extended his authority and built up a little kingdom in the heart of central Israel.

VII. Abimelech's Conspiracy. Gideon's kingdom, like that of David, suffered from the baneful effects of polygamy. At the death of his father, Abimelech, the worst of Gideon's seventy sons, slew his brothers, and, with the aid of the Shechemites, succeeded to the kingship. From this early narrative it is clear that Hebrews and Canaanites lived together side by side in this ancient city. Apparently the worshippers of Jehovah and of the local Canaanite Baal had so far affiliated that they also worshipped in the same sanctaury, which bore the significant name, *Baal of the Covenant.* Abimelech himself was a product of that process of assimilation which continued for the next century or two, until the old Canaanite population was completely absorbed. His attitude toward his subjects appears to have been that of the Canaanite tyrants, who reigned over the petty states of Palestine, and treated their subjects as slaves, rather than of the Israelites, who regarded their king as little more than a tribal sheik and demanded that he should faithfully serve and represent them. Abimelech's policy soon begat rebellion even in the friendly city of Shechem. This rebellion he put down with a cruelty which reveals the weakness of his character. At best his authority appears to have been only partially established; and his reign was characterized by a series of rebellions.

VIII. **The End of the First Hebrew Kingdom.** At last, in besieging the town of Thebez, a few miles northwest of Ophrah, Abimelech was struck by a stone thrown by a woman and mortally wounded. Thus like Sisera, the earlier oppressor of the Hebrews, Abimelech suffered the most ignominious fate known to the ancient world. Upon his own guilty head was visited the consequences of his early crimes. At his death no attempt appears to have been made to perpetuate the rule of his house. Through the inefficiency and brutal cruelty of this half-Israelite ruler, the first attempt of the Hebrews to establish a kingdom proved a sad failure. Without doubt this unfortunate example confirmed them still further in their distrust and dislike of all established authority. It illustrates, however, the problems and tendencies of the times. When at last conditions were ripe and a worthy leader was found, a permanent Hebrew kingdom was destined to rise.

§ XXXVIII. JEPHTHAH'S VICTORY OVER THE AMMONITES

1. Jephthah's early history

Now Jephthah the Gileadite was a very valiant warrior; and he was the son of a harlot; and when his father's sons by another wife grew up, they drove Jephthah out, and said to him, You shall have no inheritance in our father's house, for you are the son of another woman. So Jephthah fled from his brothers and dwelt in the land of Tob; and there gathered worthless fellows about him, and they used to go out on forays with him.

2. Request of his Gileadite clansmen

And after a time the Ammonites made war against Israel. And when the Ammonites made war against Israel, the elders of Gilead went to bring Jephthah out of the land of Tob, and they said to Jephthah, Come be our chief, that we may fight against the Ammonites. But Jephthah said to the elders of Gilead, are you not the men who hated me and drove me out of my father's house? Why then do you come to me now when you are in distress? And the elders of Gilead said to Jephthah, This is why we now turn to you, that you may go with us and fight against the Ammonites; and you shall be our chief, even over all the inhabitants of Gilead.

50

JEPHTHAH'S VICTORY OVER THE AMMONITES

Then Jephthah said to the elders of Gilead, If you bring me back to fight against the Ammonites, and Jehovah gives them over to me, shall I be your chief? And the elders of Gilead said to Jephthah, Jehovah shall be a witness between us; we swear to do just as you say. Then Jephthah went with the elders of Gilead, and the people made him head and chief over them. *3. His terms*

Then the spirit of Jehovah came upon Jephthah, and he passed over to Gilead and Manasseh. And the Ammonites were gathered together and encamped in Gilead. And Jephthah made a vow to Jehovah, and said, If thou wilt deliver the Ammonites wholly into my hand, then whoever comes from the doors of my house to meet me, when I return victorious from the Ammonites, shall be Jehovah's, and I will offer that one as a burnt-offering. *4. His vow*

So Jephthah went over to the Ammonites to fight against them; and Jehovah delivered them into his hand. *5. His victory*

And when Jephthah came home to Mizpah his daughter was just coming out to meet him with tambourines and dances; and she was his only child; beside her he had neither son nor daughter. And when he saw her he rent his garments and said, O my daughter! you have stricken me to earth: Yea, you are the cause of my woe! for, as for me, I have made a solemn promise to Jehovah, and cannot go back. And she said to him, My father, you have made a solemn promise to Jehovah; do to me what you have solemnly promised, inasmuch as Jehovah hath taken vengeance for you on your enemies, the Ammonites. *6. His return*

And she said to her father, Let this privilege be granted me: spare me two months, that I may depart, and go out upon the mountains, and lament together with my companions, because of my maidenhood. And he said, Go. So he sent her away for two months and she departed together with her companions, and lamented on the mountains because of her maidenhood. And at the end of two months she returned to her father, who did to her as he had vowed to do, she never having known a man. Thus it became a custom in Israel: yearly the daughters of Israel go four days in the year, to bewail the death of the daughter of Jephthah the Gileadite. *7. Fulfilment of his vow*

51

8. Attack and defeat of the Ephraimites

And the men of Ephraim assembled, and crossed to Zaphon; and they said to Jephthah, Why did you pass over to fight against the Ammonites, and did not call us to go with you? We will burn your house over your head. But Jephthah said to them, I and my people were parties to a great contest with the Ammonites, and when I called you, you did not deliver me from their power. So when I saw that you were not going to help me, I took my life in my hand, and passed over against the Ammonites, and Jehovah delivered them into my hand. Why then have you come up against me to-day, to make war on me? Then Jephthah gathered together all the men of Gilead, and fought with Ephraim; and the men of Gilead smote Ephraim.

9 The test and fate of the fugitives

And the Gileadites seized the fords of the Jordan to intercept the Ephraimites. And when any of the fugitives of Ephraim would say, Let me cross, the men of Gilead would say to him, Are you an Ephraimite? If he said, No, they would command him, Then say, 'shibboleth.' And if he said 'sibboleth,' and did not pronounce it exactly right, then they would lay hold on him, and slay him at the fords of the Jordan.

I. The Rôle of the East=Jordan Tribes. The deep valley of the Jordan cut off the Eastern tribes so completely that, until the days of Saul and David, these different branches of the Hebrew race had little in common. After the initial stages of the conquest, the tribes of Gad, Reuben and the half tribe of Manasseh settled down to work out independently their individual problems. On the west they were protected by natural barriers and by their kinsmen in Canaan; but from the east came the constant pressure of invasion. Throughout most of their history the Hebrews found a strong and aggressive foe in the Ammonites. The rich territory of Gilead east of the middle Jordan was also an attractive goal to the peoples living further east on the borders of the desert. Ordinarily the advance was gradual; but sometimes the invaders united in a general attack.

II. Jephthah, the Gileadite. The story of Jephthah sheds for a brief period clear light upon the condition of these Gileadite tribes. Driven from his home as a youth by his kinsmen, he had gathered about him a sturdy band of outlaws. Disorganized conditions and the almost constant state of warfare between the different tribes enabled him to subsist by means of frequent forays. His prestige became in time so great that the elders of Gilead, threatened by a determined Ammonite attack, in desperation recalled Jephthah. If successful, they promised to recognize him henceforth as their chief.

III. **Jephthah's Vow and its Consequences.** Rough warrior that he was, Jephthah was nevertheless a worshipper of Jehovah. On the eve of battle he made a solemn compact with Jehovah that, if he returned victorious, he would offer as a burnt-offering the first one who came to meet him. Later, under somewhat the same conditions, Saul made a similar vow (§ XLII).

The vow is characteristic of the early Semitic religions, and the supreme gift that a man could offer to the Deity was the life of a human being. The story of Abraham's sacrifice of Isaac reflects the same popular belief and the protest of later and more enlightened prophets (*cf.* § X¹). The significant fact is that the ancient narrator makes no protest against Jephthah's vow or its execution. He simply brings out, with dramatic vividness, the pathos of the scene, as the conqueror returns, flushed with victory, to be met by his daughter, his only child. In the thought of the early age, the calamity was the greater, because her untimely death deprived Jephthah of all hope of descendants. The solemn lamentation, observed each year by the east-Jordan maidens in memory of the event, undoubtedly kept alive the tradition of Jephthah's victories until it passed into the keeping of the early prophetic historians.

IV. **Hostility between the East and West=Jordan Tribes.** The story of Jephthah is significant, for it tells of the founding of a petty Hebrew kingdom east of the Jordan. The sequel to the account of Jephthah's victory reveals, however, the jealousy and frequent wars that were waged during this period of settlements between even the Hebrew tribes themselves. The powerful central tribe of Ephraim was evidently envious of the victory and authority of Jephthah. This envy developed into a constant state of hostility. The fords of the Jordan were the scene of many petty conflicts. Any Ephraimite captured east of the Jordan was in danger of losing his life. The inability of a stranger to pronounce correctly the test word *shibboleth*, and thus prove that he was not an Ephraimite has given to literature one of its most familiar figures.

V. **The Character of the Local Deliverers.** Jephthah well illustrates the real nature of the local deliverers, whose brave deeds are the chief events of this period of settlement and conquest. Their standards are those of the rude age in which they lived. Self interest and tribal loyalty are the chief motives which actuate them. They are local chieftains, possessed of unusual courage or daring, whom the needs of the hour call to positions of conspicuous leadership. Their authority is but local and transient. In addition to the five or six whose exploits have been recorded by tradition, there were probably many others of lesser fame. The names of certain of these local heroes and deliverers have been preserved by the compiler of the book of Judges. To this list belong Ibzan of Bethlehem, Elon the Zebulunite and Abdon the Pirathonite. Although their deeds were often cruel and their interests selfish and local, each of these deliverers was loyal to the God of his race and clearly regarded himself as the agent of the Deity in carrying on the wars of deliverance. While their faith was narrow, it was intense, as is shown by Jephthah's sacrifice even of his only child. Later experiences and later prophets were needed to broaden the religion of Israel, until, with its splendid spirit of devotion, it should become a commanding force in the life of humanity.

§ XXXIX. SAMSON'S BIRTH AND MARRIAGE

1. The announcement of Samson's birth

Now there was a certain man of Zorah, of the clan of the Danites, whose name was Manoah; and his wife was barren, and had not borne children. And the Messenger of Jehovah appeared to the woman, and said to her, Behold, thou hast been barren and not borne children, Now therefore, take heed, I pray, and drink no wine or intoxicating drink, and do not eat anything unclean; for thou art already with child, and wilt bear a son. And no razor shall be used upon his head; for the child shall be a Nazirite unto God from his birth to the day of his death.

2. Birth and childhood

And the woman bore a son, and called his name Samson; and the child grew, and Jehovah blessed him. And the spirit of Jehovah began to move him in Mahaneh-Dan, between Zorah and Eshtaol.

3. His desire to wed a woman of Timnah

Now Samson went down to Timnah, and saw in Timnah a woman of the daughters of the Philistines. When he came up, he told his father and mother, and said, I have seen a woman in Timnah a daughter of the Philistines; now therefore get her for me for a wife. Then his father and his mother said to him, Is there no woman among the daughters of your kinsmen, or among all my people, that you must go and take a wife among the uncircumcised Philistines? But Samson said to his father, Get her for me; for she pleases me. His father and mother, however, did not know that it was of Jehovah; for he was seeking an opportunity against the Philistines.

Then Samson went down to Timnah. And just as he came to the vineyards of Timnah, a young lion roared against him. And the spirit of Jehovah rushed upon him, and he tore the beast asunder as one tears a kid; and he had nothing in his hands. Then he went down and talked with the woman, and she pleased Samson. And when he returned after a while to get her, he turned aside to see the carcass of the lion; and, behold, there was a swarm of bees in the body of the lion, and honey. And he scraped it out into his hands, and went on, eating as he went; and he came to his father and mother, and gave to them, and they ate, but he did not tell them that he had taken the honey out of the body of the lion. *4. His second visit to Timnah*

And Samson went down to the woman, and gave a feast there (for so bridegrooms used to do). And it came to pass, when they saw him, that they took thirty companions and they were with him. And Samson said to them, Let me now propose to you a riddle; if you can give me the correct answer within the seven days of the feast, then I will give you thirty fine linen wrappers and thirty festal garments; but if you cannot give me the answer, then you shall give me thirty fine linen wrappers and thirty festal garments. And they said to him, Put forth your riddle, that we may hear it. And he said to them, *5. His riddle at his wedding feast*

Out of the eater came something to eat,
And out of the strong came something sweet.

But for six days they could not solve the riddle.

Then on the seventh day they said to Samson's wife, Beguile your husband, that he may explain the riddle to us, lest we burn you and your father's house with fire. Did you invite us to impoverish us? And Samson's wife wept continually before him, and said, You do not love me, you *6. Intrigues to find the answer* only hate me; you have given a riddle to my fellow-country-men and have not told it to me. And he said to her, Behold, I have not told it to my father or my mother, and shall I tell you? And she wept before him the seven days, while their feast lasted. And it came to pass on the seventh day that he told her, because she importuned him; and she told the riddle to her fellow-countrymen. Then the men of the city said to him on the seventh day before the sun went down, What is sweeter than honey? and what is stronger than a lion? And he said to them,

> If with my heifer you did not plow,
> You had not solved my riddle now.

7. His payment of the forfeit

Then the spirit of Jehovah rushed upon him, and he went down to Ashkelon, and killed thirty of their men, and took their spoil and gave the festal garments to those who had expounded the riddle. But he was very angry, and went up to his father's house. And Samson's bride was given to his companion, who had been his friend.

8. His destruction of the Philistine's grain-fields

Now it came to pass after a while, in the time of wheat harvest, that Samson went to visit his wife with a kid; and he said, Let me go into the inner apartment to my wife. But her father would not allow him to go in. And her father said, I thought that you must surely hate her, so I gave her to your friend. Is not her younger sister more beautiful than she? Take her then, instead. But Samson said to him, This time I shall not be to blame, if I do the Philistines an injury. So Samson went and caught three hundred foxes, and took torches, and turned tail to tail, and put a torch between every pair of tails. And when he had set the torches on fire, he let them go into the standing grain of the Philistines, and burned up both the shocks and the standing grain, with the olive yards besides.

9. His vengeance for the death of his wife

Then the Philistines said, Who has done this? And they said, Samson, the son-in-law of the Timnite, because he took his wife and gave her to his friend. And the Philistines went up, and burnt her and her father with fire. Then Samson said to them, If this is the way you do, I swear that I will not stop until I have had my revenge. So he smote them hip and thigh with a great slaughter; and he went down and dwelt in the cleft of the Cliff of Etam.

Then the Philistines went up and encamped in Judah, and spread themselves abroad in Lehi. And the Judahites said, Why have you come up against us? And they said, We have come up to bind Samson, to do to him as he has done to us. Then three thousand men of Judah went down to the cleft of the Cliff of Etam, and said to Samson, Do you not know that the Philistines are our rulers? What then is this that you have done to us? And he said to them, As they did to me, so have I done to them. And they said to him, We have come down to bind you, that we may deliver you into the hand of the Philistines. And Samson said to them, Swear to me, that you will not fall upon me yourselves. And they said to him, No; we will simply bind you securely, and deliver you into their hand; but we will not kill you. And they bound him with two new ropes, and brought him up from the Cliff. *10. His delivery to the Philistines*

When he came to Lehi, the Philistines shouted as they met him. Then the spirit of Jehovah rushed upon him, and the ropes that were on his arms became like flax that has been burned in the fire, and his bonds melted from off his hands. And he found a fresh jawbone of an ass, and reached out his hand and, grasping it, he killed a thousand men with it. Then Samson said, *11. His escape and slaughter of the Philistines*

> With the jawbone of an ass have I piled them, mass upon mass,
> A thousand men have I slain with the jawbone of an ass.

And when he had finished saying this, he threw away the jawbone from his hand; therefore that place was called Ramath-lehi [Throwing of the jawbone].

And he was very thirsty and called on Jehovah, and said, Thou hast given this great deliverance through thy servant, and now I shall die of thirst, and fall into the hands of the uncircumcised? Then God cleft the Mortar which is in Lehi, and water flowed from it; and when he drank, his spirits rose and he revived; therefore its name was called En-hakkore [Spring of the caller], which is in Lehi to this day. *12. Origin of the famous spring at Lehi*

57

13 Samson's escape from Gaza

Now Samson went to Gaza, and saw there a harlot, and went in unto her. When the Gazites were told that Samson was there, they set spies to lie in wait for him all night at the gate of the city, and they were quiet all the night, saying, When morning dawns, then we will kill him. And Samson lay until midnight, and at midnight he arose, and took hold of the doors of the gate of the city, and the two posts, and pulled them up, bar and all, and put them on his shoulders and carried them up to the top of the mountain which is before Hebron.

14. Delilah's attempts to betray Samson by bowstrings

Then afterward he fell in love with a woman in the valley of Sorek, whose name was Delilah. And the tyrants of the Philistines came to her and said to her, Beguile him and see why his strength is so great, and how we may overcome him, that we may bind him to torment him, and we will each one of us give you eleven hundred shekels of silver. So Delilah said to Samson, Tell me, I pray, why your strength is so great, and how you might be bound to torment you. And Samson said to her, If they should bind me with seven green bowstrings, which were never dried, then I would become weak, and be like any other man. Then the tyrants of the Philistines brought her seven green bowstrings, which had not been dried, and she bound him with them. Now she had men waiting in concealment in the inner apartment. And she said to him, The Philistines are upon you, Samson. But he snapped the bowstrings as a string of tow is snapped when it comes near the fire. So the source of his strength was not known.

15. By the new ropes

Then Delilah said to Samson, Behold, you have deceived me and told me lies; now tell me, I pray, with what you can be bound. And he said to her, If they should bind me securely with new ropes, which had never been used, then I should become weak, and be like any other man. So Delilah took new ropes, and bound him with them, and said to him, The Philistines are upon you, Samson. And the men were waiting in concealment in the inner apartment. But he snapped them from off his arms like thread.

16. By weaving his locks in a loom

And Delilah said to Samson, Hitherto you have deceived me, and told me lies; tell me with what you can be bound. And he said to her, If you should weave the seven braids of my head with the web, and fasten it with the pin, I would become weak and be like any other man. So while he was asleep, she took the seven braids of his hair and wove it with the web, and fastened it with the pin, and said to him, The Philistines are upon you Samson. And he awoke out of his sleep, and pulled up the beam and the web.

Then she said to him, How can you say, I love you, when you do not confide in me? you have deceived me these three times, and have not told me the secret of your great strength. And it came to pass when she importuned him daily, and urged him, that he was vexed to death. And he confided in her, and said to her, A razor has never come upon my head; for I have been a Nazirite to God from my mother's womb. If I should be shaved, then my strength would go from me, and I would become weak, and be like any other man. *17. His disclosure of his secret*

And when Delilah saw that he had told her all his heart, she sent and called for the tyrants of the Philistines, saying, Come up this once, for he has told me all his heart. Then the tyrants of the Philistines came up to her, and brought the money in their hands. And she put him to sleep upon her knees. Then she called for a man, and had him shave off the seven braids on his head; and she began to torment him, and his strength went from him. And she said, The Philistines are upon you, Samson. And he awoke out of his sleep, and thought, I will go out, as I have time and time again, and shake myself free; for he did not know that Jehovah had departed from him. Then the Philistines laid hold of him, and put out his eyes; and they brought him down to Gaza, and bound him with fetters of brass; and he was set to grinding in the prison. But the hair of his head began to grow again after he was shaved. *18. His capture and fate*

And the tyrants of the Philistines assembled to offer a great sacrifice to Dagon their god, and to rejoice; for they said, Our god hath delivered Samson our enemy into our power. And when the people saw him, they praised their god; for they said, *19. The Philistines' feast of triumph*

> Under our sway our god has brought low
> Our foe, —
> He who wrought our country's woe,
> He who slew many of us at a blow.

20.
Sam-
son's
death

And it came to pass, when their hearts were merry, that they said, Call for Samson, that he may make us sport. So they called Samson from the prison; and he made sport before them. And they placed him between the pillars.

Then Samson said to the young man who held him by the hand, Put me where I may feel the pillars on which the house rests, that I may lean upon them. Now the house was full of men and women, and all the tyrants of the Philistines were there; and there were upon the roof about three thousand men and women, who were looking on while Samson made sport. And Samson called on Jehovah, and said, O Lord Jehovah, remember me, I pray thee, and strengthen me, I pray thee, only this once, O God, that I may avenge myself on the Philistines for one of my two eyes. Then Samson took hold of the two middle pillars upon which the house rested, one with his right hand, and the other with his left, and leaned upon them. And Samson said, Let me myself die with the Philistines. And he bowed himself with all his might. And the house fell upon the tyrants, and upon all the people who were in it. So those whom he killed at his death were more than those whom he killed during his life.

21. His
burial

Then his brothers and all his father's household came down and took him, and brought him up and buried him between Zorah and Eshtaol, in the burying-place of Manoah his father.

I. **The Popular Character of the Samson Stories.** It is evident that the Samson stories were preserved in the book of Judges, not so much for their religious value as because of their popularity. They were doubtless retold from generation to generation, especially at the marriage feasts and festivals in ancient Israel. They contain the few examples found in the Old Testament of popular Hebrew poetry. Strangely enough it has not only the characteristic Hebrew rhythm of idea and measured beat, but also the rhyme so common in modern poetry. These primitive stories give a rare insight into the life and point of view of the common people during this period of settlement.

II. **The Character of Samson.** Samson has sometimes been held up as a worthy character. This tendency, however, is dangerous. He must, of course, be measured by the standards of his age, but even so he is far from noble. The keen admiration which the early Hebrews felt for physical strength and wit, undoubtedly explained the popularity of these stories. His contests with the Philistines, however, were but private feuds, and his great strength was never put forth for deliverance of his people. His achievements do not win for him a place even beside such a rude warrior as Jephthah. While his fellow-tribesmen admired his prowess, even they did not hesitate to deliver him to their foes in order to avoid a Philistine attack. Samson is a signal example of a man who possessed great gifts, but who failed to consecrate them to a noble cause.

III. The Nazirite Vow. According to the narrative, Samson's strength was due to the fact that he was a Nazirite. The word in its derivation appears to mean *separate, set apart*, and therefore consecrated to the Deity. The obligations assumed by the Nazirite also indicate that he was especially consecrated to Jehovah. Devotees are found in connection with most ancient religions. The Nazirite vow, however, appears to have been peculiar to that nomadic religion which the Hebrews brought from the desert. Wine was the product of the vine culture, which was characteristic of agricultural Canaan. Abstinence from wine, therefore, represented devotion to Jehovah and a refusal to have any part in the products of the corrupt Canaanite civilization. This element in the vow may also have been intended to save the devotee of Jehovah from the intoxicating power of the wine. The same vow of consecration kept him from eating or touching anything that was ceremonially unclean. As the devotee of Jehovah, his person was also sacred; therefore no razor was allowed to touch his hair. According to the narrative, Samson's strength was given him by Jehovah; hence when his hair, which symbolized his consecration to Jehovah, was cut, his strength suddenly departed. When the hair grew again it returned.

IV. Conditions at the End of the Period of Settlement. The stories regarding Samson clearly belong to the latter part of the period of settlement. Already the Philistines, whose victories are recorded in the first part of I Samuel, were beginning to invade central Canaan, and to bring the neighboring Hebrew clans into subjection. There is no evidence of any united action among the Hebrews in resisting the advance of these powerful foes. The relations between the two nations, however, were such that Samson without hesitation contracts a marriage with a Philistine woman. It was that peculiar type of marriage, common in this early age, in which the wife remained with her own clan. The stories also reveal the strength and superior civilization of the Philistines. They furnish, therefore, a natural introduction to the subsequent events which led to the establishment of the Hebrew monarchy.

V. Moral and Religious Standards. The narrative of Samson's deeds completes the picture of the moral and religious conditions of this early age. Although a devotee of Jehovah and a popular hero, Samson is lacking in the fundamental principles of morality. He is governed by his passions and selfish inclinations. His spirit of revenge makes him regardless of the rights and possessions of others. Having resorted to deception, he becomes the victim of deception. Although he attains to a certain majesty in the last scene of his life, he dies a victim of his own spirit of revenge. Samson and his contemporaries evidently believed that it was more important that he should preserve his hair intact and abstain from wine and unclean food, than that he should control his passions and observe the simple laws of justice and mercy and service. In contrast, leaders like Deborah and Barak reveal by their deeds the dawning of that nobler ideal which was destined to find full expression in the messages of the later prophets. The stories of the book of Judges vividly portray the early character of that race which, under the divine training, in time became a prophet nation with a universal spiritual message.

THE FOUNDING OF THE HEBREW KINGDOM

§ XL. THE PHILISTINE VICTORIES AND THE FORTUNES OF THE ARK

Now in those days the Philistines assembled to make war against Israel, and the battle was hard fought and they slew in the ranks on the field about four thousand men. _{1. Israel's defeat}

But when the people returned to the camp, the people sent to Shiloh and took from there the ark of Jehovah of hosts. And when the ark of Jehovah came to the camp, the earth resounded. And when the Philistines knew that the ark of Jehovah had come to the camp, they said, Woe to us! for it has not been thus before; but be men and fight. So the Philistines fought and there was a great slaughter. _{2. The second defeat}

Then the Philistines took the ark of Jehovah and brought it to the house of Dagon and set it up by the side of Dagon. And when the Ashdodites arose early the next day and came to the house of Dagon, behold there was Dagon fallen upon his face to the ground before the ark of Jehovah. And they raised up Dagon and set him in his place again. But when they arose early on the following morning, behold there was Dagon fallen upon his face to the ground before the ark of Jehovah. And the head of Dagon and both his hands were cut off upon the threshold, and only the body of Dagon was left. Therefore the priests of Dagon, and all who enter the house of Dagon, do not tread on the threshold of Dagon in Ashdod to this day, but leap over it. _{3. The ark in the temple of Dagon}

And the hand of Jehovah was heavy upon the Ashdodites, and he destroyed them, and smote them with boils, even Ashdod and its borders. And when the men of Ashdod saw that it was so, they said, the ark of the God of Israel shall not remain with us; for his hand is severe upon us, and Dagon our God. So they sent and gathered all the _{4. The plague attending the ark}

tyrants of the Philistines to them, and said, What shall we do with the ark of the God of Israel? And they answered, Let the ark of the God of Israel be brought around to Gath. So they brought the ark of the God of Israel around. But after they had brought it around, the hand of Jehovah was against the city —there was a very great panic —and he smote the men of the city, both young and old, so that boils broke out upon them. Therefore they sent the ark of God to Ekron. But when the ark of God came to Ekron, the Ekronites cried out, saying, They have brought around the ark of the God of Israel to us, to slay us and our people. They sent therefore and gathered together all the tyrants of the Philistines and said, Send away the ark of the God of Israel, that it may go back to its own place and not kill us and our people.

5. Plans for returning the ark

Then the Philistines summoned the priests and the diviners, saying, What shall we do with the ark of Jehovah? Show us how we shall send it to its place. And they said, If you are sending the ark of the God of Israel, you must not send it away empty; but you must return to him a trespass-offering. Then you will be healed, and it shall be made known to you why his hand is not removed from you. Then said they, What shall be the trespass-offering which we shall return to him? And they said, Five golden boils, and five golden mice, corresponding to the number of the tyrants of the Philistines; for one plague was upon you, as well as upon your tyrants. Therefore you shall make images of your boils, and images of your mice that mar the land; and you shall give glory to the God of Israel; perhaps he will lighten his hand from upon you and your gods and your land. Why then will you make your hearts stubborn, as the Egyptians and Pharaoh made their hearts stubborn? Was it not after he had made sport of them, that they let them go, so that they departed? Now, therefore, take and prepare a new cart, and two milch cows upon which the yoke has not come; and fasten the cows to the cart, but you shall leave their calves behind them at home. And take the ark of Jehovah and place it on the cart and put the golden objects, which you are returning to him as a trespass-offering, in a box at its side. Then send it away that it may depart.

And see, if it goes on the way to its own border to Beth-shemesh, then it is he who hath done us this great harm, but if not, then we shall know that it was not his hand that smote us; it was an accident that befell us.

And the men did so, and took two milch cows and fastened them to the cart, and shut up their calves at home. And they placed the ark of Jehovah on the cart, and the box with the golden mice and the images of their boils. And the cows took a straight course in the direction of Bethshemesh; they went along the highway, lowing as they went, and did not turn aside to the right hand or to the left. And the tyrants of the Philistines went after them to the border of Bethshemesh. And the inhabitants of Bethshemesh were harvesting their wheat in the valley. And they lifted up their eyes and saw the ark, and came rejoicing to meet it. And when the cart came into the field of Joshua the Beth-shemeshite, it stood still there. And a great stone was there. So they split up the wood of the cart, and offered the cows as a burnt-offering to Jehovah. And when the five tyrants of the Philistines saw it, they returned to Ekron on that day. And a witness is the great stone, by which they set down the ark of Jehovah. To this day it is in the field of Joshua of Bethshemesh. *6. Its restoration to the Hebrews*

The sons of Jechoniah, however, did not rejoice with the men of Bethshemesh, when they looked upon the ark of Jehovah. So he smote among them seventy men; and the people mourned because Jehovah had smitten the people with a great slaughter. And the men of Bethshemesh said, Who is able to stand before Jehovah this holy God? And to whom shall he go up from us? Then they sent messengers to the inhabitants of Kiriath-jearim, saying, The Philistines have brought back the ark of Jehovah. Come down, and bring it up to you. So the men of Kiriath-jearim came, and brought up the ark of Jehovah, and carried it into the house of Abinadab on the hill, and consecrated Eleazar his son to guard the ark of Jehovah. From the time the ark began to abide in Kiriath-jearim, many years passed. *7. The ark among the Hebrews*

I. **The Books of Samuel.** The chief record of the events which occurred during the days of Saul and David, is found in the books of

Samuel. These, together with the books of Kings, originally constituted a connected history which began with the birth of Samuel and extended to the Babylonian exile. The first book of Samuel contains two general divisions: (1) chapters 1 to 15, which give the history of Samuel and Saul; (2) 16 to 31, which tell of the rise of David and the decline and death of Saul. Second Samuel contains three general divisions. Chapters 1 to 8 deal chiefly with political events during David's reign, first over Judah and then over all Israel. Chapters 9 to 20 contain David's family history. Chapters 21 to 24 are an appendix, similar to that found at the end of the book of Judges. They record events (such as the putting to death of the sons of Saul and the achievements of David's warriors) which transpired during the earlier part of David's reign over all Israel. Chapters 22 and 23 contain later psalms associated with David. Thus the arrangement in I Samuel is in general chronological; while in II Samuel the material is grouped according to the subject-matter.

II. The Different Records of the Founding of the Kingdom. The oldest account of the founding of the united Hebrew kingdom is taken from an ancient Saul history, which probably comes from the latter part of the tenth century B.C. The extracts from this early source are found in I Samuel 9–11, 13 and 14, and are adopted as the basis of the present text. They are introduced by extracts from an equally old source, which told of the wars of the Philistines and of the fortunes of the ark. Together these ancient histories form the immediate sequel to the earliest narratives in the book of Judges.

These quotations from the older sources have been supplemented in I Samuel by extracts from what appears to have been originally an independent history, dealing with the boyhood and the work of the prophet Samuel. Like the traditional judges in the book of Judges, Samuel is thought of in this history as a judge ruling over all Israel. His personality completely overshadows that of Saul. Instead of effectively laboring for the establishment of the kingship, as in the older Saul history, Samuel is represented as bitterly opposing it. The point of view is that of Hosea and of the later prophets, who in the light of the sad experience of northern Israel, regarded the institution of the kingship as a fundamental evil. In this later Samuel history, which probably comes from some of the prophetic guilds of Northern Israel and cannot be dated before the eighth century B.C., the victory over the Philistines is won, not by the sword, but by a miracle in response to Samuel's prayer.

III. The Philistines. In the light of the Egyptian inscription it seems clear that these sturdy foes of the Israelites came from southern Asia Minor. According to Amos 9⁷ and Deuteronomy 2²³ their original home was Caphtor. This is doubtless to be identified with the Egyptian Kefto. From the Egyptian inscription it also appears that Kefto in ancient times produced works of art which were equal to those of Greece in the Mycenæan age, so that it is a mistake to regard the Philistines or Wanderers as rude barbarians.

In his inscriptions Ramses III of the twentieth Egyptian dynasty tells of a great racial movement from the north during the first half of the twelfth century B.C. He states that, "No country could withstand their arms." They advanced by land and by sea, and nearly succeeded in conquering northern Egypt. A large body of them, however, were turned back and settled on the fertile maritime plain in southwestern Palestine, where they soon built up a strong and highly developed civilization. The rich grain fields furnished the material for commerce, and their geographical position offered ample opportunity for trade with Phœnicia and Egypt.

Five walled cities, each with its independent ruler, yet bound together in a strong confederacy, ruled ancient Philistia. Ekron and Gath in the north-east were closest to the territory of the Hebrews; Ashdod, Askelon and Gaza in the south-west lay close to the sea. While the Hebrews were still struggling for homes in the uplands of central Canaan, the Philistines had already established a powerful kingdom, which extended from the sea to the western headlands of Canaan, and from a point opposite Joppa to the southern wilderness and the borders of Egypt.

IV. The Defeat of the Hebrews and the Loss of the Ark. In the limited territory of Palestine it was inevitable that the two great waves of immigration, represented by the Philistines and the Hebrews, should ultimately come into open conflict. The stories of Samson suggest the preliminary skirmishes, which took place during the latter part of the period of settlement. The western headlands of Judah, with their narrow, rocky valleys, were adapted only to border warfare. The broader valleys of central Canaan offered the natural way of approach of Philistia. Hence, when the Philistines rallied their forces to attack and subjugate the Hebrews, the decisive battles were fought in the western borders of Ephraim and Manasseh.

The first engagement revealed the weakness of the Hebrews. They apparently rallied in considerable numbers; but doubtless, as in the days of Deborah, the distant tribes were not represented. Moreover, they lacked a leader to unite them. The inevitable result was that they were ignominiously beaten by the well-organized Philistines.

In their extremity the Hebrews brought from Shiloh, north-east of Shechem, the ark of Jehovah. In their march through the wilderness they had borne with them this symbol of Jehovah's presence. In their conflicts with the hostile Arab tribes, the feeling that Jehovah was in their midst and that they were fighting for him, had strengthened their courage, kindled their zeal, and guided them on to repeated victories (*cf.* § XXVII). It was natural, therefore, that at this great crisis they should bear the ark into battle, just as the Philistines, in a later engagement with the Hebrews, carried with them the images of their gods (§ XLIX³). The popular faith in the ancient symbol was shattered, for the Hebrews suffered another signal defeat. Following up their victory, the Philistines established their rule over the Hebrews in central Canaan. It was apparently at this time that Shiloh was destroyed and disappeared from Hebrew history. Saddest of all, the ark itself was captured and borne in triumph by the Philistines to one of the temples of their gods. To the minds of the Israelites this overwhelming series of disasters seemed to mean, either that Jehovah was weaker than the gods of their foes, or else that he did not care to deliver his people. The crisis involved not only the independence, but also the faith of the Hebrew race.

V. **The Ark Among the Philistines.** The story of the ark shows traces of popular interpretation and embellishment; but clearly underlying it is the fact, that while the ark was in the hands of the Philistines a great pestilence attacked them. Sanitary conditions, which are never good in the East, are especially bad on the Philistine plain. Like Egypt, it is the home of contagious diseases. Being on the great highway which ran from north to south, it is especially open to plagues of every kind. The complete ignorance of the ancients regarding the real nature of contagious diseases left them an easy prey to its ravages. The story indicates, not only that the contagion was carried from city to city by those who bore the ark, but also suggests the nature of the disease. The golden tumors, or boils, which were sent back by the Philistines to appease the god of the Hebrews were, in accordance with ancient usage, intended to represent the peculiar form of the malady which had attacked them. This would appear to have been none other than the dread bubonic plague. Even the Hebrews themselves, who were later exposed to the contagion, were also fatally affected.

Thus again, by perfectly natural means, but with an opportuneness which clearly reveals the hand of God, the faith of the Hebrews was strengthened, and through the hardships of Philistine oppression the way was prepared for the next step forward in the development of the Hebrew nation.

§ XLI.   SAUL'S CALL AND ELECTION TO THE KINGSHIP

Now there was a man of Gibeah, whose name was Kish the son of Abiel, the son of Zeror, the son of Becorath, the son of Aphiah, a Benjamite, a man well to do. And he had a son whose name was Saul, a man in the prime of life and handsome; and there was not one among the Israelites more handsome than he. From his shoulders and upwards he was higher than any of the people.   *1. Saul's family and appearance*

Now the she-asses of Kish, Saul's father, were lost. And Kish said to Saul his son, Take now one of the servants with you and arise and go, seek the asses. And they passed through the hill-country of Ephraim, and the land of Shalishah, but did not find them. Then they passed through the land of Shaalim, but they were not there. And they passed through the land of the Benjamites, but did not find them.   *2. His search for the lost asses*

When they were come into the land of Zuph, Saul said to his servant who was with him, Come, let us return, lest my father cease thinking of the asses and become anxious for us. And he answered him, Behold now, there is in this city a man of God, and the man is held in honor; all that he says is sure to come true. Now let us go thither; perhaps he can show us the way we should go. Then Saul said to his servant, But, suppose we go, what shall we take to the man? for the bread is gone from our sacks, and there is no present to take to the man of God. What have we? And the servant answered Saul again, and said, See I have with me a fourth part of a silver shekel, and you shall give it to the man of God that he may furnish us information regarding our mission. Then Saul said to his servant, Your advice is good; come, let us go. So they went to the city where the man of God was.   *3. Appeal to Samuel*

As they were going up the ascent to the city, they met young maidens going out to draw water and said to them, Is the seer here? And they answered them and said, He   *4. Meeting with the seer* is; behold, he is before you. Make haste now, for he is come to-day into the city; for the people have a sacrifice to-day on the high place. As soon as you come to the city, you will at once find him, before he goes up to the high place to eat; for the people will not eat until he come, for he is to bless the sacrifice; and afterward the guests eat. Now therefore go up; for at this time you will meet him. So they went up to the city. When they came within the city gate, Samuel was just coming out toward them, to go up to the high place. Now Jehovah had given to Samuel, a day before Saul came, the following revelation, At this time to-morrow I will send thee a man out of the land of Benjamin, and thou shalt anoint him to be a prince over my people Israel. And he shall save my people out of the hand of the Philistines; for I have seen the affliction of my people, and their cry has come to me. And when Samuel saw Saul, Jehovah indicated to him, This is the man of whom I spoke to thee! He it is who shall rule over my people. Then Saul drew near to Samuel in the gate, and said, Tell me, if you will, where the seer's house is. And Samuel answered Saul and said, I am the seer; go up before me to the high place, for you shall eat with me to-day; and in the morning I will let you go, and will tell you all that is in your heart. And as for your asses that were lost three days ago, do not trouble yourself about them, for they have been found. And to whom belongs all that is desirable in Israel? Does it not to you, and to your father's house? And Saul answered and said, Am I not a Benjamite, of the smallest of the tribes of Israel, and is not my family the least of all the families of the tribe of Benjamin? Why then do you speak thus to me?

5. At the sacrificial meal

And Samuel took Saul and his servant and brought them into the hall and made them sit at the head of the guests (who were about thirty in number). And Samuel said to the cook, Bring the portion I gave you, which I told you to put aside. And the cook took up the leg and placed it before Saul. And Samuel said, See, the meat is served! eat! for it was kept for you until the appointed time, that you might eat with those whom I have invited. So Saul ate with Samuel that day.

And after they came down from the high place into the city, they spread a bed for Saul on the roof, and he lay down. Then at daybreak Samuel called to Saul on the roof, saying, Up, that I may send you away. So Saul arose, and he and Samuel went out into the street. As they were going down at the outskirts of the city, Samuel said to Saul, Bid the servant pass on before us, but you stand here that I may make known to you the word of God. Then Samuel took the vial of oil, and poured it on his head, and kissed him and said, Hath not Jehovah anointed you to be a prince over his people Israel? And you shall reign over the people of Jehovah and deliver them from the power of their enemies around about. And this shall be the sign that Jehovah hath anointed you to be a prince over his heritage: when you go from me to-day you shall find two men at Rachel's tomb, in the boundary of Benjamin at Zelzah; and they will say to you, 'The asses which you went to seek are found, and now your father has dismissed the matter of the asses and is anxious for you, saying, "What shall I do for my son?"' Then you shall go on from there and come to the oak of Tabor; and there three men going up to God to Bethel will meet you, one carrying three kids, and another carrying three loaves of bread, and another carrying a skin of wine. And they will salute you and give you two loaves of bread which you shall take from their hand. After that you shall come to Gibeah, where is the garrison of the Philistines; and furthermore, when you come thither to the city, you shall meet a band of prophets coming down from the high place with a lyre, a tambourine, a flute, and a harp before them; and they will be prophesying. And the spirit of Jehovah will rush upon you, and you shall prophesy with them, and shall be turned into another man. And when these signs come to you, you shall do as the occasion offers; for God is with you.

Accordingly when he turned his back to go from Samuel, God gave him another heart, and all those signs came to pass that day. And just as he came thence to Gibeah, a band of prophets met him, and he prophesied among them. And when every one who knew him saw him in the act of prophesying with the prophets, the people said to one an-

6. Public anointing by Samuel

7. Meeting with the band of prophets

71

other, What is this that has come upon the son of Kish? Is Saul also among the prophets? And one of the bystanders answered and said, And who is their father? Therefore it became a proverb, Is Saul also among the prophets? And when he had made an end of prophesying, he went to the high place.

8. Return home

And Saul's cousin said to him and to his servant, Where did you go? And he said, To seek the asses; and when we saw that they were not found, we went to Samuel. And Saul's cousin said, Tell me, I pray, what Samuel said to you. And Saul said to his cousin, He told us definitely that the asses were found. But concerning the matter of the kingdom, of which Samuel had spoken, he told him nothing.

9. The invasion of Nahash the Ammonite

Now it came to pass after about a month, that Nahash the Ammonite came up and besieged Jabesh in Gilead; and all the men of Jabesh said to Nahash, Make terms with us and we will serve you. But Nahash the Ammonite said to them, On this condition will I make terms with you: that I bore out the right eye of each of you, and thereby bring a reproach upon all Israel. And the elders of Jabesh said to him, Give us seven days respite, that we may send messengers through all the territory of Israel. Then, if there be none to save us, we will come to you.

10. Reception of the news by Saul

So the messengers came to Gibeah of Saul, and recounted the facts in the hearing of the people, and all the people wept aloud. And Saul was just coming from the field after the oxen. And Saul said, What is the trouble with the people, that they are weeping? Then they told him the words of the men of Jabesh. And the spirit of Jehovah rushed upon Saul when he heard these words, and his anger was greatly aroused. And he took a yoke of oxen, and cut them in pieces; and sent them throughout all the territory of Israel by the hand of messengers, saying, Whoever does not come forth after Saul and after Samuel, so shall it be done to his oxen.

11. The deliverance by the Israelites under Saul

Then a terror from Jehovah fell upon the people, and they rallied as one man. And he mustered them in Bezek. And they said to the messengers who came, Thus say to the men of Jabesh in Gilead, 'To-morrow, by the time the sun becomes hot, deliverance shall come to you.' So the messengers came and told the men of Jabesh, and they were glad. Therefore the men of Jabesh said, To-morrow we will come out to you, and you shall do to us whatever you please. Accordingly on the following day, Saul divided the people into three divisions; and they came into the midst of the camp in the morning watch, and smote the Ammonites until the heat of the day. And then they who remained scattered, so that no two of them were left together.

Then all the people went to Gilgal; and there they made Saul king before Jehovah in Gilgal; and there they sacrificed peace-offerings before Jehovah; and there Saul and all the men of Israel rejoiced exceedingly.

12. Saul's election as king

I. **The Need of a King.** The Philistine oppression revealed to the Israelites the absolute necessity of united action. In that early age the only known form of political organization that promised permanent independence, was the kingship. Already Gideon's kingdom had demonstrated the advantages of that form of union. The Hebrews, however, were loyal to their desert instincts, and therefore very loath to acknowledge any central authority. An exceedingly strong pressure was required to make them unite. That pressure was at last furnished by the Philistines. The bitter experiences of the period of settlement had demonstrated clearly that unless they stood shoulder to shoulder and followed a common leader, they could expect in hostile Canaan only oppression and slavery.

The Philistines energetically followed up their victories over the Hebrews. Garrisons were established at strategic points in central Canaan. All attempts at local uprisings were quickly suppressed. Tribute was doubtless exacted from the different tribal chieftains, who were permitted, on these conditions, to exercise a limited authority. The account of the later Ammonite invasion indicates that the Philistines felt no responsibility in protecting the Hebrews from foreign foes. Like the earlier Egyptian rulers of Palestine, the Philistines apparently had but one object in their conquest, and that was spoil and tribute.

For the Hebrews the Philistine rule meant an arrest of their material and social development. As has already been noted, it also threatened their faith in Jehovah. The victories of the Philistines were doubtless interpreted by the majority of the Israelites as evidence that Jehovah was powerless, or else that he did not care to arouse himself in behalf of his people. Meantime, the Israelites were being subjected to the severest temptations, not only through the Philistines, but also through the closer contact with the old Canaanite population, whose civilization and customs and institutions they were rapidly absorbing. The great danger was that in the presence of the alluring cults of Canaan the religion of Jehovah, proclaimed by the austere prophet of the desert, would be completely forgotten. To preserve that faith intact, it was absolutely essential that the Hebrews unite, and in the name of Jehovah throw off the yoke of the Philistines, and develop a kingdom which would worthily represent before the nations the God of their race. The crisis, therefore, was religious as well as political. On the battle-fields of Canaan the future faith of the race was to be decided. It was a crisis to call forth not only a patriot but a prophet.

II. **The Patriots of Israel.** The conditions resulting from the Philistine oppression probably gave rise to the bands known as *the sons of the prophets*, which appear for the first time in Israel's history. From the different references to these sons of the prophets it is evident that they were religious enthusiasts associated together in bands or guilds. These guilds were connected with the local sanctuaries, such as Bethel and Gilgal. In later times the members of these guilds lived together with their wives in communities, sharing a common table. Like the modern dervishes, ecstasy, induced by music and other external means, was a prominent element in their religious life. The exact object of these religious guilds is not revealed by the few Old Testament references to them. Throughout their history, however, the sons of the prophets are closely connected, on the one hand with the great prophetic leaders like Samuel and Elijah and Elisha, and on the other with the important political movements of their day. Like the zealots of later Jewish history, they appear to have represented an impassioned protest against the political oppressors of their race. Their patriotism and zeal for Jehovah did not deter them from resorting to intrigue or from even appealing to the sword. Their prominence at this period of Hebrew history is therefore a symptom of political unrest. Though the form in which their religious and patriotic zeal found expression was crude, there is little doubt of its sincerity. Their presence reveals one of the many powerful underlying forces at work in Israel.

Very different and yet equally hostile to the Philistine oppressors, were the Hebrew warriors and tribal chieftains. They lacked not courage but leadership. Tribal jealousies still held them apart. No great leader, like Gideon of old, had appeared to command their confidence and call forth their loyal support.

A great prophet was needed, acquainted with the men and forces in Israel, able to analyze the meaning of the situation, and, with divine authority, to suggest a definite course of action. As at every great crisis in Israel's unique history, a prophet arose at the moment of greatest need and delivered the nation from its oppressors and introduced the race to a new epoch of achievement and development.

Later traditions give an exquisite picture of the birth and boyhood and youthful training of Samuel. They also magnify his position, making him judge of all Israel, and attribute to him miraculous powers. The oldest narrative, however, pictures him as simply the local seer of Ramah, known to the servant of Saul, although not to the young Benjamite chieftain. Both groups of tradition agree in recognizing the supreme importance of his work. With divine insight he grasped the needs of the situation, realized that the moment had arrived for the birth of united Israel and found the man to lead the nation. In so doing he won a place beside Moses, Deborah, Saul and David as one of the makers of Israel.

III. Saul, the Benjamite. The situation called for a man large of stature, courageous, enthusiastic, able to bring together rival factions and to command absolute obedience in the face of the most desperate odds. These difficult conditions were met in the fullest measure by Saul, the son of Kish, a Benjamite noble, possessed of wealth and influence. Geographically, the tribe of Benjamin also stood midway between the north and south. Its comparative insignificance delivered it from the bitter jealousies which separated the larger tribes. Saul's later interview with Samuel suggests that already the sense of responsibility was strong within him, and that the other leaders in Israel were beginning to regard him as a possible deliverer. What was needed was that some one with authority sound the call to action.

IV. Saul's Meeting with Samuel. A seeming chance brought together the two men who held the key to the situation in Israel. In quest for information regarding the lost asses, Saul found Samuel presiding at the sacrificial meal in the high place at Ramah. About the prophet were gathered the elders of the city. Already Samuel was aware of Saul's approach and had made provision for his reception. The young Benjamite was accordingly assigned the seat of honor and, after the feast, was entertained overnight within the city. The reception thus accorded Saul was significant, and the words which Samuel addressed to him contained a deeper meaning, which Saul evidently understood. When Saul was about to depart, Samuel publicly anointed him with oil and told him that he was called to rule over his people. In the old Semitic symbolism, anointing with oil meant consecration to a definite task. In the case of a priest it was to minister at the sanctuary. In the case of Saul it was to represent Jehovah as the chosen leader of the nation. As he went forth, Samuel significantly commanded him to be ready to improve the opportunity when it presented itself. Also, in keeping with the prophet's statement, Saul met a band of prophets under the influence of religious ecstasy. As he joined them, rough warrior though he was, he was seized with the same religious enthusiasm. The incident gave rise to the famous proverb, "Is Saul also among the prophets." The scene revealed the depths to which the words of Samuel had stirred the soul of Saul. It symbolized his consecration to his high calling, to be Jehovah's agent in delivering his people. It also symbolized that union between the religious enthusiast and the warrior class in Israel which was necessary if the nation as a whole was to be aroused to effective action.

V. The Choice of Saul as King. The opportunity for action soon appeared. The Ammonites east of the Jordan advanced to the conquest of the Hebrew town of Jabesh in Gilead. The cruel and humiliating terms which they proposed called forth no champion from among the Israelites until the messengers came to the man whom Samuel had fired with patriotic zeal. Slaying the oxen with which he had been ploughing, Saul sent these gory reminders of battle and bloodshed to the chieftains of Israel, demanding with a grim threat that they follow him to deliver their endangered kinsmen. At last the Hebrews recognized that they had found a true leader. In taking up arms against the common foe, they encountered no opposition from the Philistines. A rapid march and an early morning attack left Saul and the Hebrews masters of the battle-field and the Ammonites in flight.

Returning either to Gilgal, beside the lower Jordan, or to that famous northern sanctuary at Gilgal near Shiloh, Saul's warriors proclaimed him king. Thus, as to Gideon of old, the Hebrews turned for leadership and protection to the one who had demonstrated on the battle-field his ability to deliver them. It was to a throne yet to be established and to a kingdom that must be won that Saul was called. His election, however, was deeply significant, for it proved that at last under the pressure of dire necessity, the Israelites were ready to lay down their tribal jealousies and to acknowledge a common leader. Out of this simple beginning rose the united Hebrew kingdom and that empire of David which left so deep an impression upon all Hebrew literature and thought.

§ XLII. THE GREAT VICTORY OVER THE PHILISTINES

Saul chose him three thousand men of Israel: two thousand were with Saul in Michmash and on the mountain of Bethel, and a thousand were with Jonathan his son in Gibeah of Benjamin. But the rest of the people he had sent each to his home. Then Jonathan smote the garrison of the Philistines that was in Gibeah. And the Philistines heard the report that the Hebrews had revolted. But Saul had meantime caused the trumpet to be blown throughout all the land. And all Israel heard the report that Saul had smitten the garrison of the Philistines, and also that Israel had brought itself into ill repute with the Philistines. *1. Outbreak of the war*

And the Philistines were gathered together to fight with Israel. When the men of Israel saw that they were in a strait (for the people were hard pressed), the people hid themselves in caves, in holes, in rocks, in tombs, and in pits. Also many people went over the Jordan to the land of Gad and Gilead. And Saul numbered the people who were with him, about six hundred men. And Saul and Jonathan his son, together with the people who were with them, were staying in Gibeah of Benjamin, while the Philistines encamped in Michmash. And the plunderers came out of the camp of the Philistines in three divisions: one division turned in the direction of Ophrah, in the land of Shual, and another division turned in the direction of Bethhoron, and another division turned in the direction of the hill that looks down over the valley of Zeboim toward the wilderness. *2. Advance of the Philistines*

And the garrison of the Philistines went out to the pass of Michmash. Now on that day Jonathan the son of Saul said to the young man who bore his armor, Come and let us go over to the Philistines' garrison, that is on the other side. But he did not tell his father. And Saul was sitting in the outskirts of Gibeah under the pomegranate tree which is by the threshing-floor, and the people who were with him numbered about six hundred men. And Ahijah the son of Ahitub, Ichabod's brother, the son of Phinehas, the son of Eli, the priest of Jehovah at Shiloh, was in charge of an ephod. And the people did not know that Jonathan had *3. Jonathan's proposal*

gone. And between the passes by which Jonathan sought
to go over to the Philistines' garrison there was a rocky
crag on the one side, and a rocky crag on the other side;
and the name of the one was Bozez [the Shining], and the
name of the other Seneh [the Thorny]. The one crag rose
up on the north in front of Michmash, and the other on the
south in front of Geba. And Jonathan said to the young
man who bore his armor, Come, let us go over to the garrison
of these uncircumcised Philistines; perhaps Jehovah will
act for us, for there is nothing that can prevent Jehovah
from saving by many or by few. And his armorbearer
said to him, Do whatever you think best; see, I am with
you; your wish is mine. Then Jonathan said, See, we will
pass over to the men and show ourselves to them. If they
say to us, 'Stand still until we can reach you,' then we will
stand still in our place, and will not go up to them. But if
they say, 'Come up to us,' then we will go up; for Jehovah
has given them into our hand; and this shall be the sign to us.

4. Jonathan's attack

Now when both of them showed themselves to the garrison
of the Philistines, the Philistines said, There are Hebrews
coming out of the holes where they have hidden themselves.
And the men of the garrison cried out to Jonathan and his
armorbearer, saying, Come up to us that we may tell you
something. Then Jonathan said to his armorbearer, Come
up after me; for Jehovah has given them into the hand of
Israel. And Jonathan climbed up on his hands and feet,
and his armorbearer after him. And they fell before
Jonathan, and his armorbearer kept despatching them after
him. And in the first attack Jonathan and his armorbearer
slew about twenty men with javelins and rocks from the
field. And there was a trembling in the camp, in the field,
and among all the people; the garrison, and even the raiders
also trembled; and the earth quaked so that it produced a
very great panic.

5. General attack and defeat of the Philistines

And the watchmen of Saul in Gibeah of Benjamin looked,
and saw a tumult surging hither and thither. Then said
Saul to the people who were with him, Investigate now and
see who is gone from us. And when they had investigated
they found that Jonathan and his armorbearer were not
there. And Saul said to Ahijah, Bring hither the ephod;

for at that time he had charge of the ephod before Israel. And while Saul was yet speaking to the priest, the tumult in the camp of the Philistines kept on increasing. Therefore Saul said to the priest, Draw back your hand. And Saul and all the people that were with him responded to the call, and came to the battle; and thereupon every man's sword was turned upon his fellow, and there was very great confusion. And the Hebrews, who were with the Philistines heretofore, who had come up into the camp, also turned to be with the Israelites who were with Saul and Jonathan. Likewise all the men of Israel, who were in hiding in the hill-country of Ephraim, when they heard that the Philistines fled, also pursued close after them in the battle. So Jehovah saved Israel that day, and the battle passed over beyond Bethhoron.

And all the people were with Saul, about ten thousand men; and the fighting was scattered over all the hill-country of Ephraim. Then Saul committed a great act of folly that day, for he laid an oath on the people, saying, Cursed is the man who shall eat any food until evening and until I avenge myself on my enemies. So none of the people tasted food. Now there was honey on the surface of the ground, and when the people came to the honeycomb, the bees had just flown away, but no one put his hand to his mouth, for the people feared the oath. But Jonathan had not heard when his father adjured the people; therefore he put forth the end of the rod that was in his hand, and dipped it in the honeycomb and put his hand to his mouth, and his eyes were lightened. Then one of the people spoke up and said, Your father adjured the people saying, 'Cursed be the man who eats food this day.' But Jonathan said, My father has brought disaster on the land. See how I have been refreshed, because I have tasted a little of this honey. If only the people had eaten freely to-day of the spoil of their enemies which they found, how much greater would have been the slaughter of the Philistines!

But they smote the Philistines that day from Michmash to Aijalon, and the people were very faint. Then the people rushed upon the spoil and took sheep and oxen and calves and struck them to the earth, and the people ate them with

the blood. When they told Saul, saying, See, the people
are sinning against Jehovah in eating with the blood, he
said to those who told him, Roll hither to me a great stone.
And Saul said, Go out among the people and say to them,
'Let each man bring to me his ox and his sheep, and slay
it here and eat; but do not sin against Jehovah in eating the
flesh together with the blood. And all the people brought
that night, each what he had in his hand, and slew them there.
So Saul built an altar to Jehovah; that was the first altar
that he built to Jehovah.

8. Penalty of the broken vow

And Saul said, Let us go down after the Philistines by
night and plunder among them until daybreak, and let us
not leave a man of them. And they said, Do whatever you
think best. Then said the priest, Let us here draw near to
God. And Saul asked of God, Shall I go down after the
Philistines? Wilt thou deliver them into the hand of
Israel? But he did not answer him that day. And Saul
said, Come hither, all you chiefs of the people and know
and see in whom is this guilt to-day. For as Jehovah liveth,
who delivereth Israel, though it be in Jonathan my son, he
shall surely die. But no one of all the people answered him.
Then he said to all Israel, You be on one side, and I and
Jonathan my son will be on the other side. And the people
said to Saul, Do what seems good to you. Therefore Saul
said, Jehovah, God of Israel, why hast thou not answered
thy servant this day? If the guilt be in me or in Jonathan
my son, Jehovah, God of Israel, give Urim; but if the guilt
is in thy people Israel, give Thummim. Then Jonathan
and Saul were taken and the people escaped. And Saul said,
Cast the lot between me and Jonathan my son. He whom
Jehovah shall take, must die. And the people said to Saul,
It shall not be so! But Saul overruled the people and they
cast the lot between him and Jonathan his son. And Jonathan was taken.

9. Jonathan's confession and deliverance

Then Saul said to Jonathan, Tell me what you have done.
And Jonathan told him, saying, I did indeed taste a little
honey with the end of the staff that was in my hand; and
here I am! I am ready to die. And Saul said, May God
do to me whatever he pleases, you shall surely die, Jonathan!
But the people said to Saul, Shall Jonathan die who has

wrought this great deliverance in Israel? Far from it! As Jehovah liveth, there shall not one hair of his head fall to the ground, for he has wrought with God this day. Therefore the people rescued Jonathan, so that he did not die. Then Saul went up from pursuing the Philistines; and the Philistines went to their own country.

But the war against the Philistines was severe all the days of Saul. And whenever Saul saw any valiant or efficient man, he would attach him to himself. The name of the commander of his army was Abner the son of Ner, Saul's cousin. And Kish the father of Saul and Ner the father of Abner were sons of Abiel. **10. Saul's military policy**

Now when Saul had taken the kingdom over Israel, he fought against all his enemies on every side: against Moab, and the Ammonites, and Edom, and Beth-rehob, the king of Zobah, and the Philistines; and wherever he turned he was victorious. And he did mighty deeds and smote the Amalekites and delivered Israel out of the hands of its plunderers. **11. His wars**

I. Jonathan's Attack upon the Philistines. Saul went forth to attack the Ammonites simply as a tribal deliverer. When he returned he had been called to the greater task of delivering the Hebrews from their Philistine oppressors. It was his son, Jonathan, however, who made the first attack, capturing the garrison of the Philistines at his native town Gibeah. This attack was the signal for a general Philistine advance. The Israelites, however, were unprepared. Instead of rallying about Saul and Jonathan, they fled before the organized forces of the Philistines. Saul and Jonathan were left with only a few hundred men, and the Hebrew cause seemed hopeless. Finding no real resistance, the Philistine army separated into three divisions and turned to plunder.

II. The Capture of the Philistine Stronghold. It was at this critical moment, when the foe were most open to attack, that Jonathan, by his prowess and courage saved his father's kingdom. The deep valley of the Michmash extends upward from the Jordan, cutting across central Canaan. On the northern side a small Philistine garrison guarded the pass. From the crags on the south Jonathan looked across the valley and conceived the bold plan of a single-handed attack. It is one of the most dramatic scenes in Israel's history. Accompanied by his brave armorbearer he descended into the valley and then mounted the cliffs to the north, amidst the taunts of the Philistines. Their taunts were changed to wonder and then to fear, when Jonathan mounted the height and boldly attacked them. A panic, possibly, as the narrative suggests, increased by an earthquake, seized the Philistine garrison and quickly spread to the marauding bands.

III. **The Pursuit of the Philistines.** News of the panic among the Philistines was soon brought to Saul. Following the custom of his age, he first turned to consult Jehovah through the priestly ephod before going out to fight with his foes. The increasing tumult, however, expelled all doubt. Without waiting for the divine response, Saul rallied his forces and was soon in hot pursuit. In their terror and confusion the Philistines turned against each other, and even the craven Israelites in their midst rose to join with Saul in the overthrow of their oppressors. Down across the hill country of Ephraim and beyond the passes of Bethhoron, the Philistines were driven in mad flight, and the Hebrews learned at last that their hated oppressors were not invincible.

IV. **Saul's Rash Vow.** In his eagerness to overcome his foes Saul, like Jephthah, made a rash vow. It was that he who tasted food until evening should die. Jonathan, however, who was in the van of the pursuit, unaware of his father's vow, transgressed the ban. When his father's vow was reported to him, with justice he condemned it.

Later when Saul failed to secure a response to the divine oracle—perhaps because the priests knew of Jonathan's act and were not ready to absolve Saul from the consequences of his vow—the king concluded that some one had disobeyed his solemn command. Accordingly he inquired through the sacred lot who was guilty. Jonathan, his son, proved to be the culprit. With a fearlessness and frankness that characterizes all that is recorded of this noble knight, Jonathan stated what he had done and declared that he was ready to die. Although he had won for Saul a throne and kingdom, he would have died to fulfil his father's rash vow had not the people redeemed him.

V. **Saul's Wars.** The initial victory over the Philistines was far from decisive; but until the end of Saul's reign the Philistines appear to have made no serious and united attempt to reconquer central Canaan. The hostilities between the two peoples took the form rather of border warfare. Hostile bands made a sudden attack on some outlying town, slaying the inhabitants and carrying away the spoil, and escaped before the pursuers could overtake them. A similar counter-attack would soon follow, and thus the petty wars of reprisal continued, apparently without intermission, throughout Saul's reign. From the south those Bedouin wanderers, the Amalekites, invaded Canaan. To prevent their repeated attacks, Saul appears to have pursued them out into their wilderness home, and for the time being to have intimidated them. The biblical narrative also states that Saul carried on similar wars with the Edomites and Moabites to the south-east and with certain Aramean tribes in the north. Thus, with the exception of the Phœnicians on the north-west, Saul's little kingdom was encircled by a close ring of active foes. His court was the camp, his sceptre the sword, and his nobles the warriors who rallied about him in defence of Israel's liberties.

THE DECLINE OF SAUL AND THE RISE OF DAVID

§ XLIII. DAVID'S INTRODUCTION TO PUBLIC LIFE

1. David's introduction to the court of Saul

Now the spirit of Jehovah had departed from Saul and an evil spirit from Jehovah tormented him. And Saul's servants said to him, See now, an evil spirit from Jehovah is tormenting you. Let your servants who are before you speak and they will seek for our lord a man skilful in playing the lyre. Then, whenever the evil spirit comes upon you, he shall play with his hands, and you will be better. Then Saul said to his servants, Provide me now a man who plays well, and bring him to me. Thereupon one of the young men answered and said, Behold, I have seen a son of Jesse the Bethlehemite who is skilful in playing and a valiant man, a soldier, judicious in speech, a man of good appearance, and Jehovah is with him. Therefore Saul sent messengers to Jesse and said, Send me David your son, who is with the flock. And Jesse took ten loaves of bread, and a skin of wine, and a kid, and sent them to Saul by David his son. So David came to Saul and entered his service; and Saul loved him so much that he became one of his armorbearers. And Saul sent to Jesse, saying, Let David enter my service, for he has found favor in my sight. And whenever the evil spirit from God came upon Saul, David would take the lyre and play with his hand and Saul would breathe freely and would feel better and the evil spirit would depart from him.

2. Goliath's challenge to the Hebrews

Now the Philistines mustered together their forces for war, and they were gathered together at Socoh, which belongs to Judah, and encamped between Socoh and Azekah, in Ephesdammim. And Saul and the men of Israel were gathered together and encamped in the valley of Elah; and they drew up in battle-array against the Philistines.

And the Philistines were standing on the mountain on the one side, and the Israelites were standing on the mountain on the other side, and the valley was between them. And there came out a champion from the camp of the Philistines, named Goliath of Gath, whose height was about ten feet. And he had a helmet of bronze upon his head, and he was clad with a bronze breast-plate of scales, the weight of which was about two hundred pounds. And he had greaves of bronze upon his legs and a javelin of bronze between his shoulders. And the shaft of his spear was like a weaver's beam, and the head of his iron spear weighed about twenty-four pounds; and his shield-bearer went before him. And he stood and cried out to the ranks of Israel and said to them, Why have you come out to draw up the line of battle? Am not I a Philistine and you Saul's servants? Choose a man for yourselves and let him come down to me. If he be able to fight with me and kill me, then we will be your servants; but if I prevail against him and kill him, then shall you be our servants and serve us. And the Philistine said, I have insulted the ranks of Israel to-day; give me a man that we may fight together. And when Saul and all Israel heard these words of the Philistine, they were terrified and greatly afraid.

But David said to Saul, Let not my lord's courage fail him; your servant will go and fight with this Philistine. And Saul said to David, you are not able to go against this Philistine to fight with him, for you are only a youth and he has been a warrior from his youth. But David said to Saul, Your servant was a shepherd with his father's flock; and when a lion, or a bear would come and take a lamb out of the flock, I would go out after him and smite him and deliver it from his mouth; and if he rose up against me, I would seize him by his beard, and slay him with a blow. Your servant smote both lion and bear. Now this uncircumcised Philistine shall be like one of them, since he has insulted the armies of the living God. David also said, Jehovah who delivered me from the paw of the lion, and from the paw of the bear, will deliver me from the hand of this Philistine. Therefore Saul said to David, Go, and may Jehovah be with you.

3. David's offer to fight with Goliath

4. The
arming

And Saul clothed David with his garments, and put a helmet of bronze on his head and clad him with a coat of mail. And David girded his sword over his coat and made a vain attempt to go, for he had not tried them. Then David said to Saul, I cannot go with these, for I have not tried them. And David put them off him.

5. The
pre-
limi-
naries

And he took his club in his hand, and chose five smooth stones out of the brook and put them in his bag, and took his sling in his hand, and he drew near to the Philistine. And when the Philistine looked and saw David, he despised him, for he was but a youth. And the Philistine said to David, Am I a dog that you come to me with a club? And the Philistine cursed David by his gods. And the Philistine said to David, Come to me that I may give your flesh to the birds of the heavens and to the beasts of the field. Then David answered the Philistine,

You come to me with a sword and a spear and a javelin,
But I come to you in the name of Jehovah of hosts,
And the God of the ranks of Israel whom you have insulted.
To-day Jehovah will deliver you into my hands,
That I may smite you and cut off your head;
And I will this day give the dead of the army of the Philistines
To the birds of the heavens and to the wild beasts of the
    earth,
That all the world may know that there is a God in Israel,
And that all this assembly may know
That not with the sword and spear doth Jehovah save,
For the battle is Jehovah's and he will give you into our hand.

6. The
duel

Then when the Philistine arose and came and drew near to meet David, David put his hand in his bag and took from it a stone and slung it and smote the Philistine on his forehead; and the stone sank into his forehead, so that he fell on his face to the earth. Then David ran and stood over the Philistine, and took his sword, and drew it out of its sheath, and slew him, and cut off his head with it.

7.
Flight
of the
Philis-
tines

When the Philistines saw that their champion was dead, they fled. And the men of Israel and Judah arose and raised the battle-cry and pursued the Philistines to the entrance to Gath and to the gates of Ekron, so that the wounded of the Philistines fell down on the way from Shaaraim, even to Gath and Ekron. And when the Israelites returned from pursuing the Philistines, they plundered their camp, but David took the head of the Philistine and brought it to Jerusalem; and he put his armor in his tent.

Now when they came back, as David returned from slaying the Philistine, the women came out dancing from all the cities of Israel to meet Saul the king with tambourines, with cries of rejoicing, and with cymbals. And the women sang to each other as they danced, and said, **8. David's popularity**

> Saul has slain his thousands,
> But David his ten thousands.

And it made Saul very angry, and this saying displeased him, and he said, They ascribed to David ten thousands, while to me they ascribed but thousands, and what can he have more but the kingdom? And Saul kept his eye on David from that day forward. And Saul was afraid of David. Therefore Saul removed him from him, and made him his commander over a thousand; and he went out and came in at the head of the people. And David acted wisely and prospered in all his ways, for Jehovah was with him. And when Saul saw that he acted wisely and prospered, he stood in dread of him. But all Israel and Judah loved David, for he went out and came in at their head. **9. Saul's fear of him**

Now the sons of Saul were: Jonathan, Ishbaal, and Malchishua. And these are the names of his two daughters: the eldest, Merab, the youngest, Michal. And the name of Saul's wife was Ahinoam the daughter of Ahimaaz. **10. Saul's family**

And Michal, Saul's daughter, loved David. And when they told Saul, he was pleased. And Saul said, I will give her to him, that she may be a snare to him and that the hand of the Philistines may be upon him. So Saul commanded his servants, saying, Communicate with David secretly and say, 'See, the king is pleased with you and all his servants love you; now therefore become the king's son-in-law.' And Saul's servants spoke these words in the ears of David. And David said, Is it an easy thing in **11. David's marriage with Michal** your opinion to become the king's son-in-law, when I am a poor man and of no reputation? And the servants of Saul told him saying, David spoke thus. And Saul said, Thus shall you say to David, 'The king desires no bride-price, but a hundred foreskins of the Philistines, in order to take vengeance on the king's enemies.' But Saul thought to make David fall by the hand of the Philistines. And when his servants told David these words, David was well pleased with the prospect of being the king's son-in-law. And the days were not yet expired; and David arose and went together with his men and slew of the Philistines a hundred men; and David brought their foreskins and paid them in full to the king, in order to become the king's son-in-law. Therefore Saul gave him Michal his daughter as wife. And when Saul saw and knew that Jehovah was with David and that all Israel loved him, Saul feared David still more.

12. Jonathan's intercession And Saul commanded Jonathan his son and all his servants to put David to death. But Jonathan, Saul's son, was very fond of David. And Jonathan spoke well of David to Saul his father, and said to him, Let not the king sin against his servant David, because he has not sinned against you and because his conduct toward you has been exceedingly good; for he took his life in his hand and smote the Philistine, and Jehovah wrought a great deliverance for Israel. You saw it and rejoiced. Why then will you sin against innocent blood, in slaying David without a cause? And Saul harkened to the voice of Jonathan; and Saul gave an oath, As Jehovah liveth, he shall not be put to death. And Jonathan called David, and Jonathan made known to him all these words. And Jonathan brought David to Saul, so that he was again in his presence as formerly.

13. Saul's attempt to kill David But when there was war again, David went out and fought against the Philistines, and slew great numbers of them, so that they fled before him. Then an evil spirit from Jehovah came upon Saul, while he was sitting in his house with his spear in his hand, and David was playing on the lyre. And Saul sought to pin David to the wall with the spear, but he slipped away out of Saul's presence, so that he smote the spear into the wall, and David fled and escaped.

And that night Saul sent messengers to David's house to watch him, so as to kill him in the morning. But Michal, David's wife, told him, saying, If you do not save your life to-night, to-morrow you will be slain. So Michal let David down through the window; and he fled away and escaped. And Michal took the household god and laid it in the bed, and put a cloth of goat's hair for its head and covered it with the garment. And when Saul sent messengers to take David, she said, He is sick. Then Saul sent the messengers to see David, saying, Bring him up to me in the bed, that I may put him to death. And when the messengers came in, there the household god was in the bed, with the cloth of goat's hair for its pillow. And Saul said to Michal, Why have you deceived me thus, and let my enemy go, so that he has escaped? And Michal answered Saul, He said to me, 'Let me go; why should I kill you?'

**14.
David's
escape**

I. **The Various Accounts of David's Achievements.** With the sixteenth chapter of I Samuel, the interest of the narrative passes from Saul to David. In a series of closely connected, graphic narratives the story of David's rapid rise to the kingship is vividly told. This ancient Judean David narrative is paralleled or supplemented by certain popular stories, evidently taken from the lips of the people. One or two stories, which magnify the work of Samuel, come from the group of prophetic traditions which were probably treasured by the later guilds of the prophets.

II. **David's Introduction to the Court of Saul.** As king of Israel, it was almost impossible that Saul should remain "among the prophets." Later tradition suggests that early in his reign he alienated the prophets. One tradition of the war against the Amalekites states that the reason was because Saul failed to carry out Samuel's demand that all the captive foes be slain. In a subsequent period, one of the sons of the prophets in the same way denounced Ahab, because he refused to slay the captive Aramean king, Benhadad. The narrative at least suggests the wide difference in point of view and policy between Saul, the war-like and patriotic king, and the sons of the prophets, who, in their religious zeal, did not hesitate to exterminate all of Jehovah's foes.

The harassing wars in which Saul was constantly involved evidently wore upon the stalwart, patriotic defender of his subjects. The sense of isolation, and of failure to unite all the varied elements in his kingdom also undoubtedly increased his malady. This disease has been diagnosed by modern medical authorities as either epilepsy or else acute melancholia. Suddenly, the strong, energetic warrior would become morose and malignant. In the popular thought of his day an evil spirit tormented him.

Following the advice of his servants, Saul consented to have them secure some one skilled in playing the lyre to soothe him, when these attacks seized him. It was thus, according to the earliest narrative, that David, the son of Jesse, was brought to the court of Saul. The picture which is given of him is remarkably clear and detailed. Far from being the stripling of the later popular tradition, David was already a famous warrior, who had won renown on the battle-field. To him the giant Saul was soon ready to intrust his life, as is shown by his making David one of his armorbearers. He was also as skilled in the use of his tongue as of his sword. Already he was famous for his tactful speech. These qualities and his attractive appearance constituted the charm which enabled David in time to win the affectionate regard of practically all the varied elements in Saul's heterogeneous kingdom. This invincible winning power and his success on the battle-field were doubtless the basis of the popular conviction that "Jehovah was with him."

III. **David's Contest with Goliath.** In the Greek text of the seventeenth chapter of I Samuel only one account of David's contest with Goliath is recorded. This version was apparently taken from the early David stories, and is the immediate sequel to the account of David's introduction to the court of Saul. In the Hebrew text, however, a popular version of the story has been closely combined with the account given in the Greek text. This later account is the more familiar because it is the more dramatic. David is here represented as a mere shepherd lad, sent by his father with provisions for his brothers in the army. Volunteering to go out and slay the Philistine champion, he is brought into the presence of Saul and Abner, who, according to this popular story, had never before heard of David.

In the popular account of the achievements of David's warriors, the slaying of Goliath, the Gittite, whose sword was like a weaver's beam, is attributed to one of David's fellow-townsmen, Elhanan. It is evident however, that Goliath was not slain three times. The close connection of the Greek (and less familiar Hebrew) version of David's victory with the preceding and following extracts from the early Judean David stories strongly favors the conclusion that it is the earliest and most authentic account of the event. Hence, there is good historical ground for believing that Goliath was slain by the hand of Saul's valiant armor-bearer.

In view of his important position in the army, it was natural that David should feel under obligation to champion the Hebrew cause. He must, like Saul, have been a man of gigantic stature, otherwise the king would not have suggested that he put on the royal armor. David refused to wear it, not because he was overpowered by its weight, but because he had had no experience in its use. He wisely employed the weapon with which he was most familiar. His gigantic opponent was armed with the sword and javelin with which men fought hand to hand. In fighting at a distance the two weapons commonly used by the Hebrew warriors were the sling and bow. A later tradition, preserved in Chronicles, states that the Benjamite warriors were famous for their effective use of the sling. In the trained hand of a skilled warrior like David, the sling and shot corresponded to the rifle of modern warfare. With this weapon of his childhood days David, the royal armorbearer, went out and slew the champion of the Philistines. According to the earliest version of the tradition, it was as the result of this valiant deed that David suddenly leaped into national prominence and popularity.

IV. Saul's Jealousy of David. The slaughter of Goliath was followed by a signal victory over the Philistines. When the Hebrew warriors returned from battle, the women came out to greet them with a song of triumph. In that song David was exalted above Israel's king. The situation was one to arouse jealousy, even in a better-balanced mind than that of Saul. The kingship was not yet a well-established institution. To maintain his position the king must be recognized as the strongest man in his realm. Saul's authority rested almost entirely on his military achievements. Suddenly his glory had been eclipsed by that of another, who not only had the support of the powerful tribe of Judah but was also endowed with a unique personal charm.

It would appear that David at this time was innocent of any deliberate attempt to undermine the authority of Saul. His moderation at a later crisis (§ XLV), and Jonathan's trust and devotion further confirm this conclusion. There was much, however, to arouse Saul's suspicion. His pathetic position calls for sympathy rather than harsh condemnation. While under the malign influence of his malady, he plotted how he might put out of the way this dangerous rival, but in each attempt he failed. That divine Providence, which was guiding the fortunes of

Israel, was also protecting and preparing the man who was destined to be its future deliverer.

V. The Importance of David's Experience at Saul's Court. David's experience as a shepherd, following the flocks among the rugged Judean hills, developed a strong, rugged physique. His contest with the wild beasts trained him for the later contests with men. At the court of Saul he became acquainted with the forces and leaders who were determining the course of Israel's history. He also gained an insight into the real needs of his nation. His brilliant achievements and fascinating personality won the favor of all ranks. It was also during this period that he attracted to himself certain adventurous souls, who followed him in his fugitive life and remained loyal to him through his many varied fortunes, until he finally became the head of a great and powerful empire. At the military court of Saul and in his numerous forays against the Philistines, he became acquainted with the military tactics of his day and learned not only how to lead, but also how to effectively direct large bodies of men.

§ XLIV.   DAVID AS A FUGITIVE

1
David's
inter-
view
with
Jona-
than

Then David came and said before Jonathan, What have I done? What is my guilt? And what is my sin before your father, that he is seeking my life? And he replied to him, Far be it! You shall not die. See, my father does nothing great or small, but that he discloses it to me; and why should my father hide this from me? Not so. And David answered and said, Your father well knows that I have found favor in your eyes, and he is saying to himself, 'Let not Jonathan know this, lest he be pained.' Nevertheless as surely as Jehovah liveth, and as you live, there is but a step between me and death. Then Jonathan said to David, What do you desire to have me do for you? And David answered Jonathan, Behold, to-morrow is the new moon and I should not fail to sit at the table with the king; therefore let me go and I will hide myself in the field until evening. If your father misses me, then say, 'David urgently asked leave of me to run to Bethlehem his city; for the yearly sacrifice is there for all the family.' If he says 'Good,' then it is well with your servant; but if it arouses his anger, then know that evil is determined upon by him. Now deal kindly with your servant, for you have brought your servant into a sacred covenant with yourself; but if there is guilt in me, slay me yourself, for why should you bring me to your father? And Jonathan said, Far be it from you! for if I should learn that my father had determined that evil should come upon you, I would tell you. Then David said to Jonathan, Who will tell me, if your father answers me harshly? And Jonathan replied to David, Come, and let us go out into the field. So the two of them went out into the field.

And Jonathan said to David, Jehovah, the God of Israel, be witness that I will sound my father about this time to-morrow, and if he is well disposed toward David, then I will send and disclose it to you. God do to Jonathan whatever he will, should my father be disposed to do you evil, and I disclose it not to you and send you away that you may go in peace. And may Jehovah be with you, as he has been with my father. And if I am yet alive, O may you show me the kindness of Jehovah! But if I should die, may you never withdraw your kindness from my house. And if, when Jehovah hath cut off the enemies of David, every one from the face of the earth, the name of Jonathan should be cut off by the house of David, may Jehovah require it at the hand of David's enemies. So Jonathan took oath again to David, because of his love to him; for with all his heart he loved him.

2. The covenant between them

Then Jonathan said to him, To-morrow is the new moon and you will be missed, because your seat will be empty. And on the third day you will be greatly missed. Then you shall come to the place where you hid yourself on the day of the affair, and you shall sit down there beside the heap of stones. And on the third day I will shoot arrows on one side of it, as though I shot at a mark. Then, I will send the lad, saying, 'Go, find the arrows.' If I say to the lad, 'See, the arrows are on this side of you; pick them up!'—then come; for it is well for you, and, as Jehovah liveth, there is nothing the matter. But if I say to the boy, 'See, the arrows are beyond you,' go, for then Jehovah sendeth you away. And as to the word which you and I

3. Their plan

have spoken, behold, Jehovah is witness between you and me forever.

4. Discovery of Saul's feeling toward David

So David hid himself in the field; and when the new moon came, the king sat down at the table to eat. And the king sat upon his seat as usual, even on the seat by the wall, and Jonathan sat opposite, and Abner sat by Saul's side; but David's place was empty. Nevertheless Saul did not say anything that day, for he thought, It is an accident, he is not ceremonially clean, for he has not been cleansed. But when on the day following the new moon, David's place was empty, Saul said to Jonathan his son, Why has not the son of Jesse come to the meal, either yesterday or to-day? And Jonathan answered Saul, David urgently asked leave of me to go to Bethlehem, for he said, 'Let me go, since our family has a sacrifice in the city; and my brothers have commanded me. Now if I have found favor in your sight, let me slip away and see my kinsmen.' Hence he has not come to the king's table. Then Saul's anger was kindled against Jonathan, and he said to him, Son of a depraved woman! Do I not know that you are associated with the son of Jesse to your own shame and to the shame of your mother's nakedness? For as long as the son of Jesse lives on the earth, neither you nor your kingdom will be established. Therefore now send and bring him to me, for he is doomed to die. Then Jonathan answered Saul his father and said to him, Why should he be put to death? What has he done? But Saul lifted up his spear at him to smite him. So Jonathan knew that his father had determined to put David to death. Therefore Jonathan rose from the table in hot anger, and ate no food the second day of the month, for he was grieved for David, because his father reviled him.

5. The warning

But in the morning Jonathan went out into the field at the time appointed with David, and a little lad with him. And he said to his lad, Run, find now the arrows which I shoot. And as the lad ran, he shot an arrow beyond him. And when the lad came to the place where the arrow which Jonathan had shot lay, Jonathan cried after the lad, and said, Is not the arrow beyond you? And Jonathan cried after the lad, Hurry, quick, do not stop! So Jonathan's lad gathered up the arrows, and brought them to his master. But the lad had no knowledge of anything; only Jonathan and David understood the matter.

And Jonathan gave his weapons to his lad, and said to him, Go, carry them to the city. And as soon as the lad had gone, David rose from beside the stone heap, and fell on his face to the ground and prostrated himself three times, and they kissed each other and wept long together. Then Jonathan said to David, Go in peace! As to what we two have sworn in the name of Jehovah—Jehovah will be between me and you and between my descendants and your descendants forever. Then David rose and departed and Jonathan went into the city. 6. The final parting

And David came to Nob, to Ahimelech the priest. And Ahimelech came trembling to meet David and said to him, Why are you alone and no one with you? And David answered Ahimelech the priest, The king has entrusted me with a matter and has said to me, ' Let no one know anything about the matter upon which I am sending you and which I have commanded you'; and I have directed the young men to meet me at a certain place. Now, therefore, if you have five loaves of bread at hand, or whatever can be found, give it to me. And the priest answered David, saying, There is no ordinary bread at hand, but there is holy bread, if only the young men have kept themselves from women. And David answered the priest and said to him, Of a truth women have been kept from us; as always when I set out on an expedition, the weapons of the young men were consecrated, though it is but an ordinary journey; how much more then to-day shall their weapons be holy! So the priest gave him holy bread, for there was no bread there but the showbread, that was taken from before Jehovah in order to put hot bread there the day it was taken away. Now one of the servants of Saul was there that day, detained before Jehovah, by the name of Doeg, an Edomite, the chief of Saul's herdsmen. And David said to Ahimelech, Have you not here at hand a spear or sword? For I brought neither my sword nor my weapons with me, because the king's matter required haste. And the priest said, The sword of Goliath, the Philistine whom you slew in the 7. David's flight to the priest at Nob valley of Elah, there it is wrapped in a garment behind the ephod. If you wish to take that, take it, for there is no other except that here. And David said, There is none like that, give it to me.

David therefore departed thence and escaped to the stronghold of Adullam. And when his brethren and all his father's clan heard it, they went down there to him. And every one who was in distress, and every one who was in debt, and every one who was embittered gathered about him, and he became their leader. And there were with him about four hundred men.

9. His
parents
with
the
king of
Moab

And David went from there to Mizpeh in Moab; and he said to the king of Moab, Let my father and my mother dwell with you, until I know what God will do for me. And he left them in the presence of the king of Moab; and they dwelt with him all the while that David was in the stronghold.

Now when Saul heard that David and the men with him were discovered (Saul was sitting in Gibeah, under the tamarisk-tree on the high place, with his spear in his hand, and all his servants were standing about him), Saul said to his servants who were standing before him, Hear O Benjamites! Will the son of Jesse likewise give you all fields and vineyards? Will he make you all commanders of thousands and commanders of hundreds, that all of you have conspired against me, and no one discloses to me that my son has made a covenant with the son of Jesse, and none of you has pity upon me or discloses to me that my son has stirred up my servant to be an enemy against me, as is now the case? Then Doeg the Edomite, who was standing by the servants of Saul, answered and said, I saw the son of Jesse coming to Nob, to Ahimelech the son of Ahitub. And he inquired of God for him and gave him provisions and the sword of Goliath the Philistine.

Then the king summoned Ahimelech the priest, the son of Ahitub, and all his father's house, the priests who were in Nob, and they came all of them to the king. And Saul said, Hear now, O son of Ahitub! And he answered, Here am I, my lord! And Saul said to him, Why have you, together with the son of Jesse, conspired against me, in that

you have given him bread and a sword and have inquired of
God for him, that he should rise against me as an enemy,
as is now the case? Then Ahimelech answered the king
and said, But who among all your servants is like David,
trusted and the king's son-in-law and captain over your
retainers and honored in your household? Is this the first
time I have inquired of God for him? Far be it from me!
Let not the king impute anything to his servant nor to any
one of my clan, for your servant did not know the slightest
thing about all this. But the king said, You shall surely
die, Ahimelech, together with all your clan. And the king
said to the runners who stood before him, Turn about and
slay the priests of Jehovah, for their hand also was with
David, and, although they knew that he was fleeing, they
did not disclose it to me. But the servants of the king
would not put forth their hands to strike down the priests
of Jehovah. Then the king said to Doeg, Turn and strike
down the priests. And Doeg the Edomite turned and himself struck down the priests. So he slew on that day eighty-
five men who wore the ephod. And the priestly city Nob
he put to the sword, both men and women, children and
infants, oxen and asses and sheep.

And one of the sons of Ahimelech the son of Ahitub,
named Abiathar, escaped and fled to David. And Abiathar
told David that Saul had slain the priests of Jehovah. And
David said to Abiathar, I knew that day, because Doeg the
Edomite was there, that he would surely tell Saul. I myself
am guilty of all the lives of your clan. Remain with me,
fear not; for whoever seeks your life must also seek mine,
since you are placed in my charge.

12. Abiathar's escape

I. **The Friendship of David and Jonathan.** The history of this
period is for the most part a record of intrigue and rivalry and bloodshed. It is this dark background that brings out in clearest relief the
noble friendship of David and Jonathan. That friendship is unique
because of the two characters who figure in it. Jonathan, the heir-
apparent, had, like his father, good ground for viewing with suspicion
David's rapid rise to popularity. It was remarkable, on the other hand,
that David could place his trust and life in the keeping of the son of
Saul. It was clearly a case of two noble souls overleaping the seemingly

insuperable barriers which separated them, and meeting under the attraction of a strong and genuine affection. Of the two friends Jonathan figures as the nobler and more unselfish, for his friendship with David cost him the more. In the face of his father's suspicion and opposition, he persisted in being loyal to him whom the course of events was rapidly carrying toward the throne.

II. The Proof of Jonathan's Friendship. Saul had clearly revealed his jealousy of David, while under the power of his evil malady. David, however, was loath to bid farewell to the court before he was sure that Saul's anger was more than a passing tempest. Accordingly the two friends agreed upon a practical plan for discovering the real state of Saul's mind. It was apparently the custom for all members of the different Hebrew clans to assemble that they might together celebrate the feast of the new moon. The reason offered for David's absence was therefore plausible. Saul's burst of anger clearly revealed his attitude toward his armorbearer. For David to have returned would have been to court death. Only one course remained, and that was to seek safety in flight. The danger of an open meeting between the two friends was obvious. Their plan of communicating secretly with each other proved effective. Tradition also gives a touching picture of their final parting.

III. David and the Priests of Nob. David naturally fled southward toward his home and kinsmen. As he fled, he found himself half famished near the priestly town of Nob, a little north of Jerusalem. To have confessed that he was fleeing from the jealous, half-insane Saul, would have been to warn the priests and to cut off all possibility of receiving food. David yielded to the strong temptation to deceive, and deliberately withheld the actual facts. To satisfy David's need, Ahimelech, the priest, disregarded the ceremonial law and gave him some of the sacred showbread, which was to be eaten only by members of the priestly families. Refreshed, and armed with the sword of Goliath the Philistine, David departed to enter upon his outlaw life.

IV. David's Followers. Adullum, with its numerous caves and its commanding position on the western headlands of Judah, which look out upon the Philistine plain, became for a time the home of David and his followers. It was within the territory of Canaan, in close touch with Saul's court and with David's kinsmen in the south, and yet on the border line just beyond the reach of Saul's sword.

Here there rallied about him a heterogeneous group of followers. They included the warriors in his father's clan—Joab probably among them—and the outcasts and refugees from Saul's court and from the neighboring tribes and kingdoms. In the later list of his valiant warriors appear the names of Hittites, Edomites, and Philistines. They joined David doubtless because of admiration for his achievements, and because he could promise them adventure and spoil. The task of leading, controlling and satisfying the rough, mixed elements that gathered about him was a severe test even for the genius of a David, and proved a valuable training for one who was destined to become king of the jealous factions of Northern and Southern Israel. As an exile from Saul's court, he was at liberty and in a position to make alliances with Israel's foes. Among the Moabites he found shelter and hospitality for his father and mother, whose lives would not have been safe in Saul's kingdom.

V. **The Fate of the Priests of Nob.** The narrative contains a striking illustration of the dangers and fatal consequences of falsehood. When David came as a fugitive to the priests at Nob, there was present by chance a certain Edomite by the name of Doeg, the Iago of early Hebrew history. He had evidently escaped the charm of David's personality. His sole aim appears to have been, by fair means or foul, to ingratiate himself into Saul's favor. Possibly he also had a personal grudge against the priests of Nob.

At the moment when Saul's suspicions were aroused against David, Doeg, with diabolical cunning, told him how the young Judean was received by Ahimelech the priest. Under the influence of his mad frenzy, Saul at once summoned the priests and charged them with conspiracy. Unfortunately, Ahimelech was unaware of the estrangement between the king and David, so that his answer only increased Saul's fury. None of the king's followers responded to his command to slay the innocent priests except the despicable Edomite. Abiathar the son of Ahimelech alone escaped and found refuge with David, who expressed deep contrition at the consequences of his deception.

Thus it was that Saul alienated still further the religious leaders of his kingdom. He presents a pathetic picture. At the moment when he was most in need of sane counsellors, he stood almost alone. In driving David from his court, he not only lost the services of his ablest warrior and leader, but also weakened the loyalty of the strong southern tribes. The better elements in his kingdom must have viewed his policy askance. Priests and prophets condemned his acts and refused to interpret to him Jehovah's will. Under the mad impulse of the moment, the patriot, who was ready to die for his people, figured in the rôle of a cruel tyrant. In the presence of his powerful pitiless foes, the shadows which suggested the coming end already began to gather about Israel's first king.

§ XLV. DAVID'S LIFE AS AN OUTLAW

1. Disclosure of David's hiding place to Saul

Now when David was told, The Philistines are fighting against Keilah and are robbing the threshing floors, David inquired of Jehovah, saying, Shall I go and attack these Philistines? And Jehovah said to David, Go, attack the Philistines, and save Keilah. But David's men said to him, Behold we are afraid here in Judah; how much more then if we go to Keilah against the armies of the Philistines. Then David inquired of Jehovah yet again. And Jehovah answered him, saying, Arise, go down to Keilah, for I will deliver the Philistines into thy hand. So David and his men went to Keilah, and fought with the Philistines and drove away their cattle and slew a great many of them. Thus David delivered the inhabitants of Keilah. Now when Abiathar the son of Ahimelech fled to David to Keilah, he came down with the ephod in his hand. And when it was told Saul that David had come to Keilah, Saul said, God has sold him into my hand; for he has entrapped himself in entering into a town that has doors and bars.

2. David's escape

And Saul summoned all the people to war, to go down to Keilah, to besiege David and his men. And when David knew that Saul was devising evil against him, he said to Abiathar the priest, Bring here the ephod. And David said, O Jehovah, the God of Israel, thy servant hath surely heard that Saul is seeking to come to Keilah, to destroy the city because of me. Will Saul come down, as thy servant hath heard? O Jehovah, God of Israel, I beseech thee, tell thy servant. And Jehovah said, He will come down. Then David said, Will the men of Keilah deliver me and my men into the hand of Saul? And Jehovah said, They will deliver thee up. Then David and his men, who were about six hundred, arose and departed from Keilah, and wandered hither and thither. And when it was reported to Saul that David had escaped from Keilah, he abandoned his expedition. So David dwelt in the wilderness in the strongholds and remained in the hill-country in the Wilderness of Ziph.

Then the Ziphites came to Saul at Gibeah, saying, Is not David hiding in the hill of Hachilah, which is east of the desert? Accordingly Saul arose, and went down to the Wilderness of Ziph, having three thousand men of Israel with him, to seek David in the Wilderness of Ziph. And Saul encamped in the hill of Hachilah, which is east of the desert on the way. But David remained in the wilderness. And when he saw that Saul was following him into the wilderness, David sent out spies and learned that Saul had come from Keilah. And David arose and came to the place where Saul had encamped. And David saw the place where Saul, with Abner the son of Ner, the commander of his army lay, and Saul lay within the barricade, and the people were encamped round about him.

3. Saul's pursuit of David

Then David spoke and said to Ahimelech the Hittite and to Abishai the son of Zeruiah, Joab's brother, saying, Who will go down with me to Saul to the camp? And Abishai said, I will go down with you. So David and Abishai came to the people by night; and Saul was lying there asleep within the barricade, with his spear stuck into the earth at his head, with Abner and the people lying round about him. Then Abishai said to David, God has delivered your enemy into your hand to-day. Now therefore let me smite him with his spear to the earth at one stroke, and I will not need to smite him twice! But David said to Abishai, Destroy him not; for who can lay his hand upon Jehovah's anointed and be innocent? And David said, As Jehovah liveth, either Jehovah shall smite him, or his day shall come to die, or he shall go down into battle and be destroyed. Jehovah forbid that I should put forth my hand against Jehovah's anointed; but now take the spear that is at his head and the jug of water and let us go. So David took the spear and the jug of water from Saul's head and they departed. And no man saw it or knew it, neither did any awake, for they were all asleep because a deep sleep from Jehovah had fallen upon them.

4. David's regard for Saul's life

Then David went over to the other side and stood on the top of a mountain at a distance, a great space being between

5. His words to Saul

them. And David cried to the people and to Abner, the son of Ner, saying, Do you make no answer Abner? Then Abner answered and said, Who are you that calls? And David said to Abner, Are you not a man? And who is like you in Israel? Why then have you not kept guard over your lord the king? For one of the people came to destroy your lord. This that you have done is not good. As Jehovah liveth, you are deserving of death, because you have not kept watch over your lord, Jehovah's anointed. And now see where the king's spear is and his jug of water that was at his head.

6. Saul's reply

Then Saul recognized David's voice and said, Is this your voice, my son David? And David said, It is my voice, my lord, O king. And he said, Why is my lord pursuing his servant? For what have I done? Or of what kind of evil have I been guilty? Now therefore let my lord the king hear the words of his servant. If Jehovah hath stirred you up against me, let him accept an offering; but if they be men, cursed be they before Jehovah, for they have driven me out to-day, so that I have no part in the inheritance of Jehovah, saying, 'Go serve other gods.' Now therefore, may my blood not fall to the earth far away from the presence of Jehovah, for the king of Israel has come out to seek my life, as one hunts a partridge on the mountains. Then Saul said, I have done wrong; return, my son David, for I will do you no more harm, because my life was regarded as sacred by you to-day. I have acted foolishly and have erred exceedingly. And David answered and said, There is the king's spear! Let one of the young men come over and take it. And Jehovah will reward each man's righteousness and fidelity; for Jehovah delivered you into my hand to-day, but I would not raise my hand against Jehovah's anointed. And just as your life was to-day of great value in my sight, so may my life be of great value in Jehovah's sight, and let him deliver me out of all affliction. Then Saul said to David, Be blessed, my son David; you shall do great things and shall surely succeed! So David went his way, but Saul returned to his place.

7. Nabal the Calebite

Then David arose and went into the wilderness of Maon. And there was a man in Maon, whose business was in Carmel. And the man was very rich, and he had three thousand sheep and a thousand goats, and he was shearing his sheep in Carmel. Now the man's name was Nabal; and his wife's name was Abigail; and the woman was sensible and comely, but the man was rough and ill-mannered; and he was a Calebite.

And David heard in the wilderness that Nabal was shearing his sheep. And David sent ten young men, and David said to the young men, Go up to Carmel and enter Nabal's house and greet him in my name; and you shall say to him and to his clan, 'Peace be to you and your house and all that you have. And now I have heard that you have shearers. Your shepherds were with us, and we did not jeer at them, and nothing of theirs was missing all the while they were in Carmel. Ask your young men and they will tell you. Therefore let the young men find favor in your eyes, for we have come on a feast day. Give, therefore, whatever you have at hand to your servants and to your son David.' And when David's young men came, they spoke to Nabal in the name of David and waited as directed. *8. David's message to him*

Then Nabal answered David's servants, and said, Who is David? And who is the son of Jesse? Many are the slaves these days who break away, each from his master! Should I then take my bread and my water and my meat that I have slain for my shearers, and give it to men of whom I know not whence they are? So David's young men turned back on their way, and came and reported all these words to him. And David said to his men, Let every man gird on his sword. And they girded on each man his sword. And David also girded on his sword; and there went up after David about four hundred men; and two hundred remained with the baggage. *9. Nabal's insulting reply*

But one of the young men had told Abigail, Nabal's wife, saying, David has just sent messengers from the wilderness to salute our master, and he railed at them. But the men have been very good to us and we have not been jeered at nor have we missed anything, as long as we went with them, when we were in the fields. They were a wall about us both by night and by day all the while we were with them keeping the sheep. Now therefore know and consider what you will do, for evil is determined against our master and *10. Abigail's prompt action* against all his house, for he is such a base scoundre*l* that no one can speak to him. Then Abigail quickly took two hundred loaves of bread and two skins of wine and five roasted sheep and three and a third bushels of parched grain and a hundred bunches of raisins and two hundred cakes of figs and laid them on asses. And she said to her young men, Go on before me; see, I am coming after you. But she said nothing about it to her husband Nabal. And just as she was riding on the ass and coming down under cover of the mountain, David and his men were also coming down toward her, so that she met them. Now David had said, Surely for nothing did I guard all that belongs to this fellow in the wilderness, so that nothing of all that belongs to him was missing, for he has returned me evil for good. God do whatever he will to David, if I leave by daybreak of all who belong to him as much as a single man.

11. Her wise counsel to David

And when Abigail saw David, she alighted quickly from her ass and fell on her face before David and bowed to the ground. And she fell at his feet and said, Upon me, my lord, upon me be the guilt. Only let your maid-servant speak in your ears, and heed the words of your maid-servant. Let not my lord pay any attention to that base scoundrel, Nabal, for as his name is, so is he; Reckless Fool is his name and folly is his master; but your maid-servant saw not the young men of my lord, whom you sent. Now my lord, as Jehovah liveth and as you live, since Jehovah hath kept you from committing an act of bloodshed and from delivering yourself by your own hand—and may your enemies and those who seek to do evil to my lord be as Nabal—let this present, which your maid-servant has brought to my lord, be given to the young men who follow my lord. Forgive, I pray, the trespass of your maid-servant, for Jehovah will certainly make for my lord a secure house, for my lord is fighting the wars of Jehovah, and no evil shall be found in you as long as you live. And should a man rise up to pursue you and to seek your life, the life of my lord shall be bound in the bundle of the living in the care of Jehovah your God, but the lives of your enemies will he sling out, as from the hollow of a sling. And when Jehovah hath done to my lord all the good that he hath promised you and hath made you prince over Israel, then this shall not be a qualm or a burden on the conscience of my lord, that you have shed blood without cause or that my lord has delivered himself by his own hand. And when Jehovah shall give prosperity to my lord, then remember your maid-servant.

And David said to Abigail, Blessed be Jehovah, the God of Israel, who sent you this day to meet me, and blessed be your discretion, and blessed be you yourself, who have kept me this day from committing an act of bloodshed and from delivering myself by my own hand. For as sure as Jehovah, the God of Israel, liveth, who hath kept me from doing you harm, except you had quickly come to meet me, verily there would not have been left to Nabal by daybreak so much as one man. So David received from her hand that which she had brought him; and to her he said, Go up in peace to your house. See, I have heeded your advice, and granted your request. *12. David's grateful response*

But when Abigail came to Nabal, he was just having a banquet in his house, like a king. And Nabal's heart was merry within him, for he was very drunk, so that she did not tell him anything at all until daybreak. But then in the morning, when the effects of the wine were gone from Nabal, his wife told him these things, and his heart died within him and he became a stone. And at the end of about ten days Jehovah smote Nabal, so that he died. *13. Death of Nabal*

Now when David heard that Nabal was dead, he said, Blessed be Jehovah who hath avenged the case of my insult at the hand of Nabal and hath kept back his servant from evil; and the evil-doing of Nabal hath Jehovah brought back upon his own head. Thereupon David sent and wooed Abigail to take her to him to be his wife. And when the servants of David came to Abigail at Carmel and said to her, David has sent us to you to take you to him to be his wife, she arose and bowed with her face to the earth and said, See, your slave is willing to be a maid-servant to wash the feet of my lord's servants. Thereupon Abigail quickly arose and mounted an ass, and five maidens followed as servants. So she accompanied the messengers of David and became his wife. *14. David's marriage with Abigail*

15. His
other
wives

David also took Ahinoam of Jezreel, and they both became his wives. But Saul had given Michal his daughter, David's wife, to Palti the son of Laish of Gallim.

I. The Relief of Keilah. Although an exile from Saul's court, David still maintained his loyalty to the Hebrew cause. When the news came that the Philistines were besieging Keilah, four or five miles southeast of Adullam, David at once consulted Jehovah through the oracle which Abiathar had brought with him. The nature of the ephod or oracle is unknown. Probably it was simply a contrivance by which to cast a sacred lot. The interpretation, however, belonged to the priest. A rare opportunity was thus given for this enlightened representative of Jehovah, under the protection of his sacred office and with divine authority, to counsel David and his followers at each crisis in their varying fortunes. Acting in accordance with the command thus received, David delivered the inhabitants of Keilah, and there made his home until the news of Saul's pursuit again drove him forth into the wilderness to the southeast of Judah.

II. David's Regard for the Life of Saul. In the rolling, rocky hill country of southern Judah, it was comparatively easy for David and his followers to elude Saul's pursuit. He was obliged, however, always to reckon with the treachery of the neighboring tribesmen. The Ziphites attempted thus to betray him. David's followers were, however, familiar with this territory and well aware of Saul's approach. Two slightly variant versions of the incident have been preserved. The older gives a vivid picture of Saul sleeping soundly on the rocky ground, with his tired warriors about him, protected from the attack of wild beasts by the usual barricade with which the Hebrew army at night was surrounded. David with one of his followers crept so quietly into the camp that Saul lay all unconscious beneath the spear point of Abishai.

The cruel laws of ancient warfare prompted David to give the signal which would free him from his malignant pursuer, and perhaps open the way for him to mount the throne; but a higher principle deterred him. In Saul he recognized the man, not only anointed by Samuel, but called by the needs of his age, his own personal ability and the divinely guided course of events to the leadership of his race. Many oriental rulers before and after David mounted the throne by murdering their predecessor; but David deliberately chose the longer and surer way. His act reveals that higher ethical standard which was already beginning to be recognized among Jehovah's people.

DAVID'S REGARD FOR THE LIFE OF SAUL

The revulsion of feeling which Saul experienced, when he learned of David's magnanimity was perfectly consistent with his character as revealed elsewhere. For the moment his old love for David returned; but the Judean chieftain had learned not to trust his life to Saul's changing moods, and therefore wisely kept himself aloof from the Hebrew court.

III. **The Meanness of Nabal.** The problem which confronted David, that of supporting his six hundred restless warriors in the thickly peopled, unproductive border-land of southern Judah, was exceedingly difficult. Occasional forays against hostile Arab tribes in part supplied their needs; but for the most part they were dependent upon the gifts of the neighboring friendly clans. From time immemorial one unwritten law of the border-land had been that the shepherds and villagers should pay the neighboring nomadic tribesmen for immunity from attack. The other well established law of hospitality required that, especially at the annual festivals, those who had possessions should share liberally with those who had not. In the code of Deuteronomy this principle is definitely expressed in the command to share the festal meal with the poor Levites and resident aliens. In demanding a liberal gift from Nabal, the wealthy Calebite, whose flocks and shepherds David's followers had protected, David was standing squarely on the customary law of the wilderness. In repudiating his obligations Nabal defied that law; but for David to have followed the impulse of the moment and turned his sword against a friendly clan would have been suicidal to his interests.

IV. **Abigail's Wise Counsel.** At this critical moment in David's history Nabal's wife, Abigail, a woman who possessed much personal charm and tact, came to his rescue. By her prompt action she saved him from committing a great crime. The abundant supply of provisions which she brought, incidentally reveals the different kinds of food known to the early Hebrews. Her gifts and wise counsel evidently not only placated David but won his heart. Nabal, perhaps as the result of a stroke of paralysis induced by intemperate habits and the unpalatable news which Abigail brought him, died soon after, and thus the way was opened for David's marriage with Abigail. By his contemporaries Nabal's sudden death was naturally regarded as a divine judgment.

V. **David's Marriages.** Throughout all their history, polygamy seems to have been the exception rather than the rule among the Hebrews. The tribal chieftains and kings were almost the only ones who appear to have indulged in this pernicious oriental institution. Their object was to extend their power and influence by means of alliances with neighboring tribes and peoples. The accepted method of sealing such alliances was by intermarriage. The fact that David, even during his outlaw life, had two wives in addition to Michal—whom Saul had given to another husband—reveals the ambition which was already beginning to stir within the mind of the young Judean leader. His marriage with Abigail was apparently prompted by true love. It brought to him a sane and devoted counsellor. It also strengthened still further his position among the tribes of the South Country. Thus at every step David was increasing his hold upon the Hebrews of the south, and preparing for the moment when they should choose their own king.

§ XLVI. DAVID AMONG THE PHILISTINES

1. David a refugee at the court of Achish

Then David said to himself, I shall be destroyed some day by the hand of Saul. There is nothing better for me than that I should escape into the land of the Philistines. Then Saul will despair of seeking me longer in all the territory of Israel, and I will escape from his hand. So David arose and went over, together with the six hundred men who were with him, to Achish the son of Maoch, king of Gath. And David dwelt with Achish at Gath, together with his men, each with his household, David with his two wives, Ahinoam the Jezreelitess and Abigail the Carmelitess, Nabal's wife. And when Saul was informed that David had fled to Gath, he sought him no more.

2. Life as a feudal lord at Ziklag

But David said to Achish, If now I have found favor in your sight, let a place in one of the towns in the open country be given me, that I may dwell there; for why should your servant dwell in the royal city with you? Then Achish gave him Ziklag at that time; therefore Ziklag belongs to the kings of Judah to this day. And the length of the time that David dwelt in the open country of the Philistines was a year and four months. And David and his men went up, and made a raid upon the Geshurites, the Girzites, and the Amalekites; for these tribes dwell in the land which extends from Telem as far as Shur, even to the land of Egypt. And as often as David smote the land, he did not leave alive man or woman, but taking the sheep, the oxen, the asses, the

camels, and the clothing, he returned and came to Achish.
Then, when Achish said, Where have you made a raid to-day? David answered, Against the South Country of
Judah, or against the South Country of the Jerahmeelites
and against the South Country of the Kenites. But David
never left alive man or woman, to bring them to Gath, for
he thought, They might give information against us and
say, 'Thus has David done.' And such was his custom all
the while he dwelt in the open country of the Philistines.
And Achish trusted David, saying, He has brought himself
into ill-repute with his people Israel; therefore he will be
my servant forever.

Now in those days the Philistines assembled their forces
to make a campaign against Israel. And Achish said to
David, Be assured that you, together with your men, must
go with me along with the forces. And David said to Achish,
Therefore you shall now know what your servant can do.
And Achish said to David, Therefore I make you my body-guard from this time on.

3. Summons to fight against Israel

And the Philistines had assembled their forces at Aphek;
and the Israelites encamped by the fountain in Jezreel.
And the tyrants of the Philistines were marching past, with
hundreds and with thousands; and David and his men
marched in the rear guard with Achish. Then the com-manders of the Philistines said, What are these Hebrews?
And Achish said to the commanders of the Philistines, This
is David, the servant of Saul, the king of Israel, who has now
already been with me two years, and I have found no fault
in him from the time that he came over to me to the present.
But the commanders of the Philistines were enraged against
him, and said to him, Send back the man that he may re-turn to the place where you have stationed him. Let him
not go down with us to battle and let him not be in the camp
an adversary to us; for with what could this fellow better in-gratiate himself with his master than with the heads of
these men? Is not this David of whom they sang respon-sively in the dances, saying,

4. Protest of the Philistine commanders

> Saul has slain his thousands,
> But David his ten thousands?

5. David's dismissal

Then Achish called to David and said to him, As Jehovah liveth, you are upright, and it is my desire that you should go out and in with me in the camp; for I have found no evil in you from the time that you came to me to the present, but you are not regarded favorably by the tyrants. Therefore now return and go in peace, that you may do nothing to displease the tyrants of the Philistines. And David said to Achish, But what have I done? And what have you found in your servant from the day that I entered into your service to this day, that I may not go and fight against the enemies of my lord the king? And Achish answered and said to David, I know that you are as good in my sight as a Messenger of God, but the commanders of the Philistines have said, ' He shall not go up with us to the battle.' Therefore now rise early in the morning, with the servants of your lord who came with you, and go to the place where I have stationed you, and do not entertain any evil design in your heart, for you are good in my sight, but rise early in the morning and as soon as it is light, depart. So David rose early, together with his men, to depart in the morning to return to the land of the Philistines. And the Philistines went up to Jezreel.

6. The Amalekite raid on Ziklag

Now when David and his men on the third day came to Ziklag, the Amalekites had made a raid on the South Country and upon Ziklag, and had smitten Ziklag and burnt it with fire, and had carried away captive the women and all who were in it, both small and great, without slaying any, and had carried them off and gone on their way. And when David and his men came to the city, there it was burned down, and their wives and their sons and their daughters had been taken captive. Then David and the people who were with him wept aloud until they were no longer able to weep. And David's two wives had been taken captive, Ahinoam the Jezreelitess, and Abigail the wife of Nabal the Carmelite.

7. The divine command to pursue the marauders

And David was in great straits, for the people spoke of stoning him, because the soul of all the people was embittered, each for his sons and for his daughters; but David strengthened himself in reliance on Jehovah his God. And David said to Abiathar the priest, the son of Ahimelech, Bring here to me the ephod. And Abiathar brought thither the ephod to David. And David inquired of Jehovah, saying,

> Shall I pursue this marauding band?
> Shall I overtake them?

And he answered him,

> Pursue,
> For thou shalt surely overtake,
> And thou shalt surely rescue.

So David went, together with the six hundred men who were with him, and came to the brook Besor, where those who were left behind remained. But David pursued together with four hundred men; while two hundred remained behind, who were too faint to cross the brook Besor. And they found an Egyptian in the field and brought him to David and gave him food to eat and water to drink; and they gave him a piece of a cake of figs, and two clusters of raisins. And when he had eaten, his spirit revived, for he had eaten no bread and drunk no water for three days and nights. And David said to him, To whom do you belong? And whence are you? And he said I am an Egyptian lad, an Amalekite's servant, and my master abandoned me because three days ago I fell sick. We made a raid upon the South Country of the Cherethites and upon that which belongs to Judah and upon the South Country of Caleb, and Ziklag we burned with fire. And David said to him, Will you bring me down to this band? And he said, Swear to me by God, that you will neither kill me nor deliver me into the hands of my master, and I will bring you down to this band. *8. The pursuit*

And when he had brought him down, there they were spread over all the land, eating and drinking and dancing, on account of all the great spoil that they had taken from the land of the Philistines and from the land of Judah. And David smote them from twilight to evening in order to destroy them completely. And none escaped except four hundred young men, who rode upon the camels and *9. The attack and recovery of the plunder* fled. And David recovered all the persons whom the Amalekites had taken; and David rescued his two wives. And there was nothing of them missing either small or great, sons or daughters, spoil or anything that they had taken to themselves—David brought back all. And he took all the flocks and the herds and drove those animals before the people, and they said, This is David's spoil.

10 The precedent regarding the division of spoil

Now when David came to the two hundred men, who had been too faint to follow him, so that he had to leave them behind at the Brook Besor, they went out to meet David, and the people who were with him. And when they came near to the people, they saluted them. Then all the wicked and base scoundrels among the men who went with David began to say, Because they did not go with us, we will not give them any of the spoil that we have recovered, except to each, his wife and his children, that he may take them away and depart. But David said, Do not so, after that which Jehovah hath given us and after he hath preserved us and delivered the marauding band that came against us into our hand. And who will give heed to you in this matter? For:

As is the share of him who goes down into battle,
So is the share of him who remains with the baggage.
They shall share alike.

And from that time on he made it a statute and precedent in Israel to this day.

11. Presents sent to the southern chieftains

And when David came to Ziklag, he sent some of the spoil to the elders of Judah, his friends, saying, See! a present for you from the spoil of the enemies of Jehovah, to them who were in Bethel, in Ramoth in the South Country, in Jattir, in Aroer, in Siphmoth, and to them who were in Eshtemoa, in Carmel, in the cities of the Jerahmeelites, in the cities of the Kenites, in Hormah, Beersheba, in Athach, in Hebron, and to those in all the places where David and his men had sojourned.

I. David as a Vassal of Achish. David's act in throwing himself upon the mercy of the Philistines shows to what difficult straits he had been reduced. The deed was in keeping with the customs of the time.

112

Refugees frequently fled from one tribe to another. The Semitic law of hospitality protected the stranger, even though he came from a hostile tribe. Between courageous foemen, such as David and the Philistines had proved themsevles on many battle-fields, a friendly alliance was easy. In welcoming the ablest champion of the Hebrews, the Philistines would naturally feel that they had won a great advantage over Saul. With David came six hundred of the most experienced Hebrew warriors. With David also went the interest and loyalty of the tribes of southern Canaan. This blow to Saul's power probably encouraged the Philistines to make that determined attack upon the Hebrews which resulted in the great disaster on Mount Gilboa.

David also doubtless trusted to his own personal charm, which had so often proved invincible. Again his expectations were not disappointed. He soon commanded the absolute confidence of the Philistine king of Gath. At his own request, David, with his followers, was assigned to Ziklag, situated somewhere on the southern Philistine border. There he was able, without close observation, to play the difficult rôle which he had assumed. Only a diplomat like David could have succeeded. It was essential to his future hopes that he should not alienate his Hebrew kinsmen. At the same time he must prove his loyalty to his Philistine master. Successful forays against the Amalekites enabled him for a time to satisfy the difficult demands of the situation.

II. **The Philistine Advance.** The course of events soon placed David in a most trying situation. The confidence of the Philistine king involved him in an almost impossible dilemma. As the body-guard of Achish, he was commanded to join the Philistine army in its march against Saul; but David's diplomacy proved equal to the test. It is difficult to determine what course he would have followed on the actual battle-field. The fears of the Philistine commanders would probably have been realized. Fortunately their lack of confidence compelled Achish to dismiss David, and he was thus delivered from his most difficult dilemma.

III. **The Pursuit and Defeat of the Amalekites.** The moment of David's return to his home at Ziklag was supremely opportune. Assuming that he would join the Philistines in their campaign, David's old foes, the Amalekites, had improved the opportunity to attack and loot Ziklag. Following the command of the divine oracle, David with his followers was soon in hot pursuit. A sudden attack at evening quickly scattered the robbers and left David in possession of their spoil. The precedent, which he established in dividing this spoil, became henceforth a binding law. The incident well illustrates the way in which the ancient Hebrew laws came into existence. A principle thus concretely laid down by a chieftain or king soon crystallized into a definite statute, which was recognized as binding by succeeding generations. Following the tendency of later Judaism, the priestly writers in Numbers 31²⁷ attribute the origin of this institution to Moses.

IV. **The Distribution of the Spoil.** David's distribution of that part of the Amalekite spoil which fell to him reveals clearly his ambition. Portions were sent to the elders of all the important towns in southern Judah and the South Country. The Bethel near Ziklag, Aroer, Carmel, Hebron, Beersheba and possibly Arad are among the towns definitely mentioned. In addition to his own tribesmen of Judah, the Jerahmeelites and the Kenites were similarly favored. These gifts clearly represent a bid for the support of the tribes of southern Canaan. In the light of the events which quickly followed, they prepared the way for that call which soon came to David to become king of Judah; and when the place sought the man, the man was fully ready for the place.

§ XLVII. SAUL'S DEFEAT AND DEATH

1. Saul's desire for a revelation

Now Samuel had died and all Israel had lamented for him and buried him in Ramah, his own city. And Saul had put the mediums and the wizards out of the land. And when the Philistines assembled and came and encamped in Shunem, Saul assembled all Israel, and they encamped in Gilboa. And when Saul saw the army of the Philistines, he was afraid and his heart was filled with apprehension. And Saul inquired of Jehovah, but Jehovah did not answer him either by dreams or by Urim or by prophets. Then Saul said to his servants, Find for me a medium who has a talisman, that I may go to her and inquire of her. And his servants said to him, Behold, there is at Endor a medium who has a talisman.

2. The midnight scene at Endor

Therefore Saul disguised himself and put on other clothes and went, taking two men with him, and they came to the woman by night. And he said, Divine for me by the talisman and bring up for me the one whom I shall name to you. And the woman said to him, Behold, you know what Saul has done, how he has cut off the mediums and the wizards from the land. Why then are you laying a snare for my

114

life, to put me to death? And Saul swore to her by Jehovah, saying, As Jehovah liveth, no guilt shall come upon you for this thing. Then the woman said, Whom shall I bring up to you? And he said, Bring up Samuel. And when the woman saw Samuel, she screamed. And the woman said to Saul, Why have you deceived me, for you are Saul? And the king said to her, Do not be afraid! What do you see? And the woman said to Saul, I see a god coming out of the earth. And he said to her, What is his appearance? And she said, An old man is coming up, and he is wrapped in a mantle. Then Saul knew that it was Samuel, and he bowed with his face to the earth and worshipped.

And Samuel said to Saul, Why have you disturbed me by bringing me up? And Saul answered, I am in great straits, for the Philistines are making war against me and God has turned from me and answers me no more, either by prophets or by dreams; so I have called you to tell me what I shall do. And Samuel said, Why do you ask of me when Jehovah hath turned from you and become your adversary? And to-morrow you and your sons with you shall fall; Jehovah will deliver the army of Israel also into the power of the Philistines. 3. The message of doom

Then Saul fell at once at full length upon the earth and was greatly afraid, because of the words of Samuel; also he had no strength in him, for he had not eaten bread during all the day and all the night. And when the woman came to Saul and saw that he was greatly troubled, she said to him, See, your maid-servant has heeded your voice, and I have taken my life in my hand and have listened to your words which you spoke to me. Now therefore, listen also to the advice of your maid-servant and let me set before you a morsel of meat, and eat that you may have strength, when you go on your way. But he refused, and said, I will not eat. But his servants, together with the woman, urged him, until he listened to their advice. So he rose from the earth and sat upon the couch. And the woman had a fatted calf in the house; and she quickly killed it, and took flour and kneaded it and baked from it unleavened bread. And she set it before Saul and his servants, and they ate. Then they rose up and went away that night. 4. Effect upon Saul

5. Defeat of the Israelites and death of Saul

Now the Philistines fought against Israel, and the Israelites fled from before the Philistines and fell down slain on Mount Gilboa. And the Philistines followed close after Saul and his sons; and the Philistines slew Jonathan and Abinadab and Malchishua, the sons of Saul. And they pressed hard upon Saul, and the archers found him out, and he was wounded by the archers. Then said Saul to his armorbearer, Draw your sword and run me through with it, lest these uncircumcised Philistines come and make sport of me. But his armorbearer would not, for he was greatly afraid. Therefore Saul took his own sword and fell upon it. And when his armorbearer saw that Saul was dead, he likewise fell upon his sword and died with him. So Saul and his three sons and his armorbearer died together on the same day.

6. Fate of Saul's body

And when the Israelites, who were in the cities of the valley and in the cities of the Jordan, saw that the Israelites had fled and that Saul and his sons were dead, they also left the cities and fled, and the Philistines came and remained in them. But when on the following day the Philistines came to strip the slain, they found Saul and his three sons fallen on Mount Gilboa. And they cut off his head and stripped off his armor and sent throughout the land of the Philistines to bring good news to their idols and to the people. And they put his armor in the temple of Ashtarte, and they fastened his body on the wall of Bethshan. And when the inhabitants of Jabesh in Gilead heard what the Philistines had done to Saul, all the valiant men arose and marched all night and took the bodies of Saul and his sons from the wall of Bethshan; and they came to Jabesh and lamented over them there. And they took their bones and buried them under the tamarisk tree in Jabesh, and they fasted seven days.

7. Arrival of the messenger

Now, after the death of Saul, when David had returned from smiting the Amalekites, David remained two days in Ziklag. Then on the third day there came a man out of the camp from Saul, with his clothes torn and with earth upon his head. And as soon as he came to David, he fell to the earth and did obeisance. And David said to him, Whence do you come? And he answered him, From the camp of Israel have I escaped. And David said to him, How was the affair? Tell me. And he answered, The people fled from the battle, and many of the people fell, and also Saul and Jonathan his son are dead.

Then David took hold of his clothes and tore them; and all the men who were with him did likewise. And they mourned and wept and fasted until evening for Saul and for Jonathan his son and for the people of Jehovah and for the house of Israel, because they had fallen by the sword. _{8. Lamentation over the fallen}

Then David sang this dirge over Saul and Jonathan his son (behold, it is written in the Book of Jashar), and said, _{9. David's dirge}

Weep, O Judah!
Grieve, O Israel!
On thy heights are the slain!
How the mighty have fallen! _{10. Greatness of the calamity}

Tell it not in Philistine Gath,
Declare it not in the streets of Askelon;
Lest the daughters of the Philistines rejoice,
Lest the daughters of the uncircumcised exult.

Ye mountains of Gilboa, may no dew descend,
Nor rain upon you, O ye fields of death!
For there was the shield of the mighty thrown down,
The shield of Saul, not anointed with oil.

From the blood of the slain, from the fat of the mighty,
The bow of Jonathan turned not back,
The sword of Saul returned not empty. _{11. Valor of the fallen}

Saul and Jonathan, the beloved and the lovely!
In life and in death they were not parted;
They were swifter than eagles, they were stronger than
    lions. _{12. Their attractiveness}

Daughters of Israel, weep over Saul,
Who clothed you daintily in finest linen,
Golden ornaments he placed on your garments,
How the mighty have fallen in the midst of battle! _{13. Saul's services to Israel}

14. David's love for Jonathan

Jonathan, in thy death me thou hast wounded!
O Jonathan, my brother, for thee I'm in anguish,
To me thou wert surpassingly dear,
Thy love were far more than the love of woman!

15. The lament.

How the mighty have fallen,
And the weapons of war perished!

I. Saul's Visit to the Medium of Endor. Samuel appears but once in the earliest narratives. The occasion was his memorable meeting with Saul. His activity at that great crisis in Israel's history rightly won for him a place beside Moses and Deborah. The fact that a large body of later traditions gather about his name confirms still further his title to greatness. From this later group of traditions apparently comes the account of Saul's visit to the medium of Endor. It throws much light on the life and thought of early Israel, and gives a tragic picture of Saul in his later days. Deprived of the counsel and support of the priests and prophets of his realm, he resorted to one of the representatives of the old heathenism, which still survived in Palestine. For the gigantic Saul disguise was futile. The medium whom he consulted regarding the outcome of the impending battle, must have recognized him from the first. Her methods are those employed by mediums of all ages. She, not Saul, claims to see the dead prophet Samuel and interprets the message to the king. The message itself was clearly suggested by the political situation. Before the organized and powerful army of the Philistines, only defeat awaited the Hebrews. As Saul goes forth to fight his last, losing battle, he commands both pity and a certain admiration.

II. The Battle on Mount Gilboa. Very briefly the early David narrative records the disastrous event. In approaching Israel along the plain of Esdraelon, the Philistines apparently aimed to separate Saul from his northern subjects. The elders of the southern Palestinian towns, who received the spoil sent them by David, had apparently not rallied about Saul. It would seem, therefore, that with only a part of his subjects, he met the Philistine attack. The heights about Gilboa on the southeastern side of the plain of Esdraelon, where the advantages would be with the defenders, were chosen by Saul as a battlefield. The Hebrews, however, were so lacking in courage that the battle soon became a mad rout. Although forsaken by their warriors, Saul and his sons and his armorbearer refused to flee. When his sons had already fallen beside him and he was himself severely wounded, Saul chose to die by his own sword rather than to fall into the hands of the pitiless foes.

The treatment of Saul's body by the Philistines reveals the brutality of the age and suggests the indignities which Saul escaped by his self-inflicted death. One bright gleam lights up the sad scene. In gratitude for the deliverance which Saul had brought them at the beginning of his reign, the citizens of Jabesh in Gilead across the Jordan rescued the body of the dead king from the walls of Bethshan and buried it under a famous tree near their city.

III. **David's Lamentation over Saul and Jonathan.** The men of Jabesh did not lament alone over the death of the fallen heroes. When at length a fugitive escaped from Saul and bore the news of the disaster to David, he and his followers joined in the universal lamentation. The desire to conciliate the northern tribes undoubtedly influenced the conduct of David, but a deeper motive, that of genuine sorrow, breathes through the dirge which tradition attributes to him. There is good ground for believing that tradition is right in ascribing this noble song of lamentation to the singer who had so often soothed Saul's perturbed spirits. The ancient minstrel appears to have improvised as he played. A part of David's charm was apparently his skill as a poet. The occasion was one which would naturally lead him to exercise this skill. The detailed references in the song fit well the lips of David. The genuine pathos and sorrow, especially over the death of the beloved Jonathan, all point to David as the author.

The artistic beauty of the poem is unsurpassed. It opens with a stanza in the quick two-beat measure, which rises in the second stanza to the three beat, and in the third to the four-beat measure, which is maintained throughout the song, until the last refrain is introduced, giving the effect of a final sob. In the first stanza the nation is called upon to join in the lamentation, in the second the cruel exultation of the Philistines is viewed with horror and in the third Nature and especially the mountains of Gilboa, the scene of the disastrous battle, are called upon to join in the universal lamentation. In the next two stanzas the courage, the prowess and the virtues of Saul and Jonathan are powerfully presented. The women of Israel, who led in the ancient lamentations, are reminded of what Saul has done for them and the nation. The culmination of the poem is reached in the pathetic stanza in which David protests his deep love for Jonathan and voices his own bitter sorrow.

IV. Saul's Strength and Weakness. The estimates regarding the character of Saul vary greatly. The task of determining the real character of Saul is complicated by the fact that we are dependent for our knowledge of the latter part of this period upon a group of narratives in which the interest is with David rather than with Israel's first king. Even in the early Saul narratives, his rash impulsiveness is revealed in the vow which he made, while in pursuit of the Philistines. His faults are especially glaring because they are so unkingly. Self-will, anger, jealousy and intemperate action are almost inexcusable in him who is called to rule others. There are suggestions in the ancient narrative that these faults were largely due to physical causes, and if so they do not represent the real Saul. At the same time physical maladies are in many cases the result of moral defects. That Saul from the first was lacking in self-control, breadth of vision and a deep religious instinct seems clear. It was perhaps too much to expect that the rude age in which he lived would produce a fully developed ruler of men. With his courage, enthusiasm and patriotic zeal Saul satisfied the demands of the moment. His natural impulses were noble and generous. There was much in his character to command admiration. David's tribute to him rests upon a substantial basis of fact. His closing years, therefore, are all the more tragic because his petty faults gained the ascendency and obscured the true nobility of his nature.

V. The Significance of Saul's Reign. David's brilliant achievements almost completely overshadow those of Saul. Yet it is important to remember that David's work would have been impossible had not Saul prepared the way. By his courage and patriotism he accomplished the almost impossible task of uniting the rival Hebrew tribes. By personal example and direction he taught the Israelites, on many a hard-fought battle-field, how to wield the sword and to win victories from their powerful foes. Against great odds, he threw off the Philistine yoke and established Israel's prestige among the nations. He also opened the highways of commerce, so that the Hebrews began to enjoy the products of that highly civilized ancient world. The simplicity and severity of his own life and court kept back for a time that wave of oriental luxury which was destined all too soon to engulf Israel. He did much to fix in the minds of the Israelites that high, democratic ideal of the kingship, which tyrants, like Solomon and Ahab, were unable to dislodge. Thus Saul established those noble precedents which David, in more favorable circumstances, followed with far greater glory and success.

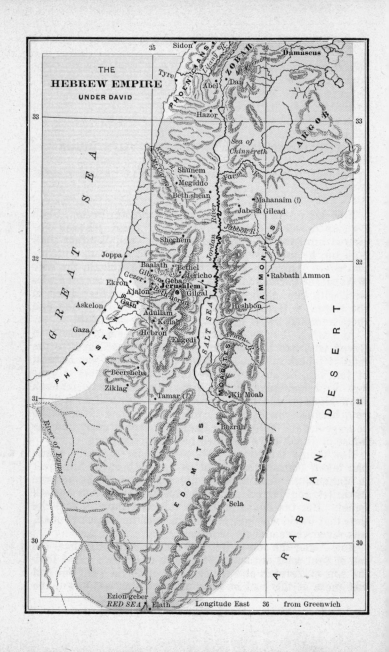

THE
HEBREW EMPIRE
UNDER DAVID

Sidon

35

36

Damascus

ZOBAH

PHOENIANS

Tyre

Abel

Dan

Mt. Hermon

33

33

Hazor

Sea of
Chinnéreth

ARGOB

Shunem

Megiddo

Beth-shean

Mahanaim (?)

Jabesh Gilead

Jabbok R.

Shechem

GREAT SEA

Joppa

32

Baalath

Bethel

32

Gezer

Gibeon

Jericho

Ekron

Geba

Jerusalem

Rabbath Ammon

Ajalon

Beth-horon

Gilgal

AMMONITES

Gath

Askelon

Adullam

Heshbon

Keilah

Gaza

Hebron

Engedi

PHILISTINES

SALT SEA

MOABITES

Arnon

Beersheba

Ziklag

Tamar (?)

Kir Moab

31

31

Bozrah

River of Egypt

EDOMITES

ARABIAN DESERT

Sela

30

30

Ezion-geber

RED SEA

Elath

Longitude East   36   from Greenwich

THE POLITICAL EVENTS OF DAVID'S REIGN

§ XLVIII. THE TWO HEBREW KINGDOMS UNDER DAVID AND ISHBAAL

Now after this David inquired of Jehovah, saying, Shall I go up to one of the cities of Judah? And Jehovah answered him, Go up. And when David said, Whither shall I go up, he said, To Hebron. So David went up with his two wives, Ahinoam, the Jezreelitess, and Abigail, the wife of Nabal the Carmelite. And David brought up the men who were with him, each with his household, and they dwelt in the towns of Hebron. And the men of Judah came and there anointed David king over the house of Judah. *1.David king at Hebron*

And when they told David about the men of Jabesh in Gilead who had buried Saul, David sent messengers to the men of Jabesh in Gilead and said to them, May you be blest of Jehovah, because you have shown this kindness to your lord Saul and have buried him. Even so may Jehovah show kindness and truth to you; and I also will do well by you, because you have done this thing. Now therefore be courageous and valiant; for Saul your lord is dead, and the house of Judah have anointed me king over them. *2. His message to the Gileadites*

Now Abner the son of Ner, commander of Saul's army, had taken Ishbaal the son of Saul, and brought him over to Mahanaim. And he made him king over Gilead and the Ashurites and Jezreel and Ephraim and Benjamin and all Israel. But the house of Judah followed David. And the time that David was king in Hebron over the house of Judah, was seven years and six months. *3. Ishbaal's kingdom*

Now Abner the son of Ner and the servants of Ishbaal the son of Saul went out from Mahanaim to Gibeon. And Joab the son of Zeruiah and the servants of David went out and met them at the pool of Gibeon. And they sat down, the *4. Battle of Gibeon* one on the one side of the pool and the other on the other side of the pool. Then Abner said to Joab, Let the young men arise and play before us. And Joab said, Let them arise. Then they arose and went over by number: twelve for Benjamin and Ishbaal the son of Saul, and twelve of the servants of David. And they each caught his opponent by the head and thrust his sword into his side, so they fell down together. Therefore that place was called, Field of the Enemies (which is in Gibeon). And the battle was very fierce that day, and Abner and the men of Israel were vanquished before the servants of David.

5. Death of Asahel

And the three sons of Zeruiah were there, Joab, Abishai, and Asahel; and Asahel was as swift of foot as one of the gazelles which are in the field. And Asahel pursued Abner; and as he went he turned neither to the right nor to the left from the pursuit of Abner. Then Abner looked behind him and said, Is it you, Asahel? And he answered, It is I. Therefore Abner said to him, Turn aside to your right or to your left and seize one of the young men and take his spoil. But Asahel would not turn aside from pursuing him. Therefore Abner said again to Asahel, Turn aside from following me. Why should I smite you to the ground? How then could I look Joab your brother in the face? But he refused to turn aside. Therefore Abner smote him with a backward stroke in the body, so that the spear came out at his back; and he fell there and died in his place. Then all who came to the place where Asahel had fallen and died, stood still.

6. Abner's escape

But Joab and Abishai pursued after Abner. And as the sun was setting, they came to the hill of Ammah, which is before Giah on the highway in the wilderness of Gibeon. And the Benjamites assembled behind Abner and formed a solid phalanx, and stood on the top of a hill. Then Abner called to Joab and said, Shall the sword devour forever? Do you not know that the end will be bitterness? How long then will it be before you command the people to turn from pursuing their kinsmen? And Joab said, As Jehovah liveth, if you had not spoken, then assuredly not until morning would the people have ceased each from pursuing his brother. So Joab blew the trumpet; and all the people stood still and pursued Israel no more, nor did they fight any more. But Abner and his men marched all that night through the Arabah and crossed the Jordan and went through the whole Bithron and came to Mahanaim.

And Joab returned from the pursuit of Abner. And when he had gathered all the people together, nineteen of David's servants besides Asahel were missing; while the servants of David had smitten of Benjamin and of Abner's men three hundred and sixty. And they took up Asahel and buried him in his father's sepulchre, which was in Bethlehem. And Joab and his men marched all night, and day dawned upon them at Hebron. *7. Losses in the battle*

And the war between the house of Saul and the house of David was prolonged; but David kept growing stronger, while the house of Saul grew gradually weaker. *8. Results of the war*

Now, while there was war between the house of Saul and the house of David, Abner made himself strong in the house of Saul. And Saul had a concubine, whose name was Rizpah, the daughter of Aiah. And Ishbaal the son of Saul said to Abner, Why do you go in unto my father's concubine? Then Abner was very angry because of the words of Ishbaal and said, Am I a dog's head, who am at this time showing kindness to the house of Saul your father, to his kinsmen, and to his friends, and have not delivered you into the hand of David, that you now charge me with guilt in connection with a woman? God do to Abner whatever he pleaseth, if, as Jehovah hath sworn to David, I do not even so to him, by transferring the kingdom from the house of Saul and by establishing the throne of David over Israel and over Judah from Dan to Beersheba. And he did not dare to make Abner any answer, for he feared him. *9. Abner's quarrel with Ishbaal*

So Abner sent messengers to David to Hebron, saying, Make your league with me, then I will co-operate with you in bringing over all Israel to you. And he said, Good, I will make a league with you, but one thing I require of you, that is, you shall not see my face unless you bring Michal, Saul's daughter, when you come to see me. Then David sent messengers to Ishbaal, Saul's son, saying, Give me my wife Michal, whom I bought for a hundred foreskins of the Philistines. And Ishbaal sent and took her from her hus- *10. Negotiations between Abner and David*

123

band, Paltiel the son of Laish. But her husband followed her, weeping as he went, to Bahurim. Then Abner said to him, Go, return; and he returned.

11. His visit to David

And when Abner came to David at Hebron, accompanied by twenty men, David gave Abner and the men who were with him a feast. And Abner said to David, I will arise and go and will gather all Israel to my lord the king, that they may make a covenant with you and that you may be king over all which you desire. Then David sent Abner away, and he went in peace.

12. His murder by Joab

Just then the servants of David and Joab came from a raid, and brought in with them great spoil; but Abner was not with David in Hebron, for he had sent him away, and he had gone in peace. So when Joab and all the band that was with him came home, they told Joab, saying, Abner the son of Ner came to the king, and he has sent him away, and he has gone in peace. Then Joab went to the king and said, What have you done? Behold, Abner came to you; why have you now sent him away, so that he is gone? Do you not know that Abner the son of Ner came to deceive you and to note your going out and your coming in and to know all that you are doing? And when Joab came out from David, he sent messengers after Abner, and they brought him back from the Cistern of Sirah without David's knowing it. And when Abner returned to Hebron, Joab took him apart to the side of the gate to speak with him quietly, and smote him there in the body. So he died for the blood of Asahel Joab's brother.

13. David's condemnation of the act

But afterward when David heard it, he said, I and my kingdom are forever guiltless before Jehovah of the blood of Abner the son of Ner. May it fall upon the head of Joab and upon all his father's house, and may there not fail from the house of Joab one who has an issue, or who is a leper, or who is effeminate, or who falls by the sword, or who lacks bread.

14. His lamentation over Abner

And David said to Joab, and to all the people who were with him, Tear your clothes, and gird yourselves with sackcloth, and mourn before Abner! And King David followed the bier. And when they buried Abner in Hebron, the king wept with a loud voice at the grave of Abner, and all the people wept. And the king sang a dirge for Abner and said,

> Must Abner die as dies the impious fool?
> Thy hands were not bound,
> Thy feet were not put into fetters;
> As one falls before ruthless men, thou didst fall.

Then all the people wept still more over him. Afterward all the people came to urge David to eat bread while it was yet day; but David took oath, saying, God do to me whatever he will, if I taste bread or anything else before the sun goes down. And when all the people observed it, they were pleased; for everything that the king did pleased all the people. So all the people and all Israel understood that day that the king had nothing to do with the slaying of Abner the son of Ner. And the king said to his servants, Do you not know that a prince and a great man has fallen to-day in Israel? And I am this day weak, though anointed king, for these men, the sons of Zeruiah, are too strong for me. May Jehovah requite the evil-doer according to his wickedness!

Now when Ishbaal, Saul's son, heard that Abner was dead in Hebron, his hands became limp and all the Israelites were thrown into confusion. And Ishbaal, Saul's son, had two men who were captains of guerilla bands: the name of one was Baanah, and the name of the other Rechab, sons of Rimmon the Beerothite, of the Benjamites (for Beeroth is also reckoned to Benjamin, and the Beerothites fled to Gittaim and have been sojourners there until this day). And the sons of Rimmon the Beerothite, Rechab and Baanah, went and came about mid-day to the house of Ishbaal, as he was taking his rest at noon. And just then the doorkeeper of the palace was cleaning wheat, and she became drowsy and slept. So Rechab and Baanah his brother slipped in and thus entered the house, while the king was lying on his bed in his sleeping room, and they smote and killed him and cut off his head. *15. Assassination of Ishbaal*

Then they took his head and went all night by the way of the Arabah. And they brought the head of Ishbaal to David to Hebron and said to the king, Here is the head of Ishbaal, the son of Saul your enemy, who sought your life. But *16. David's attitude toward it*

Jehovah hath avenged my lord the king this day on Saul and his descendants. Then David answered Rechab and Baanah his brother, the sons of Rimmon the Beerothite, and said to them, As Jehovah liveth, who hath delivered my life out of all adversity, when one told me, saying, 'Behold, Saul is dead,' thinking to have brought good news, I took hold of him, and slew him in Ziklag, to give him the reward for his news. How much more, when wicked men have slain a righteous person in his own house upon his own bed, shall I not now require his blood from you and destroy you from the earth? Then David commanded his young men, and they slew them and cut off their hands and their feet, and hanged them up beside the pool in Hebron. But the head of Ishbaal they took and buried in the grave of Abner at Hebron.

17. David king of all Israel Then all the tribes of Israel came to David to Hebron and said, See, we are your bone and your flesh. In times past when Saul was king over us, it was you who led out and brought in Israel, and Jehovah hath said to you, 'Thou shalt be shepherd of my people Israel, and thou shalt be prince over Israel.' And all the elders of Israel came to the king to Hebron, and King David made a covenant with them in Hebron before Jehovah, and they anointed David king over Israel.

18. Length of David's reign David was thirty years old when he became king, and he reigned forty years. In Hebron he reigned over Judah seven years and six months, and in Jerusalem he reigned thirty-three years over all Israel and Judah.

I. **David, King of Hebron.** The overwhelming disaster on Mount Gilboa led the Hebrew and allied tribes of southern Palestine to look to David for leadership. As a vassal of the Philistines, he was in a position to deliver them from the danger which they most feared. They had evidently never been strongly loyal to the house of Saul. It was, therefore, easy for them to transfer their allegiance to a chieftain who came from their own ranks, and especially so, since David had proved his ability in many different crises.

The message which David sent to the men of Jabesh suggests that he aspired at this time to the kingship of all Israel; but Saul's able commander, Abner, still lived, and succeeded in saving certain fragments of the dismembered kingdom and in placing Saul's son, Ishbaal, on the throne. By later generations Ishbaal was called Ishbosheth, *the man of shame,* because his name contained the hated word, *Baal.*

✗ **II. Hostilities between the Two Kingdoms.** Both David and Ishbaal appear to have ruled as vassals of the Philistines and to have paid yearly tribute to these powerful foes, whose authority was again reëstablished in central Canaan. The fact that they were subject to an outside power did not prevent the two rival kingdoms from making war upon each other. It was a war, however, inspired not by the desire for conquest but by the jealousy of the rival leaders, Abner and Joab. It is in this connection that Joab first comes into prominence. As a kinsman of David, he had evidently shared his leader's outlaw experiences. He was a man without fear or conscientious scruple. Pity and forgiveness were also foreign to his nature. His one virtue and also his fault was his supreme devotion to David's cause. Unfortunately for Abner, Joab soon became involved in a blood feud with this rival commander of the northern forces.

III. Abner's Negotiations with David. Of the two men, Abner appears to have been much the nobler character. His endeavor to avoid bloodshed and his loyalty to the unworthy son of Saul are virtues rare in this early age. When at last it became evident that the rule of the jealous and incompetent Ishbaal could no longer be maintained, Abner entered into negotiations with David with the aim of uniting the two kingdoms. A peaceful union seemed imminent, when Joab, prompted by the spirit of jealousy and blood-revenge, treacherously slew Abner. The act was prompted by such personal and unworthy motives that no palliation is possible.

IV. David's Election as King. On the eve of its realization David's fondest ambition was endangered. The treacherous murder of the popular northern leader in David's territory and by his own kinsman and commander-in-chief was a crime difficult to overlook. David's supreme tact and that marvellous fortune, which followed him throughout his career, are well illustrated at this crisis, but the real explanation of his ability to escape this seemingly impossible dilemma lies deeper. His upright record and the personal confidence, which he had inspired even in his foes, alone enabled him to dispel suspicion. His lament over Abner might have been deemed mere hypocrisy, but it was evidently not so regarded by the people of Israel. His frank confession of his own weakness in the hands of Joab and his ruthless kinsmen perhaps also carried great weight before the bar of public opinion.

The news, which quickly came of the assassination of Ishbaal, undoubtedly aided much in turning the tide in David's favor. His prompt action in slaying the assassins, who came expecting reward, still further confirmed the people in their belief that David was sincere. Back of the action of the elders of Israel, as they came to Hebron to anoint David king over all Israel, was the fact that the only choice which remained for them was to endure the Philistine yoke or else to accept the leadership of the one man who was able to restore their freedom. Through perils at the hands of friend and foe, through many crises and temptations, David had passed unscathed. By his reserve and moderation, as well as by his courage and diplomacy, he had at last won the highest honor that his race could confer. Israel had also, in divine providence, at last found the man supremely fitted to lead it on to the realization of its highest material hopes.

§ XLIX. THE LIBERATION AND CONSOLIDATION OF ALL ISRAEL

1 The Philistine advance

Now when the Philistines heard that they had anointed David king over Israel, all the Philistines went up to seek David; and when David heard of this he went down to the stronghold.

2. Brave deed of the warriors at Bethlehem

And three of the Thirty went down, and came to the rock to David to the stronghold of Adullam, while a force of the Philistines was encamped in the valley of Rephaim. And David was then in the stronghold, and the garrison of the Philistines was in Bethlehem. And David longed and said, O that one would give me water to drink from the well of Bethlehem, which is by the gate! And the three famous warriors broke through the camp of the Philistines and drew water out of the well of Bethlehem, that was by the gate, and took and brought it to David; he would not drink of it, however, but poured it out to Jehovah. And he said, Jehovah forbid that I should do this. It is the blood of the men who went at the risk of their lives. Therefore he would not drink it. These things did the three mighty men.

3. The first victory in the valley of Rephaim

Now the Philistines had come and spread themselves out in the valley of Rephaim. And David inquired of Jehovah, saying, Shall I go up against the Philistines? Wilt thou deliver them into my hand? And Jehovah said to David,

Go up; for I will certainly deliver the Philistines into thy hand. And David came to Baal-perazim, and David smote them there; and he said, Jehovah hath broken down mine enemies before me, like the breaking of waters. Therefore he called the name of that place Baal-perazim [Lord of the breakings through]. And they left their gods there, and David and his men carried them away.

And the Philistines came up yet again and spread themselves out in the valley of Rephaim. And when David inquired of Jehovah, he said, Thou shalt not go up; go about to their rear and come upon them opposite the balsam trees. And when thou hearest the sound of marching in the tops of the balsam trees, make haste, for then Jehovah hath gone out before thee to smite the camp of the Philistines. And David did as Jehovah commanded him, and smote the Philistines from Gibeon as far as Gezer. *4. The second victory*

Then the king and his men went to Jerusalem against the Jebusites, the inhabitants of the land, who spoke to David, saying, You shall not come in here, but the blind and the lame shall turn you away, thinking, David cannot come in here. *5. Advance against Jebus*

Nevertheless David took the stronghold of Zion (that is the city of David). And David said on that day, Whoever smites the Jebusites, let him get up through the watercourse and smite the lame and the blind, whom David's soul hates. Then David dwelt in the stronghold, and called it the City of David. And David constructed an encircling wall from Millo and inward. *6. Its capture and fortification*

And David kept on growing greater, for Jehovah of hosts was with him. And Hiram king of Tyre sent messengers to David, and cedar trees and carpenters and masons and they built David a palace. Thus David perceived that Jehovah had established him king over Israel, for his kingdom had been exalted for the sake of his people Israel. *7. David's prestige*

Then David again assembled all the chosen men of Israel, thirty thousand. And David arose and went with all the people who were with him, to Baal-Judah, to bring up from there the ark of God which is called by the name of Jehovah of hosts who sits enthroned upon the cherubim. And they set the ark of God upon a new cart, and brought it out of the house of Abinadab, that was on the hill, with Uzzah and *8. The first attempt to bring up the ark*

Ahio the sons of Abinadab guiding the cart: Uzzah went with the ark of God, while Ahio went before the ark. And David and all the house of Israel were dancing before Jehovah with all their might and with songs and harps and lyres and cymbals.

9. Death of Uzzah

And when they came to the threshing-floor of Nacon, Uzzah stretched out his hand to the ark of God to hold it, for the oxen slipped. Then the anger of Jehovah was aroused against Uzzah and God smote him there because he had stretched out his hand to the ark, so that he died there in the presence of God. And David was angry because he had broken forth upon Uzzah. Therefore that place is called Perez-uzzah [Breach of Uzzah] to this day. And David was afraid of Jehovah that day, so that he said, How can the ark of Jehovah come to me? And David was unwilling to remove the ark of Jehovah to the city of David, but carried it aside into the house of Obed-edom the Gittite. So the ark remained in the house of Obed-edom the Gittite three months. And Jehovah blessed Obed-edom and all his house.

10. Transfer of the ark to Jerusalem

And when the report came to King David: Jehovah hath blessed Obed-edom and all his house because of the ark of God, David went and brought up with joy the ark of God from the house of Obed-edom to the city of David. And when the bearers of the ark of Jehovah had gone six paces, he sacrificed an ox and a fatling. And David was dancing before Jehovah with all his might, and David was girded with a linen ephod. So David and all the house of Israel brought up the ark of Jehovah with shouting, and the sound of the trumpet.

11. Its reception

Now when the ark of Jehovah was coming into the city of David, Michal the daughter of Saul looked out of the window, and when she saw King David leaping and dancing before Jehovah, she despised him in her heart. And when they brought in the ark of Jehovah and set it in its place in the midst of the tent that David had pitched for it, David offered burnt-offerings and peace-offerings before Jehovah.

12. Gifts to the people

And when David had finished sacrificing the burnt-offerings and the peace-offerings, he blessed the people in the name of Jehovah of hosts. And he distributed to all the people, even among the whole multitude of Israel, both men and women, to each a cake of bread, a portion of meat, and a bunch of raisins. Then all the people departed each to his home.

But when David returned to greet his family, Michal the daughter of Saul came out to meet David and said, How glorious was the king of Israel as he exposed himself to the eyes of his servants' maids, as one of the vain fellows shamelessly exposes himself! And David said to Michal, It was before Jehovah that I was dancing. Blessed be Jehovah, who chose me rather than your father and rather than any of his family to appoint me as prince over the people of Jehovah, over Israel. Therefore I will sport before Jehovah and I will be yet more lightly esteemed than this and I will be despised by you. But of the maids of whom you have spoken I shall indeed be held in honor. And Michal the daughter of Saul had no child to the day of her death. _{13. David and Michal}

And David was king over all Israel. And David administered justice and righteousness to all his people. And Joab the son of Zeruiah was in command of the army, and Jehoshaphat the son of Ahilud was chancellor, and Zadok and Abiathar the son of Ahimelech were priests, and Shousha was scribe, and Benaiah the son of Jehoiada was in command of the Cherethites and the Pelethites, and David's sons were priests; Ira the Jairite was also a priest of David, and Adoniram was in charge of the forced labor. _{14.-David's state officials}

I. The Wars with the Philistines. The account of David's wars with the Philistines is exceedingly brief. Apparently David's acceptance of the kingship of all Israel was the signal for a general Philistine attack. The war seems to have continued for some years. The incidental references in the popular stories regarding the achievements of David's warriors indicate that at first David was obliged to take refuge in his old stronghold at Adullam and to resort to the method of warfare of his outlaw days. His past experiences and the character of the battle-field gave him a great advantage over his foes. Gradually the people rallied about him, until he was able to meet the Philistines in open battle. In the valley of Rephaim, which led up from the Philistine plain to the west or southwest of Jerusalem, two decisive engagements were fought, and in both cases the Hebrews won a sweeping victory. **After**

the final battle they drove the Philistines out upon the western plain, as far as the Canaanite city of Gezer.

Henceforth the two rival nations settled down on peaceful terms, and for many years neither made an attempt to conquer the other. Ittai, David's most honored friend and trusted counsellor, came from the Philistine town of Gath. The king's body-guard of six hundred, which at a later crisis was effective in preserving the integrity of the empire, was enlisted from the ranks of his old friends and foes, the Philistines.

II. **The Capture of Jebus.** The capture of the strong fortress of Jebus appears to have followed soon after David's victory over the Philistines. In the famous el-Amarna letters, Urusalamu figures as one of the most important towns of southern Canaan. The letters written by its governor to the kings of Egypt are the most interesting documents in that ancient correspondence. This fortress was so strong that it had remained in the hands of the Canaanite tribe, known as the Jebusites, until David sought a capital midway between the rival Hebrew tribes of the north and the south. Jerusalem also possessed the important advantage of being a city which belonged originally to neither the tribes of the north nor the south, but had been conquered by their united forces. It was, therefore, common ground.

Its retired position up among the hills of the central plateau protected it from foreign attack. Its natural strength also gave good ground for the note of defiance with which its ancient Jebusite inhabitants met the advance of David's forces. According to the parallel account in I Chronicles the daring of Joab and his followers was alone equal to the task of taking the city. Crawling up through the water courses, a few of them found entrance into the otherwise impregnable citadel. With this capture of Jebus the conquest of the Canaanites was complete; in a generation or two the older native population was entirely absorbed by the Israelites.

III. **The Situation of Jebus.** Recent excavations leave little doubt that the original city of David and the Jebusites was the hill of Ophel, on the eastern side of the present city. It was bounded on the east by the deep ravine of the Kidron, which met the valley of Hinnom on the south. Originally the valley of the Tyropoean bounded the hill of Ophel on the west, cutting through the centre of the present city just west of the temple area. Although the *debris*, which has come from the many sieges of Jerusalem, has filled this valley to a depth of from forty to ninety feet, its presence is still marked by a slight depression. The fortress of Jebus apparently stood on the southern slope of the hill.

A slight cutting in the sloping rocky hillside furnished a practically impregnable defence on three sides. On its northern side the hill rises to the present temple area and further on broadens out into a level plateau. On the north, therefore, the fortress was doubtless protected by a strong wall. It was probably not until the days of Solomon or later that the western hill, which extends to the valley of Hinnom, was included in Jerusalem.

IV. The Transfer of the Ark. Like Gideon before him, David evidently desired to make his new capital a religious centre. During the early part of the period of settlement, the ark had been kept at Shiloh, in the territory of the strong northern tribe of Ephraim. In bringing the ark to Jerusalem, therefore, David aimed to enlist still further the loyalty of these strong northern tribes. The ark stood for the presence of Jehovah among his people and recalled the military glories of their early history. In transferring it to Jerusalem, David attracted to his new capital not only the patriotism but the religious zeal of all his subjects. The act was far reaching in its consequences. Many other sanctuaries throughout the land of Israel enjoyed the homage and loyalty of the different tribes and clans, but Jerusalem came to be regarded more and more as the special abiding place of Jehovah.

The account of the transfer of the ark to Jerusalem reveals the current beliefs of that early day. While it was being carried up the hill of Ophel, one of its attendants stretched out his hand to keep it from falling. The act was prompted by a worthy motive, and there was apparently nothing in the ceremonial usage of the day to condemn it. His sudden death, however, was interpreted as a clear signal of Jehovah's displeasure, and the ark was left in the home of one of David's Philistine body-guard. The prosperity which came to this Philistine soon influenced the Hebrews again to attempt to carry the ark to Jerusalem. Amidst song and oriental dancing, in which the king participated with great religious zeal, it was borne in triumph to the city of David. There it was deposited in a tent especially prepared for it. Rich offerings to Jehovah were also presented by David, and food was distributed from the royal bounty among the assembled people in commemoration of this event which symbolized the entrance of the God of Sinai and the wilderness into the capital of his united people.

V. David's Court. At his new capital David established his simple court. He himself stood as the supreme judge and court of appeal of the nation. To him, as to Moses, all difficult cases were referred. Joab, his loyal, fearless kinsman was in command of the army. The needs of the growing kingdom led to the establishment of the office of chancellor or grand vizier. Another official kept the state records and conducted the royal correspondence. Abiathar, the priest of the house of Eli, continued in charge of the oracle. His priestly duties, however, were shared by a certain Zadok of unknown origin, who in time became the head of the Jerusalem priesthood. Certain of David's sons also acted as priests. All these officials were appointed by David and were probably supported from the royal exchequer. Benaiah, one of David's valiant warriors was at the head of the royal body-guard, whose presence reveals the well-founded fear with which David regarded the rivalry between the different factions in his nation. It is significant that, like the popes of to-day, he preferred to entrust the protection of his person to aliens, who were influenced by no personal or factional feeling, but were responsible only to himself and supported directly by him.

David's establishment on the throne of united Israel marks another important stage in Hebrew history. At last a king, who was able not only to lead but to organize, was at the head of the confederacy of tribes. It was during David's reign that the foundations were firmly laid for Israel's future growth and greatness. For the next four centuries the dynasty which he founded continued on the throne at Jerusalem. Israel had finally found its place in the assembly of nations.

§ L.   THE INTERNAL EVENTS OF DAVID'S REIGN

1. Demand of the Gibeonites

Now in the days of David there was a famine three years, year after year, And when David sought the face of Jehovah, Jehovah said, Upon Saul and upon his house there is blood-guilt, because he put to death the Gibeonites (now the Gibeonites were not of the Israelites, but of the remnant of the Amorites; nevertheless the Israelites had sworn to them; and Saul sought to slay them in his zeal for the Israelites and the Judahites), and David said to the Gibeonites, What shall I do for you? And wherewith shall I make the expiation, that you may bless the heritage of Jehovah? And the Gibeonites said to him, It is not a matter of silver and gold between us and Saul or his house; neither is it for us to put any man to death in Israel. And he said, What do you say that I shall do for you? And they said to the king, The man who consumed us, and who planned to destroy us that we should not remain in any of the borders of

Israel—let seven men of his sons be given to us, and we will hang them up to Jehovah in Gibeon in the mount of Jehovah. And the king said I will give them.

So the king took the two sons of Rizpah the daughter of Aiah, whom she bore to Saul, Armoni and Meribaal, and the five sons of Merab the daughter of Saul, whom she bore to Adriel the son of Barzillai the Meholathite. And he delivered them over to the Gibeonites, and they hung them in the mountain before Jehovah, so that the seven of them fell together; and they were put to death in the first days of harvest.

2. Execution of the sons of Saul and Rizpah

Then Rizpah the daughter of Aiah took sackcloth, and spread it for her upon the rock, from the beginning of the barley harvest until water was poured upon them from heaven; and she did not permit the birds of the heavens to settle down upon them by day nor the wild beasts by night. And when it was reported to David what Rizpah the daughter of Aiah, the concubine of Saul, had done, David went and took the bones of Saul and the bones of Jonathan his son from the men of Jabesh in Gilead, who had stolen them from the citizens of Bethshan, where the Philistines had hanged them, on the day that the Philistines slew Saul in Gilboa. And he brought up from there the bones of Saul and the bones of Jonathan his son and they gathered the bones of those who were hanged. And they buried the bones of Saul and the bones of Jonathan his son in the territory of Benjamin in Zela in the sepulchre of Kish his father, and they did all that the king commanded. And after this God was propitiated toward the land.

3. Rizpah's devotion to the dead

Now Jonathan, Saul's son, had a son who was lame in his feet. He was five years old when the news came from Jezreel regarding Saul and Jonathan. And his nurse took him up and fled, and while she was hastily fleeing, he fell and became lame. And his name was Meribaal.

4. Meribaal's lameness

And David said, Is there left of the house of Saul any to whom I may show kindness for Jonathan's sake? Now there was of the house of Saul a servant whose name was Ziba; and they called him to David. And the king said to him, Are you Ziba? And he said, Your servant am I. The king said, is there no one else belonging to the house of

5. David's search for descendants of Saul

Saul to whom I may show the kindness of God? And Ziba said to the king, Jonathan has still a son, who is lame in his feet. And the king said to him, Where is he? And Ziba said to the king, Behold he is in the house of Machir the son of Ammiel, in Lodebar. Then King David sent and brought him from the house of Machir the son of Ammiel, from Lodebar. And when Meribaal the son of Jonathan, the son of Saul, came to David, he fell on his face and did obeisance. David said, Meribaal! And he answered, Behold your servant! Then David said to him, Fear not, for I will surely show you kindness for the sake of Jonathan your father and will restore to you all the land of Saul your ancestor; and you shall eat at my table continually. And he did obeisance and said, What is your servant that you should look favorably upon such a dead dog as I am?

6. His provision for Meribaal

Then the king called to Ziba, Saul's servant, and said to him, All that belongs to Saul and all his house have I given to your master's son. And you shall cultivate the land for him, together with your sons and servants, and bring in the fruits that your master's son may have food to eat; but Meribaal your master's son shall always eat bread at my table. Now Ziba had fifteen sons and twenty servants. Then said Ziba to the king, Just as my lord the king commands his servant, so will your servant do. So Meribaal ate at David's table like one of the sons of the king. And Meribaal had a young son, whose name was Mica. And all who dwelt in the house of Ziba were Meribaal's servants. So Meribaal dwelt in Jerusalem, for he ate continually at the king's table, being lame in both feet.

7. The taking of the census

Then Jehovah's anger was again aroused against Israel, and he instigated David against them, saying, Go number Israel and Judah! So the king said to Joab and the commanders of the army who were with him, Go now about among all the tribes of Israel, from Dan even to Beersheba, and muster the people that I may know the number of the people. Then Joab answered the king, May Jehovah your God add to the people, a hundred times as many as they are, while the eyes of my lord the king are looking on! But why has my lord the king a desire for such a thing? But the king's command prevailed against Joab and the commanders of the army. And Joab and the commanders of the army went out from the presence of the king to number the people of Israel. And they crossed the Jordan, and began from Aroer and from the city that is in the midst of the torrent valley, toward Gad and on to Jazer. Then they came to Gilead and to the land of the Hittites, toward Kadesh; and they came to Dan, and from Dan they went around to Sidon, and came to the fortress of Tyre and all the cities of the Hivites, and of the Canaanites; and they went out to the South Country of Judah at Beersheba. So when they had gone about through the land, they came to Jerusalem at the end of nine months and twenty days. And Joab gave to the king the number of the people who had been enrolled, and there were in Israel eight hundred thousand able-bodied, fighting men; and the men of Judah were five hundred thousand.

Then David's conscience smote him after he had numbered the people. And David said to Jehovah, I have sinned greatly in what I have done. But now, O Jehovah, pardon, I beseech thee, the iniquity of thy servant, for I have done very foolishly. *8. David's remorse*

Then the word of Jehovah came to the prophet Gad, David's seer, saying, Go and speak to David, 'Thus saith Jehovah, " Three things I offer thee; choose one of them, that I may do it to thee." ' So when David rose up in the morning, Gad came to David and told him, and said to him, Shall three years of famine come over your land? Or will you flee three months before your foes, while they pursue you? Or shall there be three days' pestilence in your land? Now take counsel and consider what answer I shall return to him who sent me. And David said to Gad, I am in a great strait. We would rather fall into the hand of Jehovah, for his mercy is great, but let me not fall into the hand of man. *9. His choice*

So David chose the pestilence. And when it was the time of wheat harvest, the plague began among the people and slew of the people from Dan to Beersheba seventy thousand men. And when the Messenger stretched out his hand toward Jerusalem to destroy it, Jehovah repented of the evil, and said to the Messenger who was destroying the people, *10. The pestilence*

Enough, now stay thy hand! and the Messenger of Jehovah was by the threshing-floor of Araunah.

And Gad came that day to David, and said to him, Go up, rear an altar to Jehovah on the threshing-floor of Araunah the Jebusite. So David went up at the command of Gad, as Jehovah commanded. And when Araunah looked down and saw the king and his servants crossing over to him, Araunah went out and bowed before the king with his face to the ground. And Araunah said, Why has my lord the king come to his servant? And David said, To buy the threshing-floor of you, to build an altar to Jehovah, that the plague may be averted from the people. And Araunah said to David, Let my lord the king take and offer what he pleases, the oxen for the burnt-offering, and the threshing-sledges and the implements of the oxen for the wood. All this has your servant, my lord the king, given to the king. And Araunah said to the king, Jehovah your God accept you! And the king answered Araunah, No, but I will surely buy it of you at a price. I must not offer burnt-offerings to Jehovah my God which cost me nothing. So David bought the threshing-floor and the oxen for fifty shekels of silver. Then David built there an altar to Jehovah, and offered burnt-offerings and peace-offerings. So Jehovah was entreated for the land and the plague was averted from Israel.

I. **The Ancient Doctrine of Evil.** From earliest times the dogma that calamity was the sign of divine displeasure was widely accepted. It was one of the fundamental doctrines of ancient theology. Hence when Israel was afflicted with a severe famine, the one question raised by all was, In what has the nation sinned to be thus afflicted with the mark of Jehovah's displeasure? The survivors of the old Canaanite town of Gibeon appeared with an explanation which was accepted not only by the Israelites but by David himself. It was that Jehovah was punishing the crime of Saul, who, disregarding the ancient covenant (§ XXXII), had put to death many of the Gibeonites. Their proposal that the two surviving sons of Saul and his five grandsons be hung up before Jehovah, as an expiation for the crime of their ancestor, was adopted. The relief from the famine which followed was interpreted as evidence that Jehovah had accepted the bloody sacrifice. The devotion of

THE ANCIENT DOCTRINE OF EVIL

Rizpah, Saul's wife, to her sons at last aroused the sympathy of the nation, and moved David honorably to inter the bones of Saul and his descendants in the family sepulchre in Benjamin.

II. The False and the True Doctrine of Human Sacrifice. This ancient story reveals the imperfect belief of the age. The later prophetic teaching that Jehovah was a righteous God and that all his acts were prompted by justice and love had not yet dawned upon the popular consciousness. In common with their heathen neighbors, they still thought of their Deity as a God whose anger could be appeased by sacrifice of an innocent human being. Later and more enlightened prophets recognized the act, even though it was inspired by religious zeal, as simple murder. They also saw clearly that God's attitude toward men was that of love, and that he was ever ready to forgive the nation or individual who came to him with true penitence. No bloody sacrifice was required to win God's favor. Indeed they declared that he desired not sacrifice, but only "a broken and contrite heart." The later theologies, therefore, which clung to the old heathen doctrine, were far removed from the nobler teachings of the early prophets.

In the suffering, discordant life of humanity, human sacrifice plays its essential part. To be effective, however, the sacrifice must be voluntary, and it is effective, not in changing the attitude of God toward men, but of men toward God. The noble self-giving of parents for their children, of friend for friend, of patriot for his country, of reformer and philanthropist for the down-trodden and suffering, is absolutely essential for the salvation of humanity.

III. David's Treatment of Jonathan's Son. Possibly as a reaction for the cruel penalty that was visited upon the descendants of Saul, David made earnest search, and succeeded in finding the crippled son of his beloved friend Jonathan. Upon him David bestowed Saul's family estates and the honor of eating at the royal table. Thus Meribaal remained a pathetic reminder of David's noblest passion and of the departed glories of the house of Saul.

IV. The Census of All Israel. As a part of David's policy and in order to ascertain upon how many warriors he could rely in his foreign campaigns, command was given to number all Israel. The royal order was carried out in the face of Joab's earnest protestation. Nearly ten months were required for the task. The report revealed one million, three hundred thousand warriors in all Israel. It is interesting to note that the population of Judah, which doubtless included the tribes of the south, at this time nearly equalled that of Northern Israel.

V. The Pestilence. A vivid, picturesque, popular tradition tells of a pestilence which swept through Israel about this time, and connects the calamity with David's numbering the Israelites. The old Semitic belief that a census was displeasing to the Deity was accepted, and the pestilence was interpreted as a direct punishment. At the direction of his prophetic adviser, Gad, David purchased from Araunah the Jebusite, a threshing-floor, which was probably on the northern extension of the hill of Ophel. There he reared an altar to Jehovah and sacrificed burnt-offerings. The ancient story was apparently preserved because it told of the acquisition of the sacred site on which Solomon later reared the temple. Possibly David's sacrifice was offered on the same jagged native rock, which later figured as the great altar before Solomon's temple, and is to-day covered by the quaint Mosque of Omar.

VI Israel's Faith in the Days of David. These popular stories lay bare the beliefs held by the Hebrews at this early period. Their faith, like their civilization, was a blending of the beliefs, which their ancestors brought from the wilderness, with the new and very different ideas which they found regnant in Canaan. It was inevitable that their theology should contain many heathen superstitions. Ceremonial correctness was evidently still regarded as more important than ethical righteousness. Man continued to bargain with his God in order to attain cherished ends. Jehovah was regarded more with fear than with love. He was the supreme King, who demanded the absolute loyalty and devotion of his subjects, very much as did their human king. David reigned as Jehovah's viceroy, consulting his divine King through the priestly oracle before deciding any important question of state. The consolidation of all the tribes under one ruler not only rendered their beliefs more uniform, but also fixed their faith on one God supreme throughout all the nation. Thus it was that the institution of the united Hebrew kingdom represents an important step forward in the development of Israel's religion from the crude polytheism of the desert into the exalted monotheism of the later prophets.

§LI. DAVID'S FOREIGN WARS AND CONQUESTS

1. David's warriors

These are the names of David's mighty heroes: Ishbaal the Hachmonite, leader of the Three; he swung his spear over eight hundred slain at one time.

2. Eleazar

And next to him among the three mighty heroes was Eleazar the son of Dodo, the Ahohite. He was with David at Pasdammim when the Philistines gathered there for battle. But when the Israelites retreated, he stood up and smote the Philistines until his hand was weary and clave fast to the sword. Thus Jehovah brought about a great deliverance that day; and the people returned after him only to take spoil.

And next to him was Shammah the son of Agee, a Hararite. And the Philistines gathered together at Lehi. And there was a plot of ground full of lentils. But when the people fled from the Philistines, he stood in the middle of the plot and defended it and slew the Philistines. Thus Jehovah brought about a great deliverance.

3. Shammah

And Abishai, the brother of Joab the son of Zeruiah, was leader of the Thirty. And he swung his spear over three hundred slain, so that he was renowned among the Thirty. He was honored more than the Thirty, so that he became their commander, but he did not attain to the Three.

4. Leader of the Thirty

And Benaiah the son of Jehoiada was a valiant man of Kabzeel, who had done great deeds; he slew the two sons of Ariel of Moab. He also went down and slew a lion in the midst of a pit in time of snow. And he slew a tall Egyptian, who had a spear in his hand, but he went down to him with a club and snatched the spear out of the Egyptian's hand and slew him with his own spear. These things did Benaiah the son of Jehoiada, and he was renowned among the thirty mighty heroes. He was honored more than the Thirty, but he did not attain to the Three, And David set him over his body-guard.

5. Deeds of Benaiah

Then David smote Moab and measured them off with a line, making them lie down on the ground; and he measured two lines: one full line to put to death and one full line to save alive. And thus the Moabites became subject to David, and brought a present.

6. Conquest of Moab

Now it came to pass after this, that the king of the Ammonites died and Hanun his son became king in his place. And David said, I will show kindness to Hanun the son of Nahash as his father showed kindness to me. So David sent by his servants to condole with him concerning his father. But when David's servants came to the land of the Ammonites, the princes of the Ammonites said to Hanun

7. Cause of the war with the Ammonites

their lord, Do you suppose that David is honoring your father in sending comforters to you? Has not David sent his servants to you to search the city and to spy it out and to overthrow it? So Hanun took David's servants, and shaved off the one half of their beards, cut their robes in two, even to their hips, and sent them away. When David was informed regarding the men, he sent to meet them, for the men were greatly ashamed. And the king said, Stay at Jericho until your beards are grown and then return.

8. First victory of the Israelites under Joab

Now when the Ammonites saw that they had become odious to David, the Ammonites sent and hired the Arameans of Beth-rehob, and the Arameans of Zobah, twenty thousand footmen, and the king of Maacah and of Ishtob with twelve thousand men. And when David heard of it, he sent Joab and all the army and the trained warriors. And the Ammonites came out, and drew up in battle-array at the entrance of the city. And the Arameans of Zobah and Rehob, and Ishtob and Maacah, were by themselves in the open country. But when Joab saw that he was being attacked both in front and in the rear, he selected the picked men of Israel, and put them in array against the Arameans. And the rest of the people he placed under the command of Abishai his brother; and he put them in array against the Ammonites. And he said, If the Arameans should be too strong for me, then you shall help me, but if the Ammonites should be too strong for you, then I will come to your aid. Be courageous and let us show ourselves men for the sake of our people and for the cities of our God; and may Jehovah do that which seems good to him. Now when Joab and the people who were with him drew near for battle against the Arameans, they fled before him. And when the Ammonites saw that the Arameans had fled, they likewise fled before Abishai, and entered into the city. Then Joab returned from the Ammonites, and came to Jerusalem.

9. The second campaign and victory over the Arameans

But when the Arameans saw that they had been defeated by the Israelites, they gathered themselves together, and Hadadezer sent, and brought out the Arameans who were beyond the River [Euphrates], and they came to Helam with Shobach, the commander of the army of Hadadezer, at their head, And when it was reported to David, he gathered all Israel together and crossed over the Jordan and came to Helam. And the Arameans set themselves in array against David and fought with him. And the Arameans fled before Israel; and David slew of the Arameans seven hundred horsemen and forty thousand footmen and smote Shobach the commander of their army, so that he died there. And when all the kings who were subject to Hadadezer saw that they were defeated by Israel, they made peace wth Israel and were subject to them. Therefore the Arameans feared to help the Ammonites any more.

And David took the shields of gold that were on the servants of Hadadezer, and brought them to Jerusalem. And from Tibhath and from Berothai, cities of Hadadezer, King David took a great amount of brass. 10. The spoil

And when Tou king of Hamath heard that David had smitten all the army of Hadadezer, Tou sent Hadoram his son to King David, to greet him and to wish him good fortune, because he had fought against Hadadezer and smitten him, for Hadadezer was Tou's military antagonist. And he brought with him vessels of silver, of gold, and of brass. Thus David made a reputation for himself. 11. Gifts of Tou, king of Hamath

Now, a year later, at the time when kings are accustomed to go forth, David sent Joab and his servants with him, even all Israel; and they destroyed the Ammonites, and besieged Rabbah. But David remained at Jerusalem. And Joab fought against Rabbah of the Ammonites and took the water city. Then Joab sent messengers to David, saying, I have fought against Rabbah; also I have taken the water city. Now therefore gather the rest of the people together, and encamp against the city, and take it, lest I take the city and it should be called by my name. So David gathered all the people together and went to Rabbah and fought against it and took it. And he took the crown of Milcom from his head; and its weight was about one hundred and forty pounds of gold, and in it was a precious stone; and it was set on David's head. And he brought away the great amount of spoil that was in the city. And he brought away the people who were in it, and put them at the saws and picks and axes of iron and made them work at the brickmoulds. 12. Victorious conclusion of Ammonite war

Even thus he did to all the cities of the Ammonites. Then David and all the people returned to Jerusalem.

13. Defeat of the Edomites

On his return, he smote of the Edomites in the Valley of Salt, eighteen thousand men. And he put garrisons in all Edom; and all the Edomites became subject to David. And Jehovah helped David wherever he went.

I. **David's Warriors.** During David's outlaw period he gathered about him a trained and tested body of valiant knights. The relative honors which they enjoyed were measured simply by their bravery and achievement. It was an age when a powerful, brave, far-famed warrior could successfully meet and put to flight a company of ordinary soldiers. On many a hard-fought battle-field David had proved himself a brave and chivalrous knight, and his example was imitated by his followers. Three of these warriors stood preëminent above all others. There was also another group of thirty knights of the second class whose names have been preserved in the narratives of Samuel and Chronicles. The personality of these warriors and the accounts of their bold achievements undoubtedly did much to inspire courage and enterprise in the rank and file of David's army.

II. **The Organization of David's Army.** David's regular army seems to have consisted simply of his chosen knights and the Philistine body-guard, which numbered six hundred trained fighting men. These could be absolutely depended upon at every crisis. From their ranks were doubtless drawn commanders to lead the different divisions of the militia, which could be quickly called out in the event of a foreign invasion or war.

As in olden times, the Hebrew warriors rallied under their tribal and local leaders, who were thus able intelligently to direct and command the obedience of their followers. During the winter and spring time the rank and file of the army returned to their homes to attend to their private interests, to follow their flocks, or to till their fields. Foreign campaigns were not undertaken until the crops had been gathered in and the men were free to respond to the call of the camp and battle-field. The simple habits and diet of the early Hebrews called for few provisions beyond what each individual could himself furnish. In this way it was possible for David to rally at short notice most of the able-bodied men in his realm, and to carry on protracted wars without seriously draining the resources of his kingdom.

THE AMMONITE WARS

III. The Ammonite Wars. There is a brief and apparently late reference to a campaign against the Moabites, according to which they were completely subjugated and two-thirds of their men were put to death. If the narrative is historical it was a strange requital of their hospitality toward David's parents unless, perchance, the Moabites later did some violence to the refugees thus entrusted to their care.

The first extensive foreign campaign to be undertaken by David appears to have been against the Ammonites, the old foes of the east-Jordan tribes. On his accession to the throne the son of Nahash treated David's ambassadors shamefully and thereby took the initiative in declaring war. The Ammonites called in as their allies a large body of Arameans from the north and north-east of Israel. Joab was despatched against them with an army of picked warriors. To anticipate an attack in his rear, he divided his forces into two divisions, placing one under the command of his brother, Abishai. The battle was evidently fought in the open, and both divisions of the Hebrew army put to flight the opposing forces.

Under the leadership of David a campaign was next conducted against the Arameans. At a certain east-Jordan point, not yet identified, he won a decisive victory. The Aramean princes, whose kingdoms lay nearest to Israel, hastened to make peace with David and to pay tribute.

A year later Joab was sent out with a new army to besiege the Ammonite capital Rabbah. He first captured the water city, thus cutting off the water supply. David was then summoned to be present at the final conquest of the capital, and he soon returned laden with rich spoil. The crown of gold was taken from the head of the Ammonite god, Milcom (or Milk), and its chief jewel was added to David's diadem. The Ammonites were enslaved and set at forced labor, and their territory was annexed to the rapidly growing Hebrew empire.

IV. The Extent of David's Kingdom. Another campaign, with a bloody victory, was carried on by David against his southern foes, the Edomites. Hebrew garrisons were established throughout the land and the people were completely subjugated. Thus apparently within a few years David built up a little empire which extended from the territory of the Phœnicians and Philistines on the west to the desert on the east, and from the eastern arm of the Red Sea in the south to the neighborhood of Damascus in the north.

V. The Significance of David's Conquests. Later prophets like Amos condemned, even in their heathen foes, the barbarous cruelty with

145

which David treated the conquered peoples. It was a brutal age and the warfare between the kindred tribes of southwestern Asia had always been characterized by great cruelty and disregard of human life. Each petty nation fought in the name of its god and in the name of its god slaughtered its conquered foes. The cause was partially because the struggle for the limited territory in the ancient Semitic world was so intense, and partially because the ethical motives of justice and mercy had not as yet found a central place in the religions of the day.

In the light of existing conditions it was clear that, if David's kingdom was to enjoy peace and prosperity, he must subdue the persistent foes to the south and east, who were constantly pressing the Hebrews from behind, and who never lost a favorable opportunity for attack. David's conquests not only gave him a unified empire, but also opened on every side the highways for foreign commerce. From Philistia, Phœnicia, Damascus and Arabia came those products and ideas which, in the days of Solomon, transformed the simple, rude Hebrew state into an opulent, ambitious monarchy. Under David the Israelites also ceased to be a race of struggling, hunted peasants and suddenly became the masters of the eastern Mediterranean. The Hebrews never forgot the proud achievements of David's reign. Their fondest hopes for the future were moulded by the memories of the conquests and achievements of this early period, which represented the zenith of their national glory.

§ LII. DAVID'S CRIMES AND THEIR PUNISHMENT

1. David's children born in Hebron

Now in Hebron sons were born to David: his eldest was Amnon the son of Ahinoam the Jezreelitess; and his second, Chileab the son of Abigail, the wife of Nabal the Carmelite; and the third, Absalom the son of Maacah, the daughter of Talmai king of Geshur; and the fourth, Adonijah the son of Haggith; and the fifth, Shephatiah the son of Abital; and the sixth, Ithream the son of Eglah, David's wife. These were born to David in Hebron.

2. In Jerusalem

And in Jerusalem David took for himself more concubines and wives, after he came there from Hebron; and more sons and daughters were born to David. And these are the names of those who were born to him in Jerusalem: Shammua, Shobab, Nathan, Solomon, Ibhar, Elishua, Nepheg, Japhia, Elishama, Baaliada, and Eliphelet.

146

Now once at eventide, while Joab was besieging Rabbath-Ammon, David arose from his bed, and walked upon the roof of the king's palace; and from the roof he saw a woman bathing. And the woman was very beautiful. And David sent to inquire concerning the woman. And one said, Is not this Bathsheba, the wife of Uriah the Hittite? Then David sent messengers to take her; and she came to him, and he lay with her—she having been purified from her uncleanness. Then she returned to her house. And the woman conceived; and she sent to tell David, saying, I am with child. *3. David's sin with Bathsheba*

Then David said to Joab, Send me Uriah the Hittite. And Joab sent Uriah to David. And when Uriah had come to him, David asked him concerning the welfare of Joab and the people and the progress of the war. Then David said to Uriah, Go down to your house and wash your feet. And Uriah departed from the king's house, and there followed him a portion from the king. But Uriah slept at the door of the king's house with the servants of his lord and did not go down to his house. Now when it was told David, Uriah did not go down to his house, David said to Uriah, Have you not come from a journey? Why did you not go down to your house? But Uriah said to David, The ark and Israel and Judah are abiding in huts, and my master Joab, and the servants of my lord are camping in the open fields; shall I then go to my house to eat and drink and to lie with my wife! As Jehovah liveth and you live, I cannot do this. Then David said to Uriah, Stay here to-day also, and to-morrow I will let you go. So Uriah remained in Jerusalem that day. But on the next day David invited him and he ate and drank before him, so that he made him drunk. Then in the evening he went out to lie on his couch with the servants of his lord, but went not down to his house. *4. His attempt to conceal it*

And in the morning, David wrote a letter to Joab, and sent it by Uriah. And he wrote in the letter saying, Set Uriah in the face of the fiercest fighting, then retreat from behind him, that he may be smitten and die. So in keeping guard over the city, Joab assigned Uriah to the place where he knew valiant men were. And when the city went out to fight with Joab, there fell some of the soldiers of David, and *5. His murder of Uriah*

Uriah the Hittite fell also. Then Joab sent to tell David all the facts concerning the war. And he instructed the messenger, saying, When you have finished telling all the facts concerning the war to the king, then if the king's wrath is aroused, and he say to you, ' Why did you go so near to the city to fight? Did you not know that they would shoot from the wall? Who smote Abimelech the son of Jerubbaal? Did not a woman cast an upper millstone upon him from the wall, so that he died at Thebez? Why did you go near the wall?' then shall you say, 'Your servant Uriah the Hittite is dead also.'

6. Joab's report

So the messenger of Joab went to the king at Jerusalem and came and told David all that Joab commanded him concerning the war. Then the messenger said to David, The men boldly attacked us and came out to us in the open field, and so we drove them back even to the entrance of the gate. And the archers shot at your servants from the wall; and some of the king's servants are dead. Then David was very angry with Joab, and he said to the messenger, Why did you go near the city to fight? Did you not know they would shoot you from the wall? Who smote Abimelech, the son of Jerubbaal? Did not a woman cast an upper millstone upon him from the wall, so that he died in Thebez? Why did you go near the wall? But the messenger said, Your servant Uriah the Hittite is dead also. Thereupon David said to the messenger, Thus shall you say to Joab, ' Let not this thing displease you, for the sword devours one as well as another; persist in your attack upon the city, and overthrow it,' and encourage him.

7. David's marriage with Bathsheba

Now when the wife of Uriah heard that Uriah her husband was dead, she made lamentation for her husband. But when the mourning was over, David sent and took her home to his house, and she became his wife and bore him a son. But the thing that David had done displeased Jehovah.

8. Nathan's parable

Then Jehovah sent the prophet Nathan to David. And he came to him, and said to him, There were two men in one city, the one rich, the other poor. The rich man had very many flocks and herds. But the poor man had nothing, except one little ewe lamb, which he had bought. And he nourished it and it grew up with him and with his children. It used to eat of his own morsel, and drink out of his own cup, and lay in his bosom, and was to him as a daughter. But there came a traveller to the rich man, and he spared his own flock and did not take from it nor from his own herd to make ready for the traveller who had come to him, but took the poor man's lamb and prepared it for the man who had come to him. Then David's anger was greatly aroused against the man, and he said to Nathan, As Jehovah liveth, the man who has done this is worthy of death, and he shall restore the lamb sevenfold, because he showed no pity.

Therefore Nathan said to David, You are the man! Thus saith Jehovah, the God of Israel, ' I anointed thee king over Israel and I delivered thee out of the hand of Saul, and I gave thee thy master's house and thy master's wives into thy bosom, and gave thee the house of Israel and of Judah, and if that were too little, I would add to you as much again.' Why have you despised the word of Jehovah by doing that which is evil? You have smitten Uriah the Hittite with the sword, and have taken his wife to be your wife, and have slain him with the sword of the Ammonites. Now therefore the sword shall never depart from your house, because you have despised me and have taken the wife of Uriah the Hittite to be your wife. Thus saith Jehovah, ' Behold, I will raise up evil against thee out of thine own house, and I will take thy wives from before thine eyes and give them to thy neighbor, and he shall lie with thy wives in the sight of this sun, for thou didst it secretly; but I will do this thing before all Israel, and before the sun.' Then David said to Nathan, I have sinned against Jehovah. And Nathan said to David, Jehovah also put away your sin; you shall not die. Yet, because by this deed you have scorned Jehovah, the child also that is born to you shall surely die. And Nathan departed to his house.

9. Condemnation of David

And Jehovah smote the child which Uriah's wife bore to David, so that it fell sick. Then David besought God for the child, and fasted and went in and lay all night in sackcloth upon the earth. And the elders of his house stood over him in order to raise him up from the earth; but he would

10. Death of David's first son by Bathsheba

not arise, neither would he eat bread with them. But on the seventh day the child died. And the servants of David feared to tell him that the child was dead, for they said, Behold while the child was yet alive, we spoke to him, and he hearkened not to our voice; how can we say the child is dead, for he will do some harm! But when David saw that his servants were whispering together, David perceived that the child was dead, and David said to his servants, Is the child dead? And they said, He is dead. Then David arose from the earth, and washed and anointed himself, and changed his garments; and he came into the house of Jehovah and worshipped. Then he went to his own house; and he asked for bread and they set it before him and he ate. Then his servants said to him, What is this you have done? You fasted and wept for the child, while it was alive, but when the child died, you arose and ate bread. And he said, While the child was yet alive, I fasted and wept; for I said, ' Who knows whether Jehovah will have mercy, so that the child will live? ' But now he is dead; why should I fast? Can I bring him back again? I am going to him, but he will not come back to me.

11. Birth of Solomon

Then David comforted Bathsheba his wife, and went in unto her and lay with her, and she conceived and bore a son whose name he called Solomon. And Jehovah loved him, and sent a message through Nathan the prophet; and he called his name Jedidiah [The Beloved of Jehovah], according to the command of Jehovah.

I. **David's Family History.** A mere historian would have dismissed David's domestic experiences with a sentence or two. The author of the parallel history of Chronicles, who wrote from the point of view of the third century before Christ, entirely ignores this side of David's character and reign. By him, as by later generations, David was simply regarded as a king after God's own heart, who laid the foundations for the temple and sang Israel's most deeply spiritual songs. It was only the prophetic historian who had the courage and desire to present in their hideous realism David's odious crimes and their consequences. These stories constitute the major part of the book of II Samuel (chaps. 9–20). In a vivid, detailed narrative they present the pathetic tragedy of David's closing years. The problems there treated are of universal and vital significance. Their importance amply justifies the frankness with which they are presented. Their message is supremely applicable to the present age in which the great social evil threatens to undermine our vaunted Christian civilization.

II. David's Household.

The dark background of these stories is an oriental court, with its degrading institution of polygamy. Before he became king of united Israel, David had married seven wives. Later, still others were added to his harem. The subsequent history shows that his household was by no means free from the usual vices which flourish in an eastern harem: luxury, the pursuit of pleasure, petty jealousies and intrigues. The king, therefore, lived in an atmosphere in which it was almost impossible to develop strong moral fibre.

III. David's Double Crime.

At the zenith of David's popularity and success the fatal weakness in his character was disclosed. All ancient codes, including those of the Hebrews, were very strenuous in their punishment of adultery. The avenging of murder was left to the kinsmen of the murdered man. The adulterer, however, committed an unpardonable sin against society; therefore the Hebrew law enacted that he should be publicly stoned to death by the community (§ LIX[5]). In thus condemning social immorality even more severely than the act of murder, primitive society was but following the example of Nature. No crime to-day involves more sudden and terrible consequences in the life of the individual; no crime is capable of exerting as malign an influence upon the innocent family and later descendants of the culprit; no crime leaves in its wake as many physical and moral ills.

With true intuitions the ancient Hebrews punished adultery as they did blasphemy. In the ultimate analysis the two crimes are closely akin. No diviner function is given to man than that of becoming, like God himself, a creator. No human relation is more sacred than that of parenthood; no institution is more basal to the welfare of society than that of the family. Therefore, he who perverts this divine gift allies himself with the impious fool who tramples upon his noblest religious impulses and defies God himself.

David must always be judged by the standards of his age, and yet his own generation did not hesitate to condemn his act, as is well illustrated by the story itself. Like many a culprit David tried to cover his act by a treacherous murder. Under the dominance of a misguided passion, the brave, the chivalrous, the magnanimous idol of his people suddenly fell to the level of an unprincipled oriental tyrant.

IV. **Nathan's Parable.** In the original David narratives,[10] was apparently the immediate sequel of [7]. The story of Nathan's parable bears the marks of a later prophetic age. The parable itself is one of the classics of the Old Testament. In simple, concise, highly poetical form, the prophet set forth the principles, which he forthwith called upon David not only to accept but to apply. The appeal was to David's strong sense of justice and pity. The analogy between the crime of the rich man and the royal culprit was complete. David's response was in harmony with his character as revealed, for example, when he listened in silence and humiliation to the revilings of the Benjamite, Shemei (§ LIV[8,9]).

V. **David's Punishment.** If David confessed his sin in the presence of the prophet Nathan, as the later tradition affirms, his subsequent acts indicate that the repentance lacked many of the qualities demanded by the great ethical prophets of later generations. He was sorry for the act and its consequences, but there is no evidence that his repentance was deep enough to allow the diviner qualities within him to reassert themselves. His sorrow and petitions were that God might spare the child whom Uriah's wife bore him. Henceforth, Bathsheba, with her malign influence, remained the dominant power in his heart and court. Upon Solomon, the later offspring of this unfortunate alliance, he centred his affection and hope for the future of his realm. Thus it was that David's crime left its fatal influence not only upon his own character and family, but also upon the history of his race.

§ LIII. THE CRIMES OF DAVID'S SONS

1. Amnon's base passion for Tamar

Now afterwards it came to pass that Absalom the son of David had a beautiful sister, whose name was Tamar; and Amnon the son of David loved her. And Amnon was so distressed that he became sick because of his sister Tamar —for she was a virgin—and it seemed to Amnon impossible to do anything to her. But Amnon had a friend whose name was Jonadab the son of Shimeah, David's brother; and Jonadab was a very shrewd man. And he said to him, Why are you, a king's son, so ill every morning? Will you not tell me? And Ammon said to him, I love Tamar, my brother Absalom's sister. And Jonadab said to him, Lie down on your bed, and pretend to be sick. Then when your father comes to see you, say to him, ' Let my sister

Tamar come and give me bread to eat, and prepare the food
in my sight, that I may see it and eat from her hand.'
So Amnon lay down and pretended to be sick. And when
the king came to see him, Amnon said to the king, Let my
sister Tamar come and make a few heart-shaped cakes in
my sight, that I may eat from her hand.

So David sent home to Tamar, saying, Go now to your
brother Amnon's house, and prepare food for him. So
Tamar went to her brother Amnon's house while he lay in
bed. And she took dough and kneaded it and made cakes
as he looked on, and baked the cakes. And she took the
pan and poured them out before him, but he refused to eat.
And Amnon said, Let all go out from me. And they all
went out from him. And Amnon said to Tamar, Bring the
food into the inner room, that I may take from your hand.
And Tamar took the cakes which she had made, and brought
them into the inner room to Amnon her brother. And when
she had brought them to him to eat, he took hold of her and
said to her, Come, lie with me, my sister. And she answered
him, No, my brother, do not force me, for it is not so done
in Israel; do not commit this impious act of folly. And as
for me, whither could I carry my shame? and as for you,
you would become one of the impious fools in Israel. Now
therefore, I beg you, speak to the king, for he will not withhold me from you. But he would not hearken to her, but
being stronger than she, he violated her and lay with her.

Then Amnon hated her with great hatred, for the hatred
with which he hated her was greater than the love with
which he had loved her. And Amnon said to her, Arise,
be gone! But she said to him, No, my brother; far greater
is the second wrong in sending me away than the first that
you did to me. And he would not listen to her, but called
his servant who was standing in front of the house and said,
Put this woman out from my presence, and bolt the door
after her. And she wore a long-sleeved tunic, for thus the
royal maidens were formerly wont to be clad. Then his
servant put her out and bolted the door after her. And
Tamar put ashes on her head, and rent her long-sleeved
tunic which she wore; and she put her hand on her head,
and went her way, crying aloud as she went.

2. His
treach-
erous
assault

3. His
refusal
to
make
amends
for his
crime

4. David's inaction

And Absalom her own brother said to her, Has Amnon your brother been with you? But now, my sister, be silent, for he is your brother; do not take this thing to heart. So Tamar dwelt desolate in her brother Absalom's house. But when King David heard of all these things, he was very angry, but he did not discipline Amnon his son, for he loved him, because he was his eldest. And Absalom spoke to Amnon neither good nor bad; for Absalom hated Amnon, because he had violated his sister Tamar.

5. Absalom's revenge

Now it happened after two years, that Absalom had sheep-shearers in Baal Hazor near Ephraim, and Absalom invited all the king's sons. And Absalom came to the king and said, See your servant has sheepshearers; let the king, I pray, and his servants go with your servant. But the king said to Absalom, No, my son, let us not all go, lest we be burdensome to you. And he pressed him; however, he would not go, but bade him farewell. Then Absalom said, If not, then let my brother Amnon go with us. And the king said, Why should he go with you? But when Absalom pressed him, he let Amnon and all the king's sons go with him. Then Absalom commanded his servants, saying, See to it: when Amnon's heart is merry with wine, and when I say to you, 'Smite Amnon,' then kill him. Fear not; have not I commanded you? Be brave and show yourselves valiant men! And the servants of Absalom did to Amnon as Absalom had commanded. Then all the king's sons arose and each mounted his mule and fled.

6. David's reception of the news

And while they were on the way, the news came to David: Absalom has slain all the king's sons so that there is not one of them left. Then the king arose and tore his clothes and lay on the earth; and all his servants who were standing by him tore their clothes and stood with torn clothes. And Jonadab the son of Shimeah, David's brother, answered and said, Let not my lord suppose that they have killed all the young men, the king's sons, for Amnon only is dead, since by the statement of Absalom this was decided from the day of the violation of his sister Tamar. Now therefore let not my lord the king take this thing to heart, to think that all the king's sons are dead; for Amnon only is dead. And when the watchman lifted up his eyes and looked, there were many people coming down the descent on the Bethhoron road. And the watchman came and told the king, saying, I have seen people coming down from the Bethhoron road by the side of the hill. And Jonadab said to the king, There the king's sons are coming, as your servant said, so it has come to pass. As soon as he had finished speaking, the king's sons came and lifted up their voices and wept; and the king also and all his servants wept loudly.

And David mourned continually for his son. But Absalom fled and went to Talmai the son of Amihud, king of Geshur, and remained there three years. And the spirit of King David longed to go out to Absalom, for he was comforted for the death of Amnon. 7. Absalom's flight

Now when Joab the son of Zeruiah perceived that the king's heart was favorable towards Absalom, Joab sent to Tekoa and brought from there a wise woman and said to her, Pretend to be a mourner and put on mourning garments, and do not anoint yourself with oil, but become like a woman who has been many days mourning for one dead, and go to the king and speak thus with him. So Joab put the words in her mouth. 8. Joab's intrigue

And the Tekoite woman came to the king, and prostrated herself upon the ground and did obeisance, crying, Help, O king, help! And the king said to her, What is wrong with you? And she said, Verily, I am a widow and my husband is dead. And your maid-servant had two sons, and these two quarrelled in the field when there was no one to part them, and one smote the other and killed him. And now the whole clan has risen up against your maid-servant and they say, 'Deliver up the slayer of his brother, that we may put him to death for the life of his brother whom he has killed, and we will destroy the heir.' Thus they will quench my remaining coal, so as to leave to my husband neither name nor remnant on the face of the earth. 9. Fictitious petition of the Tekoite woman

Then the king said to the woman, Go to your house and I will give orders regarding you. And the woman of Tekoa said to the king, My lord, O king, the guilt be on me and on my father's house; and the king and his throne be innocent. And the king said, Whoever saith anything to you bring 10. David's decision him to me and he shall not touch you again. Then she said, I pray, let the king swear by Jehovah thy God, not to let the avenger of blood destroy and not to let them exterminate my son. And he said, As Jehovah liveth, not one hair of your son shall fall to the ground.

11. Application of the principle to the royal judge

Then the woman said, Let your maid-servant, I pray you, speak a word to my lord the king. And he said, Speak. And the woman said, Why then do you devise such a thing against the people of God? For in rendering this decision the king is as one that is guilty, in that the king does not bring back his banished one. For we die and are as water spilt on the ground, which cannot be gathered up again; and God will not take away the life of him who devises means not to keep in banishment one who is banished. Now the reason why I have come to speak this word to my lord the king is because the people made me afraid, and your maid-servant said, ' I will now speak to the king; it may be that the king will perform the request of his servant.' For the king will hear, to deliver his servant out of the hand of the man who seeks to destroy me and my son from the heritage of Jehovah. Then your maid-servant said, ' Let the word of my lord the king be a comfort, for like the Messenger of God is my lord the king to hear good and evil.' And Jehovah thy God be with you.

12. His appreciation of Joab's purpose

Then the king answered and said to the woman, Do not conceal from me, I pray, anything that I may ask you. And the woman said, Let my lord the king now speak. And the king said, Was the hand of Joab with you in all this ? And the woman answered and said, As sure as you live, my lord the king, I cannot turn to the right hand or to the left from all that my lord the king has spoken, for your servant Joab bade me put all these words in the mouth of your maid-servant; in order to change the face of affairs has your servant done this thing. But my lord is wise, according to the wisdom of the Messenger of God, so that he knows all things that are in the earth.

13. Absalom's return

And the king said to Joab, See now, I have granted this request; go, therefore, bring the young man Absalom back. Then Joab fell to the ground on his face and did obeisance and blessed the king. And Joab said, To-day your servant knows that I have found favor in your sight, my lord, O king, in that the king has granted the request of his servant. So Joab arose and went to Geshur, and brought Absalom back to Jerusalem. And the king said, Let him live apart in his own house, but my face he shall not see. So Absalom lived apart to his own house, but he did not see the king's face.

Now no man in Israel was so praiseworthy for his beauty as Absalom: from the sole of his foot even to the crown of his head there was no blemish in him. And when he shaved his head—at the end of every year he cut it, because it was heavy on him, therefore he cut it—he would weigh his hair, about six pounds according to the royal standard of weight. And to Absalom there were born three sons and one daughter, whose name was Tamar—she was a beautiful woman. *14. His personal beauty*

And Absalom dwelt two years in Jerusalem, without seeing the king's face. Then Absalom sent for Joab to send him to the king; but he would not come to him. Then he sent again a second time, but he would not come. Therefore he said to his servants, See Joab's field is near mine, where he has barley; go and set it on fire. Then Joab arose, and came to Absalom at his house and said to him, Why have your servants set my field on fire? And Absalom answered Joab, Behold, I sent to you, saying, ' Come here that I may send you to the king, to say, " Why have I come from Geshur? It were better for me to be there still." ' Now therefore let me see the king's face, and if there be guilt in me, let him kill me. And when Joab went to the king and told him, he called Absalom. And he came to the king and bowed himself with his face to the ground before the king. Then the king kissed Absalom. *15. Restoration to royal favor*

I. **Amnon's Brutal Crime.** The consequences of David's crime appear in the character and deeds of his own children. Amnon, his oldest son, was one of the pitiable products of the oriental harem. He was ruled by the same ungovernable passions that overmastered his kingly father. An unprincipled friend was at hand to advise him how he could gratify his mad passion. Even David himself was made an agent in the ghastly tragedy. The hideous wrong to the victim of Amnon's lust is brought out with a frankness and realism that everywhere characterizes the teaching of those early champions of righteousness, the Hebrew prophets. Amnon's brutality, even after the lapse of centuries, arouses the hot indignation of the reader. One's sympathy goes out to the desolate Tamar, and David's paternal weakness in neglecting his duty as a father stands clearly revealed. Many of the world's worst criminals are thus trained in a home where pure love is wanting, or else where the fond parents are too weak or selfish to teach by impartial justice, discipline and plain instruction those vital lessons which must be learned, if the children are to successfully resist the inevitable temptations of life.

II. **Absalom's Revenge.** As is so often the case in the tangled lives of men, the crime against social morality was quickly followed by murder. David's weakness in not punishing his oldest son left Tamar's brother, Absalom, with a real grievance. In the ancient East the responsibility of avenging a great crime was assumed by the nearest of kin. The fact that Amnon stood in the way of Absalom's ambition doubtless also strengthened his murderous purpose. In the method which Absalom employed, he but imitated his father's treachery in dealing with Uriah, and proved himself an apt pupil in the school of David and Joab. He also evidently counted upon his father's weakness in punishing the crimes of his sons.

III. **The Wise Woman of Tekoa.** Evidently Absalom's act received Joab's secret approval. At first the young prince won the support of that hardy warrior, even though he was unable at a later time to shake Joab's loyalty to David.

In connection with Absalom's recall, a representative of that class in Israel, known as "the wise," first emerged on the horizon of Hebrew history. It is interesting to note that it was a woman whom Joab summoned from the town of Tekoa, a little south-east of Bethlehem, on the borders of the wilderness looking toward the Dead Sea. At a later time from this same town came the sage prophet, Amos. The wise woman's pathetic story appealed, like that of Nathan, to the sympathy of David, so that he again stood committed to a principle which he was asked to apply to his own case.

The king at once recognized the strong hand of Joab, and yielded to the combined influence of his own heart and that of his trusted commander. Absalom's pardon, however, was only partial, until he appealed, in a way well calculated to attain its end, for Joab's further intercession. Then he was restored and found himself free to develop his heartless conspiracy.

IV. **The Shadow of David's Crimes.** In reading these stories one is reminded of certain of the old Greek tragedies; and yet there is no doubt that the historian is recounting actual facts. The stories are a supreme illustration of the scientific as well as biblical truth that in life and history the sins of the fathers are visited upon the children of succeeding generations. The close and fundamental relation between moral causes and effects can be traced at each stage. The faults of David reproduce themselves in even more glaring forms in the lives of his sons. The memory of his guilt and disgrace led the king to withdraw more and more from public life into the seclusion of the harem, and therefore to neglect his duty as judge and administrator. This gave Absalom a free field for the carrying out of his intrigues. The open secret that David intended to pass over his oldest son, Absalom, and to put Bathsheba's son, Solomon, on to the throne, perhaps also goaded the prince on to his desperate venture. In its ultimate consequences the sin of Israel's beloved king involved his nation in bloody civil war. "The wages of sin are death," but unfortunately the innocent share the wages.

§ LIV. ABSALOM'S REBELLION

Now later Absalom prepared a chariot and horses and fifty men to run before him. And Absalom used to rise early and stand beside the way which led to the gate, and every man, who had a suit to come before the king for judgment, Absalom would call to himself and say, Of what city are you? And when he replied, Your servant is of one of the tribes of Israel, Absalom said to him, Evidently your claims are good and right; but there is no man appointed by the king to hear you. Absalom said moreover, O that some one would make me judge in the land, that to me might come every man who has any suit or cause, and I would give him justice! And whenever a man came near to do obeisance, he would put out his hand and take hold of him and kiss him. And in this way Absalom did to all the Israelites who came to the king for judgment. So Absalom stole the hearts of the men of Israel.

At the end of four years, Absalom said to the king, I would like to go and pay my vow, which I have vowed to Jehovah, in Hebron. For your servant vowed the following vow

1. Absalom's intrigues

2. The conspiracy

while I abode at Geshur in Aram: 'If Jehovah shall indeed bring me back to Jerusalem, I will serve Jehovah in Hebron.' Then the king said to him, Go in peace. So he arose and went to Hebron. But Absalom sent emissaries into all the tribes of Israel, saying, As soon as you hear the sound of the trumpet, then say, ' Absalom has become king in Hebron.' And with Absalom went two hundred men from Jerusalem, who were invited and went in their innocence and knew nothing at all. And Absalom sent and called Ahithophel the Gilonite, David's counsellor, from his city Giloh, while he was offering the sacrifices. And the conspiracy was strong, for the people with Absalom kept increasing.

3. David's flight from Jerusalem
And when a messenger came to David, saying, The heart of the men of Israel has gone after Absalom, David said to all his servants who were with him at Jerusalem, Up, let us flee; for otherwise there will be for us no escape from Absalom. Make haste to depart, lest he quickly overtake us and bring down evil upon us and put the city to the edge of the sword. Then the king's servants said to the king, Just as our lord the king decides, we are your servants. So the king went out, and all his household with him. And the king left behind ten concubines to keep the palace. And the king and all the people who followed him went out and stood at the last house, while all his officers passed beside him, and all the Cherethites and all the Pelethites and all the men of Ittai the Gittite, six hundred who had followed him from Gath, passed on before the king.

4. Loyalty of Ittai the Gittite
Then said the king to Ittai the Gittite, Why will you also go with us? Return and stay with the king; for you are a foreigner and an exile from your own land. Yesterday you came, and to-day shall I make you wander with us, while I go whither I may? Return, and take your fellow countrymen back with you; and Jehovah will show you kindness and faithfulness. But Ittai answered the king, and said, As Jehovah liveth and as my lord the king liveth, wherever my lord the king shall be—whether for death or for life— there will your servant be. And David said to Ittai, Well then, go, and pass on. So Ittai, the Gittite, passed on with all his men and all the little ones that were with him.

160

And all the inhabitants of the land were weeping loudly as all the people passed on. While the king stood in the Kidron valley, the people were passing by before him toward the olive tree in the wilderness. And there was Zadok and Abiathar with him, bearing the ark of God, until all the people had all passed out of the city. And the king said to Zadok and Abiathar, Carry back the ark of God into the city. If I shall find favor in the eyes of Jehovah, he will bring me back, and show me both it and his dwelling. But if he say, 'I have no delight in thee'; then here am I, let him do to me as seemeth good to him. The king also said to Zadok and Abiathar the priests, Behold, return to the city in peace and your two sons with you, Ahimaaz your son and Jonathan the son of Abiathar. See, I am going to delay at the fords of the wilderness, until word comes from you to inform me. Therefore Zadok and Abiathar carried the ark of God again to Jerusalem, and they remained there. *5. David's directions to the priests*

But David went up the ascent to the Mount of Olives, weeping as he went, and with his head covered and his feet bare. All the people who were with him also covered each his head, and also went up, weeping as they went. And when David was told, Ahithophel is among the conspirators with Absalom, David said, O Jehovah, I pray, turn the counsel of Ahithophel to foolishness. And when David came to the summit, where one worships God, there came to meet him Hushai the Archite with his garment rent and earth upon his head. And David said to him, If you go on with me you will be a burden to me. But if you return to the city, and say to Absalom, 'Your brothers have gone away and the king your father has gone away after them, I will be thy servant, O king; I have been your father's servant in the past, so now I will be your servant,' thus you can defeat for me the counsel of Ahithophel. And have you not there with you Zadok and Abiathar the priests? Everything that you hear from the king's palace tell it to Zadok and Abiathar the priests. See, they have there with them their two sons, Ahimaaz, Zadok's son, and Jonathan, Abiathar's son; and by them you shall send to me everything that you shall hear. So Hushai, David's friend, came into the city, when Absalom came to Jerusalem. *6. To his friend Hushai*

7. Ziba's protestations of loyalty

And David was a little past the summit, when Ziba the servant of Meribaal met him with a pair of asses saddled, and on them two hundred loaves of bread, and a hundred bunches of raisins, and a hundred cakes of preserved fruits, and a skin of wine. And the king said to Ziba, Why do you have these? And Ziba answered, The asses are for the king's household to ride on, and the bread and the preserved fruit for the young men to eat, and the wine, that those who are faint in the wilderness may drink. And the king said, And where is thy master's son? And Ziba answered the king, He remains there at Jerusalem, for he thinks, 'To-day will the house of Israel give me back my father's kingdom.' Then said the king to Ziba, All is now yours that belongs to Meribaal. And Ziba said, I do obeisance. Let me find further favor in your sight, my lord, the king.

8. Shimei's curses

And when King David came to Bahurim, there came out from there a man of the family of the house of Saul, whose name was Shimei the son of Gera, constantly cursing as he came. And he cast stones at David and all the officers of King David and at all the people and all the mighty warriors at his right hand and at his left. And thus Shimei said as he cursed, Begone, begone, bloody and vile scoundrel! Jehovah has brought back upon you all the blood of the house of Saul, in whose place you have reigned; and Jehovah hath delivered the kingdom into the hand of Absalom your son; and behold now you are in your misfortune, for you are a bloody man!

9. David's humility

Then Abishai the son of Zeruiah said to the king, Why should this dead dog curse my lord the king? Let me go over now and take off his head. But the king said, What have I in common with you, you sons of Zeruiah? If he curses when Jehovah hath said to him, 'Curse David!' then who shall say, 'Why have you done so?' And David said to Abishai and to all his officers, See, my son who came from my bowels seeks my life; how much more this Benjamite! Let him curse, for Jehovah hath bidden him. Perhaps Jehovah will look on my affliction and repay me good instead of this cursing that he hath sent to-day. So David and his men went along the way; but Shimei went along on the hillside parallel with him, cursing as he went, and threw stones and continually cast dust at him. Then the king and all the people who were with him, arrived weary at the Jordan and he refreshed himself there.

And Absalom with all the men of Israel, came to Jerusalem, and Ahithophel was with him. Now when Hushai the Archite, David's friend, came to Absalom, Hushai said to Absalom, May the king live, may the king live! But Absalom said to Hushai, Is this your love for your friend? Why did you not go with your friend? Then Hushai answered Absalom, No! for whom Jehovah and his people and all the men of Israel have chosen, to him will I belong, and with him will I remain. And in the second place, whom should I serve? Should it not be his son? As I have served your father, so will I serve you. *10. Hushai's protestations of loyalty to Absalom*

Then Absalom said to Ahithophel, Give your counsel as to what we shall do. And Ahithophel said to Absalom, Go in unto your father's concubines whom he has left to keep the palace; and all Israel will hear that you have made yourself abhorrent to your father, and the hands of all who are on your side will be strengthened. So they pitched for Absalom the tent on the top of the house; and Absalom went in unto his father's concubines in the sight of all Israel. And the counsel of Ahithophel, which he gave in those days, was regarded as if one inquired of the word of God—so was all the counsel of Ahithophel regarded by David and Absalom. *11. Absalom's formal usurpation of his father's rights*

Moreover Ahithophel said to Absalom, Let me now choose out twelve thousand men, and I will arise and pursue after David to-night; thus I will come upon him when he is tired and weak and will storm him into a panic, and all the people who are with him will flee; and I will smite the king alone, and I will bring back all the people to you as the bride returns to her husband. You seek only the life of one man, and all the people shall be at peace. And the advice pleased Absalom, and all the elders of Israel. *12. Ahithophel's advice*

Then Absalom said, Call now Hushai the Archite also, and let us hear likewise what he has to say. And when Hushai came to Absalom, Absalom spoke to him, saying, Thus Ahithophel has spoken; shall we act upon his advice? *13. Hushai's advice*

If not, you give advice. Then Hushai said to Absalom,
The counsel that Ahithophel has given this time is not good.
Hushai said moreover, You know your father and his men,
that they are mighty warriors and of angry temper, like a
bear robbed of her cubs in the field. Furthermore your
father is a man of war and will not remain at night with
the people. Even now he has hidden himself in one of the
caves or in some other place. And in case some of the
people fall at the first, whoever hears it will say, 'There is a
slaughter among the people who follow Absalom.' Then
even he that is valiant, whose heart is like the heart of a lion,
will completely lose courage; for all Israel knows that your
father is a mighty warrior, and they who are with him are
valiant men. But I counsel, Let all Israel be gathered to
you, from Dan to Beersheba, as many as the sand that is
by the sea, with you yourself marching in the midst of them.
So shall we come upon him in some place where he has been
discovered, and we will light upon him as the dew falls on the
ground; and of him and of all the men who are with him
there shall not be left even one. But if he has withdrawn
into a city, then all Israel will bring ropes to that city, and
we will draw it to the valley, until not even a small stone is
found there. And Absalom and all the men of Israel said,
The counsel of Hushai the Archite is better than the counsel
of Ahithophel. For Jehovah had ordained to defeat the
good counsel of Ahithophel, in order that Jehovah might
bring evil upon Absalom.

14. His
secret
mes-
sage to
David

Then Hushai said to Zodak and to Abiathar the priests,
Thus and thus did Ahithophel counsel Absalom and the
elders of Israel; and thus and thus have I counselled. Now
therefore send quickly and tell David, saying, Do not spend
this night at the fords of the wilderness, but by all means
cross over, lest the king and all the people with him be
swallowed up. Now Jonathan and Ahimaaz were staying
at Enrogel; and a maid-servant was to go and bring them
news, and they were to go and tell King David, for they
must not be seen to come into the city. But a lad saw them,
and told Absalom. Then they both went away quickly and
entered into the house of a man in Bahurim, who had a
well in his court into which they descended. And the

woman took and spread the covering over the mouth of
the well, and strewed dried fruit upon it, so that nothing
was known. And when Absalom's servants came to the
woman to the house and said, Where are Ahimaaz and
Jonathan? the woman answered them, They are gone over
the water brook. And when they had sought and could
find nothing, they returned to Jerusalem. But as soon as
they had gone away, Ahimaaz and Jonathan came up out of
the well, and went and told King David and said to David,
Arise, cross quickly over the water, for thus has Ahithophel
counselled in regard to you. Then David and all the people
who were with him arose and they crossed over the Jordan.
By daybreak there was not one left behind who had not
gone over the Jordan.

But when Ahithophel saw that his counsel had not been
carried out, he saddled his ass and arose, and went to his
house, to his city. And when he had given command concerning his house, he strangled himself, and he died and was
buried in his father's sepulchre. 15. Suicide of Ahithophel

Then David came to Mahanaim. And Absalom passed
over the Jordan, together with all the men of Israel. And
Absalom set Amasa over the army in the place of Joab.
Now Amasa was the son of an Ishmaelite by the name of
Jether, who had come in marriage to Jesse's daughter
Abigail, the sister of Zeruiah, Joab's mother. And Israel
and Absalom encamped in the land of Gilead. But when
David came to Mahanaim, Shobi the son of Nahash of the
Ammonite Rabbah, and Machir the son of Ammiel of
Lodebar, and Barzillai the Gileadite of Rogelim, brought
couches, rugs, bowls, and earthen vessels, and wheat, barley,
meal, parched grain, beans, lentils, honey, curds, sheep,
and calves for David, and for the people who were with him,
to eat; for they thought, The people are hungry and weary
and thirsty in the wilderness. 16. David's reception at Mahanaim

Then David mustered the people who were with him,
and appointed over them commanders of thousands and of
hundreds. And David divided the people into three divisions,
one third was under the command of Joab, another third
under Abishai the son of Zeruiah, Joab's brother, and another third under the command of Ittai the Gittite. And 17. The battle

the king said to the people, I also will surely go out with you. But the people said, You shall not go out; for if we flee away, no one will care for us, or if half of us die, no one will care for us, for you are equal to ten thousand of us. Also it is now better for you to be ready to help us from the city. And the king said to them, I will do what you think best! So the king stood by the side of the gate, while all the people went out by hundreds and by thousands. And the king commanded Joab, and Abishai, and Ittai, saying, Deal gently for my sake with the young man, with Absalom! And all the people heard when the king gave all the commanders the order regarding Absalom. So the people went out into the field against Israel. And the battle was in the forest of Ephraim. And the people of Israel were smitten there before the servants of David, so that the slaughter on that day was great—twenty thousand men. And the battle was spread out over the whole country; and the forest devoured more that day than the sword.

18. Absalom's death

And Absalom happened to meet the servants of David. And Absalom was riding upon his mule, and the mule went under the thick boughs of a great oak and his head caught fast in the oak, and he was hung between heaven and earth, while the mule that was under him went on. And when a certain man saw it, he told Joab and said, Behold, I saw Absalom hanging in an oak. Then Joab said to the man who told him, So you saw him! Why did you not smite him there to the ground? And my part would have been to give you ten shekels of silver and a girdle. But the man said to Joab, If I were to feel the weight of a thousand shekels of silver in my hand, I would not put forth my hand against the king's son, for in our hearing the king charged you and Abishai and Ittai, saying, 'Take care of the young man Absalom.' Or if I had treacherously taken his life, nothing would have been hidden from the king, and you yourself would have stood aloof. Then Joab answered, I will not tarry thus with you. And he took three spears in his hand, and thrust them into Absalom's heart, while he was still alive in the midst of the oak. And ten young men who bore Joab's armor gathered about and smote Absalom and put him to death.

Then Joab blew the trumpet, and the people returned from pursuing Israel; for Joab held back the people. And they took Absalom and cast him into the great pit in the forest, and raised over him a heap of stones. And all Israel fled each to his home. But Absalom had already in his lifetime taken and reared up for himself the pillar which is in the King's Dale; for he said, I have no son to keep my name in remembrance; and he named the pillar after his own name. Therefore it is called ' Absalom's Monument,' to this day. 19. Burial of Absalom

But when Ahimaaz the son of Zadok said, Let me now run and bring the news to the king that Jehovah hath pronounced judgment for him against his enemies, Joab said to him, You are not the man to bring news to-day. On another day you may bring news, but not to-day, for the king's son is dead. Then said Joab to the Cushite, Go, tell the king what you have seen. And the Cushite bowed before Joab and ran off. But Ahimaaz the son of Zadok said yet again to Joab, However it may be, I would like also to run after the Cushite. And Joab said, Why is it that you would run, my son, seeing that no reward will be paid out? And he said, However it may be, I would like to run. So he said to him, Run. Then Ahimaaz ran by the way of the plain of the Jordan and outran the Cushite. 20. Ahimaaz's eagerness to bear the news

Now David was sitting between the two gates; and the watchman had gone up to the roof of the gate by the wall. And when he lifted up his eyes and looked, he saw there a man running alone. Then the watchman cried and told the king. And the king said, If he be alone, good news are in his mouth. And he kept coming and was drawing near, when the watchman saw another man running; and the watchman called toward the gate, and said, See, another man running alone! And the king said, He also is bringing good news. And the watchman said, I see that the running of the first is like the running of Ahimaaz the son of Zadok. And the king said, He is a good man and comes with good news. Then Ahimaaz drew near and said to the king, All is well. And he bowed before the king with his face to the earth, and said, Blessed be Jehovah your God, 21. David's reception of the news who hath delivered up the men who lifted up their hand against my lord the king. And the king said, Is it well with the young man Absalom? And Ahimaaz answered, When Joab sent your servant, I saw a great tumult, but I did not learn what it was. And the·king said, Turn aside and stand here, and he turned aside and stood still. And, just then, the Cushite said, Let my lord the king receive the good news that Jehovah hath pronounced judgment for you this day upon all those who rose up against you. And the king said to the Cushite, Is it well with the young man Absalom? And the Cushite answered, may the enemies of my lord the king and all who rise up against you for evil be as that young man!

22. David's sorrow for Absalom

Then the king was greatly moved and went up to the chamber over the gate and wept. And thus he said, as he kept on weeping, My son Absalom, my son, my son Absalom! O that I had died instead of you, Absalom, my son, my son! And it was told Joab, The king is weeping and lamenting for Absalom. So for all the people the victory that day was turned to mourning, since the people heard that day, The king is grieving for his son. Therefore the people stole away into the city, as people who are ashamed when they have fled in battle steal away. But the king covered his face, and cried aloud, My son Absalom, Absalom, my son, my son!

23. Joab's rebuke

Then Joab came to the king in the palace and said, You have to-day shamed the face of all your servants, who have saved your life and the lives of your sons, your daughters, your wives, and your concubines, by loving them who hate you and hating them who love you. For you declared to-day that princes and brave officers are nothing to you, for now I know if Absalom had lived and all of us had died to-day, then you would be pleased. Now therefore come, go forth, and reassure your followers; for I swear by Jehovah, if you do not go forth, not a man will remain to you, and that will be worse for you than all the evil that has befallen you from your youth until now. Then the king arose, and sat in the gate. And the rumor spread among all the people, See the king is sitting in the gate; and all the people came before the king.

Now Israel had fled every man to his tent. And all the people were at strife throughout all the tribes of Israel, saying, The king delivered us out of the hand of our enemies, he saved us out of the hand of the Philistines, but now he has fled out of the land from Absalom. And Absalom, whom we anointed over us, has fallen in battle. Now therefore why do you say nothing about bringing the king back? And the word of all Israel came to the king.

24. Uncertainty of the people

Then King David commanded Zadok and Abiathar the priests, Speak to the elders of Judah, saying, ' Why are you the last to bring the king back to his palace? You are my bone and my flesh; why then are you the last to bring back the king?' Say to Amasa, 'Are you not my bone and my flesh? God do to me whatever he will if you shall not henceforth be commander of the army before me in the place of Joab.' And he turned the heart of all the men of Judah as one man, so that they sent to the king saying, Return with all your servants. So the king returned, and arrived at the Jordan. And Judah came to Gilgal to meet the king and bring him across the Jordan.

25. David's liberal overtures to the elders of Judah

And Shimei the son of Gera the Benjamite, who was of Bahurim, hastened down with the men of Judah to meet King David, with a thousand men of Benjamin; and with him was Ziba the servant of the house of Saul, with his fifteen sons and his twenty servants; and they dashed into the Jordan before the king. And they kept crossing the ford to bring over the king's household and to do what would please him. Meanwhile Shimei the son of Gera prostrated himself before the king, when he was about to cross the Jordan. And he said to the king, Let not my lord consider me guilty nor remember what your servant did perversely the day that my lord the king went out of Jerusalem, that the king should take it to heart. For your servant knows that I have sinned; therefore, see, I have come down first of all the house of Joseph to meet my lord the king. But Abishai the son of Zeruiah spoke and said, Should not Shimei be put to death for this, because he cursed Jehovah's anointed? But David said, What have I to do with you, you sons of Zeruiah, that you should this day oppose me? Should anyone be put to death to-day in Israel?

26. His pardon of Shimei

And the king said to Shimei, You shall not die. And the king swore it to him.

27. Concessions to Meribaal

And Meribaal the son of Saul came down to meet the king; and he had neither dressed his feet nor trimmed his beard nor washed his clothes from the day the king departed until the day he came home safe and sound. And so when he came to Jerusalem to meet the king, the king said to him, Why did you not go out with me, Meribaal? And he answered, My lord, O king, my servant deceived me: for your servant said, 'Saddle me an ass, on which I may ride and accompany the king, because your servant is lame.' But he has slandered your servant to my lord the king. My lord the king is as a Messenger of God; do therefore what seems good to you. For though all my father's house were only deserving of death before my lord, the king set your servant among those who eat at your table. What right have I now, that I should continue to cry to the king? And the king said to him, Why do you continue to speak? I say, You and Ziba divide the land. And Meribaal said to the king, Rather let him take all, inasmuch as my lord the king has come home safe and sound.

28. Parting with the aged Barzillai

Then Barzillai the Gileadite came down from Rogelim, and he went over the Jordan with the king to bid him good-by at the Jordan. Now Barzillai was a very aged man, eighty years old, and he had provided the king with food while he remained at Mahanaim; for he was a very great man. And the king had said to Barzillai, Come over with me, and I will support you during your old age with me in Jerusalem. But Barzillai said to the king, How many years have I still to live, that I should go up with the king to Jerusalem? I am now eighty years old. Can I distinguish good from evil? Can your servant taste what I eat or what I drink? Can I hear any more the voice of singing men and singing women? Why then should your servant be a burden to my lord the king? Your servant would merely go over the Jordan with the king, and why should the king give me this recompense? Only let your servant return, I pray you, that I may die in my own city, by the grave of my father and my mother. But there is your servant Chimham; let him go over with my lord the king; and treat him as shall seem good to you. And the king answered, Chimham shall go over with me, and I will do to him as you would desire; and whatever you shall request of me, that will I do for you. Then all the people went over the Jordan. The king also went over after he had kissed Barzillai, and blessed him; so he returned to his home.

And the king passed by Gilgal, Chimham being with him; and all the people of Judah were escorting the king, and also half the people of Israel. Therefore all the men of Israel came to the king, and said to the king, Why have our clansmen, the men of Judah, stolen you away, and brought the king and his household over the Jordan, when all of David's men are his people? Then all the men of Judah answered the men of Israel, Because the king is near of kin to us. Why are you angry at this thing? Have we eaten anything at the king's cost? or has he been carried away by us? And the men of Israel answered the men of Judah, and said, I have ten shares in the king, furthermore I am the firstborn rather than you; why then did you despise me? And was not our advice first to bring back the king? But the words of the men of Judah were fiercer than the words of the men of Israel. *29. Strife between Israel and Judah*

Now there chanced to be there a vile scoundrel, whose name was Sheba, the son of Bichri, a Benjamite. He blew on a trumpet and cried, *30. Rebellion of the northern tribes*

> We have no share in David,
> And we have no claim in the son of Jesse!
> Each to his tents, O Israel!

So all the men of Israel ceased to follow David, and followed Sheba the son of Bichri; but the men of Judah remained loyal to their king, from the Jordan even to Jerusalem.

And when David came to his palace at Jerusalem, he took care of his ten concubines, whom he had left to take charge of the palace, and put them in a guarded house and supported them, but went not in unto them. So they were shut in until the day of their death, living as widows. *31. Fate of David's concubines*

32. Reinstatement of Joab

Then the king said to Amasa, Summon in my name the men of Judah within three days, and also be present yourself. So Amasa went to summon Judah. But when he delayed longer than the time which David had appointed him, David said to Abishai, Now will Sheba the son of Bichri do us more harm than did Absalom; take your lord's servants, and pursue after him, lest he find for himself fortified cities and escape out of our sight. So there went out after Abishai, Joab and the Cherethites and the Pelethites, and all the mighty heroes. They set out from Jerusalem to pursue Sheba the son of Bichri.

33. The death of Amasa

And while they were at a great stone which is in Gibeon, Amasa came to meet them. And Joab was girt with a sword under his warrior's cloak, and also over it was a girdle with a sword fastened upon his loins in its sheath; and as he went forth it fell out. And Joab said to Amasa, Is it well with you, my brother? And Joab took Amasa by the beard with his right hand to kiss him. But Amasa did not notice the sword that was in Joab's hand; so he smote him with it in the body, and shed his bowels to the ground, and he did not strike a second blow; but he died. And Joab and Abishai his brother pursued Sheba the son of Bichri. And one of Joab's young men stood by him and said, Whoever favors Joab and is for David, let him follow Joab. But Amasa lay wallowing in his blood in the middle of the highway. And when the man saw that all the people stood still, he carried Amasa out of the highway into the field, and cast a garment over him, inasmuch as he saw that every one who came to him stood still. When he was removed out of the highway, all the people went on after Joab, to pursue Sheba the son of Bichri.

34. Pursuit of Sheba

But he passed through all the tribes of Israel to Abel-beth-maacah. And all the Bichrites gathered together, and entered also after him. And they came and besieged him in Abel-beth-maacah, and they cast up a mound against the city, and it stood even with the wall; and all the people with Joab were devising how to throw down the wall.

35. Counsel of the wise woman of Abel

Then a wise woman out of the city, cried, Hear, hear! Say, I pray, to Joab, 'Come near that I may speak with you.' And he came near her; and the woman said, are you Joab?

and he answered, I am. Then she said to him, Hear the words of your maid-servant. And he said, I am listening. Then she spoke, saying, They used to say formerly, 'Let them ask in Abel and Dan whether what the faithful in Israel have established has ceased to be.' I am of those who are peaceful and faithful in Israel. You seek to destroy a city and a mother in Israel; why will you consume the inheritance of Jehovah?

And Joab answered and said, Far be it, far be it from me, that I should consume or destroy. That is not at all our errand. But a man of the hill-country of Ephraim, Sheba the son of Bichri by name, has lifted up his hand against the king, even against David; only deliver him, and I will leave the city. And the woman said to Joab, Behold his head shall be thrown to you over the wall. Then the woman went and advised all the people in her wisdom. And they cut off the head of Sheba the son of Bichri and threw it out to Joab. So he blew the trumpet, and they were dispersed from the city, each to his home. And Joab returned to the king at Jerusalem.

36. Death of Sheba and the end of the rebellion

I. **Absalom's Intrigues.** In his endeavor to place himself on the throne of Israel, Absalom showed himself an adept in the use of the methods of a demagogue. His appeal was to selfish individual interests. David's astonishing ignorance of the trend of events indicates how completely he had withdrawn from public life and cut himself off even from his faithful advisers. Later events, however, show that the hearts of the great majority of the nation were still loyal to David. By a crafty deception Absalom succeeded in implicating the majority of the royal court in his conspiracy. In raising the standard of rebellion at the old capital of Hebron he bid strongly for the support of the Judahites. Strangely enough, most of his supporters appear to have come from David's own tribe; while the king's support came from his body-guard and immediate followers, and the militia of the northern and eastern tribes.

II. **David's Flight.** Absalom's rebellion had gained such headway before it was discovered by David that the king was obliged to flee from Jerusalem before he had time to arouse the loyal elements in his kingdom. The prominent men in his court remained faithful: Joab, the priests Zadok and Abiathar, Hushai, his able adviser, and his Philistine friend Ittai.

In the face of the great danger, David's early energy and skill as a leader reasserted themselves. His piety forbade him, even at this great crisis, to carry away with him in his flight the sacred ark of Jehovah. He wisely provided for a method of communication whereby he might learn of Absalom's movements. With that shrewd diplomacy which had ever characterized him, he sent back Hushai to undermine the counsel of the acute Ahithophel, who for the time had the ear of Absalom. Through Hushai's diplomacy, the danger that the rebel would strike an immediate blow before David could rally his forces was averted.

The sullen resentment and hatred of the Benjamites, who still remained loyal to the house of Saul, found expression in the revilings of a certain Shimei. David's characteristic moderation was again revealed. He seemed to have also hoped that the magnitude of his misery would influence Jehovah to interpose in his behalf. At the Jordan, however, his friends rallied about him and brought ample provisions for the rapidly increasing body of his followers.

III. **The Decisive Battle.** The decisive battle was fought east of the Jordan. David divided his forces into three divisions, placing them under the command of Abishai, Joab and Ittai. With the trained bodyguard, the experienced commanders and a large army on David's side, it was not surprising that the rebels, inspired by no exalted patriotism, were quickly put to flight.

Joab, as often before, disregarded David's personal wishes and acted in accordance with his own personal conviction. In his eyes Absalom was a rebel and a menace to the integrity of the empire; therefore he was put to death. David's sorrow and lamentations over the death of his rebellious son are indeed pathetic, but they are doubly sad because the great calamity was but one of the many indirect fruits of the king's own sin and weakness.

IV. **David's Return to Jerusalem.** David's failure to recognize the loyalty of his subjects, who appear to have sympathized with the act of Joab, nearly led to a disruption of his kingdom at the moment of victory. The words of the people reveal their appreciation of the fact that the David of the later years was very different from the valiant champion who had successfully led them in their early struggles for freedom. His appeal, however, to the dissatisfied men of Judah quickly won their support. A universal amnesty was granted to all the rebels. Even Shimei the Benjamite was spared. The tribes of the north and the south vied with each other in their zeal to escort the king back to his capital.

V. Sheba's Rebellion. David's personal feelings again overruled his kingly sense of justice. In his desire to free himself from the iron hand of Joab, he made the serious mistake of appointing Amasa, an Ishmaelite, who had led Absalom's rebellious army, commander-in-chief of the forces of Israel. It was inevitable that this rebel leader should make no headway in suppressing the remnants of Absalom's rebellion in the north. A certain Benjamite by the name of Sheba, with his clansmen, had fled to the town of Abel-beth-maacah. Joab, as David might well have anticipated, improved the first opportunity to put his rival out of the way. Then rallying the forces of Israel, he marched against the rebels. Through the intercession of a wise woman the city was saved and the rebellion quickly suppressed. Having put down two rebellions, Joab returned to Jerusalem, to continue the grim, invincible power behind the throne.

These rebellions reveal the deep-seated jealousy between the tribes of the north and south, and show how weak were the bonds which bound the Hebrews together. The old danger of Philistine attack had passed away. Even the prestige of David was dimmed. The ancient tribal and sectional interests were beginning to assert themselves. Only the sense of common race and religion, and the iron hand of Joab, kept the empire intact.

§ LV. SOLOMON'S ELECTION AS KING

Now King David was advanced in years, and although they covered him with clothes, he was not warm. Therefore his servants said to him, Let there be sought for my lord the king a young virgin and let her attend the king and constantly take care of him; and let her lie in your bosom, that the lord, my king, may be warm. So they sought for a beautiful maiden throughout all the territory of Israel, and found Abishag the Shunammite and brought her to the king. And the maiden was surpassingly beautiful; and she took care of the king and ministered to him; but the king knew her not. *1. The aged king*

Then Adonijah the son of Haggith exalted himself, saying, I will be king. Therefore he prepared for himself chariots and horsemen and fifty men to run before him as runners. And his father had never in his life troubled him by saying, Why have you done so? And he was also an exceedingly *2. Adonijah's conspiracy* good-looking man, and he was by birth next after Absalom. And he entered into negotiations with Joab the son of Zeruiah and with Abiathar the priest, so that they espoused Adonijah's cause. But Zadok the priest and Benaiah the son of Jehoiada and Nathan the prophet and Shimei and Rei and David's famous heroes were not with Adonijah. And Adonijah slew sheep and oxen and fatlings by the Serpent's Stone, which is beside the Fuller's Spring, and he invited all his brothers, the king's sons, together with all the royal officials of Judah; but the prophet Nathan and Benaiah and the famous heroes and Solomon his brother, he did not invite.

3. Nathan's plan to insure Solomon's succession

Then Nathan said to Bathsheba the mother of Solomon, Have you not heard that Adonijah the son of Haggith has been made king without David our lord knowing it? Now therefore come, let me counsel you that you may save your own life and the life of your son Solomon. Go at once to King David and say to him, 'Did you not, my lord, the king, swear to your maid-servant, saying, "Solomon your son shall be king after me, and he shall sit on my throne? Why then has Adonijah been made king?"' Just as you are talking with the king, I also will come in after you, and confirm your words.

4. Bathsheba's message to David

And Bathsheba went in to the king into his apartment; and the king was very old, and Abishag the Shunammite was ministering to the king. And Bathsheba bowed and did obeisance to the king. And the king said, What do you wish? And she said to him, My lord, you swore to your maid-servant by Jehovah God, 'Solomon your son shall be king after me and he shall sit upon my throne.' And now, see, Adonijah has been made king, without my lord, the king, knowing it. And he has slain oxen and fatlings and sheep in abundance, and has invited all the sons of the king and Abiathar the priest and Joab the commander of the army; but Solomon your servant he has not invited. And now, my lord, the king, the eyes of all Israel are on you, that you should tell them who shall sit on the throne of my lord the king after him. Otherwise, the result will be, when my lord the king shall sleep with his fathers, that I and my son Solomon will be regarded as criminals.

And, while she was still talking with the king, Nathan the prophet came in. And they told the king, saying, Nathan the prophet is here. And he came in before the king and did obeisance before the king with his face to the ground. And Nathan said, My lord the king, have you said, 'Adonijah shall be king after me and shall sit on my throne?' For he has gone down this day and slain oxen and fatlings and sheep in abundance, and has called all the king's sons and the commanders of the army and Abiathar the priest; and there they are eating and drinking before him, and saying, 'May King Adonijah live!' But me, even me, your servant, and Zadok the priest, Benaiah the son of Jehoiada, and your servant Solomon, has he not invited. Has this been brought about by my lord the king, and have you not showed your servants who should sit on the throne of my lord the king after him? 5. Nathan's confirmatory words

Then King David answered and said, Call Bathsheba to me. And she came into the king's presence and stood before the king. Then the king took an oath and said, As Jehovah liveth, who hath redeemed me out of all adversity, as I have sworn to you by Jehovah, the God of Israel, saying, 'Solomon your son shall be king after me and he shall sit on my throne in my place;' verily so will I do to-day. Then Bathsheba bowed her face to the earth, and did obeisance to the king and said, May my lord King David live forever. 6. David's declaration that Solomon should be king

Then King David said, Call to me Zadok the priest, Nathan the prophet, and Benaiah the son of Jehoiada. And when they came before the king, the king said to them, Take with you the servants of your lord, let Solomon my son ride upon my own mule, bring him down to Gihon, and there let Zadok the priest and Nathan the prophet anoint him king over Israel; and blow the trumpet, and say, 'May King Solomon live!' Then you shall go up after him, and he shall enter in and sit upon my throne, for he shall be king in my place; and I have appointed him to be leader over Israel and Judah. And Benaiah the son of Jehoiada answered the king and said, So may it be! thus may Jehovah establish the words of my lord the king. As Jehovah hath been with my lord the king, even so may he be with Solo- 7. Command to proclaim him king mon, and make his throne greater than the throne of my lord King David!

8. Public anointing and acceptance of Solomon

Then Zadok the priest, Nathan the prophet, and Benaiah the son of Jehoiada, together with the Cherethites and the Pelethites, went down and set Solomon on King David's mule, and brought him to Gihon. And Zadok the priest took the horn of oil out of the tent and anointed Solomon. Thereupon they blew the trumpet; and all the people said, May Solomon live! Then all the people went up after him and the people played on flutes and rejoiced so loudly that the earth seemed to be rent with their voice.

9. Announcement to the conspirators

Now Adonijah and all the guests who were with him heard it just as they had finished eating. And when Joab heard the sound of the trumpet, he said, Why is there the noise of the city in an uproar? While he was still speaking, Jonathan the son of Abiathar the priest came. And Adonijah said, Come in, for you are a valiant man and bring good news. And Jonathan answered and said to Adonijah, Nay, but our lord King David has made Solomon king. And the king has sent with him Zadok the priest, Nathan the prophet, and Benaiah the son of Jehoiada, together with the Cherethites and the Pelethites, and they have set him on the king's mule, and Zadok the priest and Nathan the prophet have anointed him king in Gihon, and they have come up from there rejoicing, so that the city is thrown into an uproar. That is the noise which you heard. And Solomon also has taken his seat on the royal throne! And moreover the king's servants have already come to congratulate our lord King David, saying, 'May God make the name of Solomon better than your name, and his throne greater than your throne!' and the king bowed himself on his bed. And furthermore thus said the king, 'Blessed be Jehovah the God of Israel, who hath given one of my descendants to sit on my throne this day, my eyes even seeing it.'

10. Pardon of the conspirators

Then all the guests of Adonijah were seized with terror and rose up and each went his way. But Adonijah in his fear of Solomon arose, and went and caught hold of the horns of the altar. And it was reported to Solomon, See, Adonijah fears King Solomon, for behold he has caught

178

hold of the horns of the altar, saying, Let King Solomon swear to me first that he will not slay his servant with the sword. Solomon said, If he shall show himself a worthy man, not a hair of him shall fall to the earth, but if wickedness be found in him, he must die. So King Solomon sent to bring him away from the altar. And he came and did obeisance to King Solomon. And Solomon said to him, Go to your house.

Then David slept with his fathers and was buried in the city of David. And the period that David reigned over Israel was forty years: seven years in Hebron, and thirty-three years he reigned in Jerusalem. 11. David's death

I. **The Law of Succession in Israel.** Inasmuch as David was but the second king to rule over all Israel, the law of succession had not yet been firmly established. The traditions of the Hebrew kingship went back to the old tribal life. Israel's earliest rulers were but local chieftains or sheiks, with no authority that extended beyond their own tribe and lifetime. In the tribal life of the desert, the oldest son of the sheik succeeded his father, provided he had the requisite qualifications. If, however, a younger son revealed superior ability, the law of primogeniture was frequently set aside. Only the ablest man was called to rule. The two decisive elements in determining the succession were the nomination by the dying chief of the one who was to follow him, and the acceptance of this choice by the people. The same usage apparently continued in force in the days of David, so that Solomon's succession was entirely legitimate.

II. **Adonijah's Attempted Usurpation.** After his return to Jerusalem, David does not appear to have left the seclusion of his harem. While the spark of life still flickered in the body of the aged warrior-king, his court was the scene of constant intrigue. The royal promise to Bathsheba that her son should succeed the throne was probably known to the members of the court. Joab and the priest Abiathar evidently did not view the proposed succession with approval. With their support, Adonijah, the oldest surviving son of David, made a desperate attempt to secure the kingship. Like all the sons of David, he was of attractive appearance, ambitious and fond of display. He accordingly called an assembly of the nobles at the Serpent's Stone, probably not far from the Pool of Siloam, to the south of Jerusalem where the valleys of the Kidron and Hinnon unite. He made the fatal mistake of not inviting to this assembly—the object of which was to proclaim him king—Nathan the prophet, Zadok the priest, Benaiah the commander of the body-guard and other famous warriors. Possibly this oversight was because he was aware that they were loyal not to himself, but to the son of David's choice.

III. **The Counter Conspiracy.** Adonijah's plans failed because of the prompt action of Nathan. Communicating the news to Bathsheba, the prophet arranged that they should go in to David and win his consent to have Solomon at once proclaimed king. Their plot was successful. Solomon was nominated by David as his successor, placed upon the royal mule and led by Zadok and Nathan to the spring of Gihon on the side of the Kidron valley east of the Hill of Ophel. There, a few hundred yards above the spot where the assembled banqueters were crying, "May King Adonijah live!" Solomon was anointed king by Zadok, the priest. The trumpet was then blown, and Solomon was presented to the people and formally accepted as their king. The conspirators about Adonijah were rudely awakened from their dream by the shouts of the people. Adonijah took advantage of the ancient right of altar asylum, thus putting himself under the protection of Jehovah. Solomon, however, in the hour of his triumph granted full pardon to his rival and to those who had opposed his succession.

IV. **David's Dying Injunctions.** The original David stories apparently ended with the account of Solomon's accession. In the subsequent context the author of the books of Kings has given a brief reference to David's death and the duration of his reign. The popular Solomon traditions, which have been quoted in the earlier part of I Kings, attribute to David certain dying injunctions which were apparently intended to palliate Solomon's action in putting to death Shimei and Joab. It is, of course, possible that these grim commands were laid upon Solomon by his dying father. If so, they but reveal the vindictiveness of an old man in his dotage. They are certainly not in harmony with the character of David as portrayed in the earlier narratives. Although a man of war, he had ever showed himself averse to the unnecessary shedding of blood. Loyalty to his supporters and readiness to pardon those who had wronged him were among his most marked characteristics.

V. **The Character of David.** No character in all the Old Testament is as fully portrayed as that of David. Almost contemporary traditions throw light upon his life at every important stage from boyhood to the grave. His faults are pictured as faithfully as his virtues. They are the faults peculiar to a versatile genius: a lack of absolute truthfulness, a failure in the face of sudden and powerful temptation to control his passions, a selfish fondness for his children, which made him a weak father; these are the glaring faults which overshadow the brilliant virtues of David's earlier days. Like many another man in the world's history, he developed rapidly and nobly in the face of hardship and opposition, and fell in the moment of prosperity and success. His life history, therefore, is a tragedy because it failed to realize the promise of his earlier years.

That David was truly religious is amply illustrated at every stage in his history. No important act was undertaken without consulting the Deity. His dominant aim was to rule over the people as Jehovah's representative. His religion, however, was of a conventional and superficial, rather than a profound, type. His conceptions of Jehovah and of his obligations to him were those of his age. Through the priestly oracle he sought to know the will of God. To win his approval, he transferred the ark to Jerusalem and danced before it as an expression of his religious zeal. By the sacrifice of animals, and even by the sacrifice of innocent human beings, he sought to win and retain the approval of the God whom his age worshipped; but for traces of the profound faith of the later prophets and psalmist one seeks in vain.

David's virtues are many. He was brave, chivalrous, magnanimous and patriotic. He genuinely loved his friends and followers and was passionately loved by them. Tact, insight, excellent organizing ability, made him a successful king, as well as an able leader. He was ambitious for personal glory, but he was also equally ambitious for his race and nation. As poet, patriot, warrior and devout worshipper of Jehovah, he embodied the highest ideals of his age. It is, therefore, not strange that he was idolized by his own and idealized by succeeding generations. His love for Jehovah and his people left little place in his heart for pride and tyranny. He kept always before him the noble Hebrew ideal of the kingship. Except on the one memorable occasion, when he yielded to his own base passion, he ever showed himself the loyal servant of the people. Thus, as a king, he proved, as did no other ruler in early Hebrew history, "a man after God's own heart."

VI. David's Work. In the perspective of history, Saul figures as the great pioneer; but David built well on the foundations which Saul had laid. Under his leadership united Israel became a fixed reality. By closer organization, by sharing together a common capital, by uniting in successful wars against their common foes, rival tribes were led to forget their jealousies and to recognize the bond of common race, ideals and religion. By his foreign conquests David gave to his people peace and prestige, and prepared the way for that development of the resources of the empire and of commerce which quickly followed in the days of Solomon. David also inspired those ideals of kingly justice, as well as of world-wide dominion, which were ever after cherished by the Hebrews and which find frequent echoes in the Messianic predictions of later prophets. In uniting all Israel under one king he also impressed upon his subjects the conception of Jehovah as the one Supreme Ruler over all the different tribes. In conquering the neighboring nations and building up a great empire he laid the foundations of that later monotheism which was proclaimed by the great prophets of the Assyrian period.

THE SPLENDORS OF SOLOMON'S REIGN

§ LVI. SOLOMON'S POLICY AND FAME

Now Solomon sat upon the throne of David his father and his kingdom was firmly established. Then Adonijah the son of Haggith came to Bathsheba the mother of Solomon and bowed before her. And she said, Do you come in a friendly manner? And he replied, Yes, and added, I have something to say to you. And she said, Speak. And he said, You know that the kingdom was mine and that all Israel looked upon me as the coming king, but now the kingdom has been taken away from me and has become my brother's, for it was his from Jehovah. Now, however, I would ask one thing of you; do not refuse me. And she said to him, Speak. And he said, Then request Solomon the king—he will not refuse you—to give me Abishag the Shunammite as wife. And Bathsheba said, Good, I will speak for you to the king.

1. Adonijah's solicitations for Abishag

Bathsheba went therefore to King Solomon to speak to him for Adonijah. And the king rose up to meet her and bowed before her, and sat down on his throne, and a seat was placed for the king's mother, and she sat on his right. Then she said, I would make a small request of you; do not refuse me. And the king said to her, Make your request, my mother, for I will not refuse you. And she said, Let Abishag the Shunammite be given to Adonijah your brother as wife. Then King Solomon answered and said to his mother, Why then do you ask Abishag the Shunammite for Adonijah? Ask for him the kingdom also! for he is my elder brother, and on his side are Abiathar the priest and Joab the son of Zeruiah.

2. Solomon's indignation

3. Execution of Adonijah

Thereupon King Solomon swore by Jehovah, saying, God do to me whatever he pleaseth, if Adonijah has not spoken this word against his own life. Now therefore as Jehovah liveth, who hath established me and caused me to mount the throne of David my father, and who hath, as he promised, given me posterity, Adonijah shall surely be put to death this day. Then King Solomon sent Benaiah the son of Jehoiada; and he struck him down, so that he died.

4. Banishment of Abiathar

And to Abiathar the priest the king said, Go to Anathoth to your estate; for you are to-day condemned to die, but I will not put you to death, because you bore the ark of Jehovah before David my father and because you shared all the afflictions which my father experienced. Thus Solomon sent away Abiathar, so that he was no longer Jehovah's priest.

5. Joab's bloody end

But when the report came to Joab—for Joab had upheld Adonijah, and had not upheld Absalom—Joab fled to the tent of Jehovah, and caught hold of the horns of the altar. And it was told King Solomon, Joab has fled to the tent of Jehovah and is there beside the altar. Thereupon Solomon sent to Joab, saying, How comes it that you have fled to the altar? Joab replied, Because I was afraid of you and so I fled to Jehovah. Then Solomon sent Benaiah the son of Jehoiada, saying, Go, strike him down. And Benaiah went to the tent of Jehovah and said to him, The king commands, 'Come forth.' But he said, No; I will rather die here. And Benaiah brought the king word again, saying, Thus said Joab and thus he answered me. And the king said to him, Do as he has said: strike him down and bury him, that you may take away the innocent blood which Joab shed from me and from my father's clan. And Jehovah will requite his bloody act upon his own head, because he struck down two men more honorable and better than he, and slew them with the sword without the knowledge of my father David: Abner the son of Ner, commander of the army of Israel, and Amasa the son of Jether, commander of the army of Judah. So shall their blood come back upon the head of Joab and the head of his descendants forever; but to David, and to his descendants, and to

his house, and to his throne may there be peace forever
from Jehovah. Then Benaiah the son of Jehoiada went
up and struck him down and slew him; and he was buried
in his own house in the wilderness. And the king put
Benaiah the son of Jehoiada in his place over the army,
and the king put Zadok the priest in the place of Abiathar.

Then the king summoned Shimei and said to him, Build
a house in Jerusalem, there you may live, but you shall
not go forth from there to any place whatever. For as soon
as you go away and cross the Brook Kidron, know for certain that you shall surely die; your blood shall be upon your
own head. And Shimei said to the king, The statement is
fair; Your servant will do as my lord the king has said.
And Shimei lived in Jerusalem a long time.

6. Shim-ei's sentence

But at the end of three years, two of Shimei's slaves ran
away to Achish son of Maacah king of Gath. And when it
was reported to Shimei, Your slaves are in Gath, Shimei
rose and saddled his ass and went to Gath to Achish to seek
his slaves. And Shimei went and brought his slaves from
Gath. And it was told Solomon that Shimei had gone from
Jerusalem to Gath and had come back again. Then the
king summoned Shimei, and said to him, Did I not cause
you to take an oath by Jehovah and solemnly admonish
you, saying, 'Know for certain that as soon as you go away
to any place whatever, you shall surely die'? And you
said to me, 'The statement is fair.' Why then have you
not kept the oath of Jehovah and the command that I laid
upon you? The king also said to Shimei, You are aware of
all the wickedness which you yourself alone know, that you
did to David my father; now Jehovah hath brought your
wickedness upon your own head. But King Solomon shall
be blessed and the throne of David shall be established before Jehovah forever. So the king gave command to Benaiah the son of Jehoiada, and he went out and struck him
down, and thus he died. So the kingdom was brought
completely under the control of Solomon.

7. Shim-ei's fate

Now Solomon was king over all Israel. And these were
the princes whom he had: Azariah the son of Zadok was
priest; Elihoreph and Ahijah, the sons of Shisha, were
scribes; Jehoshaphat the son of Ahilud was chancellor;

8. Solomon's court officials

185

and Benaiah the son of Jehoiada was the head of the army;
and Azariah the son of Nathan was at the head of the officers; and Zabud the son of Nathan was a priest and the
king's friend; and Ahishar was prefect of the palace; and
Adoniram the son of Abda was in charge of the forced levy.

9. Commissary officers And Solomon had twelve officers over all Israel, who provided food for the king and his household: each man had
to make provision for a month in the year. And these are
their names: Ben-hur, in the hill-country of Ephraim;
Ben-deker, in Makaz, Shaalbim, Bethshemesh, and Elon-
beth-hanan; Ben-hesed, in Arubboth; to him belonged
Socoh and all the land of Hepher; Ben-abinadab, in all the
highland of Dor (he had Tapath the daughter of Solomon as
wife); Baana the son of Ahilud, in Taanach and Megiddo
and all Bethshean, which is beside Zarethan, beneath Jezreel, from Bethshean to Abel-meholah, as far as the other
side of Jokneam; Ben-geber in Ramoth in Gilead; to him
belonged the region of Argob, which is in Bashan, sixty
great cities with walls and brazen bars; Ahinadab the son
of Iddo in Mahanaim; Ahimaaz, in Naphtali (he also took
Basemath the daughter of Solomon as wife); Baana the son
of Hushai, in Asher and Bealoth; Jehoshaphat the son of
Paruah, in Issachar; Shimei the son of Ela, in Benjamin;
Geber the son of Uri, in the land of Gad, the country of
Sihon king of the Amorites and of Og king of Bashan; and
one officer was over all the officials who were in the land.

10. Amount of the provisions And these officers provided food for King Solomon and
for all who came to King Solomon's table, each in his month.
They let nothing be lacking. Barley also and straw for
the horses and swift steeds they brought to the proper place—
each according to his individual charge. And Solomon's
provision for one day was about six hundred bushels of
fine flour, and about one thousand, two hundred bushels
of meal, ten fat, and twenty meadow-fed oxen, and a hundred sheep, besides harts, gazelles, roebucks, and fatted fowls.

11. Alliance with Egypt And Solomon allied himself by marriage with Pharaoh,
king of Egypt, and took Pharaoh's daughter, and brought
her into the city of David, until he had completed the building of his own palace and the temple of Jehovah and the
wall around Jerusalem.

Then Pharaoh king of Egypt went up, captured Gezer, and burnt it with fire, slew the Canaanites who dwelt in the city, and gave it as a portion to his daughter, Solomon's wife. And Solomon rebuilt Gezer. 12. Capture of Gezer

And the king went to Gibeon to sacrifice there; for that was the great high place; a thousand burnt-offerings did Solomon offer upon that altar. 13. Solomon's sacrifice

In Gibeon Jehovah appeared to Solomon in a dream by night. And God said, Ask what I shall give thee. And Solomon said, Thou hast showed to thy servant David my father great kindness. And now, O Jehovah my God, thou hast made thy servant king in the place of David my father, although I am but a child, not knowing how to go out or come in. Give thy servant therefore an understanding mind to judge thy people, that I may discern between good and evil; for who is able to judge this thy great people? 14. His request for wisdom to rule justly

And it pleased Jehovah that Solomon had asked this thing. And God said to him, Because thou hast asked this thing and hast not asked for thyself long life nor riches nor the life of thy enemies, but hast asked for thyself insight to discern justice; behold, I have done according to thy request: I have given thee a wise and discerning mind. And I have also given thee that which thou hast not asked: both riches and honor. And when Solomon awoke, behold it was a dream. Then he returned to Jerusalem. 15. Jehovah's promise

Then two harlots came to the king and stood before him. And the one woman said, O, my lord, this woman and I dwell in the same house; and I was delivered of a child in her presence within the house. Now on the third day after I was delivered, this woman was also delivered and we were together, there being no one else with us in the house: we two being alone in the house. And this woman's child died in the night, because she lay upon it. And she arose at midnight and took my son from beside me, while your maid-servant slept, and laid it in her bosom and laid her dead child in my bosom. And when I rose in the morning to nurse my child, there it was dead; but when I looked at it in the morning, behold, it was not my son whom I had borne. Then the other woman said, No; but the living is my son, and the dead child is your son. And the first 16. An example of Solomon's wisdom woman was saying, No; but the dead is your son and the living child is my son. Thus they contended before the king.

17. His sagacious decision

Then the king said, This one says, 'This is my son, the living, and your son is the dead.' And the other says, 'No; but your son is the dead, and my son is the living!' Thereupon the king said, Bring me a sword. And they brought a sword before the king. And the king said, Divide the living child in two and give half to the one and half to the other. Then the woman to whom the living child belonged, spoke to the king—for her heart yearned over her son—and she said, O, my lord, give her the living child and on no account put it to death. But the other said, It shall be neither mine nor yours! Divide it! Then the king answered and said, Give her the living child, and on no account put it to death; she is his mother. And when all Israel heard of the judgment which the king had rendered, they revered the king, for they saw that divine wisdom to execute justice was in him.

18. Impression made upon the queen of Sheba

Now when the queen of Sheba heard of the fame of Solomon through the name of Jehovah, she came to test him with riddles. So she came to Jerusalem with a very great retinue, with camels that bore spices and very much gold and precious stones. And as soon as she came to Solomon, she told him all that was on her mind. And Solomon answered all her questions; there was nothing hid from the king which he could not answer her. And when the queen of Sheba had seen all the wisdom of Solomon, the house that he had built, the food of his table, the seating of his courtiers, the attendance of his waiters, their clothing, his cupbearers, and his burnt-offering which he used to offer at the temple of Jehovah, there was no more spirit in her. And she said to the king, True was the report that I heard in my own land of your acts and of your wisdom. But I would not believe the words until I came and saw with my own eyes; the half was not told me; you exceed in wisdom and prosperity the report which I heard. Happy are your wives! Happy are these your courtiers who stand continually before you and hear your wisdom! Blessed be Jehovah your God who delighted in you and hath set you on the throne of Israel! Because Jehovah loved Israel forever, he hath made you king that you may do justice and righteousness. Then she gave the king a hundred and twenty talents of gold and a very great store of spices and precious stones; never again came so many spices as these which the queen of Sheba gave to King Solomon.

And King Solomon gave to the queen all that she wished and asked, aside from that which she had brought to Solomon, according to his royal bounty. So she returned and went to her own land, together with her servants.

19. His gifts to her

I. The Removal of Solomon's Foes. Solomon's policy was clearly revealed at the beginning of his reign. The occasion was the request of Adonijah that he be allowed to marry Abishag, the Shunammite, who had attended David in his old age. Bathsheba, to whom he appealed, evidently regarded it as an innocent request, for she at once presented it to her son Solomon. According to the custom of the East, a new monarch on his accession entered into the possession of the harem of his predecessor. Marriage with the wife of a deceased king was regarded as a step toward the throne. Thus Abner's marriage with Rizpah, Saul's concubine, was considered an act of treason by Ishbaal. A similar interpretation was placed on Adonijah's request. At Solomon's command, Adonijah was forthwith put to death.

Adonijah's supporters next became the victims of Solomon's policy of absolutism. Abiathar, the descendant of Eli, who had shared David's outlaw life, was deposed from the priesthood and banished from Jerusalem. Zadok and his family were established in that position at the head of the royal priesthood which they continued to hold for the next seven or eight hundred years. Even the right of altar asylum was denied the aged Joab. Beside the altar of Jehovah this aged warrior, who had been so blindly loyal to the interests of David and who had contributed more than any other to the building up of Israel's prestige, was cut down as a common criminal, and Benaiah, the captain of the body-guard, was placed at the head of the army. Shemei the Benjamite was brought to Jerusalem under pledge that he would remain within the precincts of the city. When, in his eagerness to recover two runaway slaves, he broke his oath, Solomon showed no mercy, but caused to be slain by the sword the last of the foes of his house.

II. The Organization of Solomon's Kingdom. The readiness with which Solomon, on the least pretext, put to death his foes indicates that he was determined to tolerate no rival. The methods which he employed to establish his absolute authority were those of the ordinary oriental despot. The same policy is apparent in the organization of his court. Few of the officials who had served under his father retained their office. The sons of Nathan, the prophet, who had been so active in securing Solomon's accession, were assigned to high positions of trust.

A prefect of the palace appears now for the first time among the court officials. Elaborate provisions were also made for the collection of the king's tribute. In that minute description of Solomon's policy which is placed by the later prophetic narrator of I Samuel 8[10-18] in the mouth of Samuel, it is stated that this tribute amounted to one-tenth of the entire product of the fields and vineyards and of the offspring of the flocks. Twelve officials, each charged with the task of collecting sufficient food to supply the royal court for one month, were placed in charge of the different districts of Northern Israel. The old tribal divisions were apparently disregarded. The absence of any reference to the territory of Judah suggests that perhaps this southern tribe, from which came the reigning dynasty, was exempted from taxation.

The elaborate provisions, which were thus collected from his subjects, were required for the large and magnificent court which Solomon gathered about him. All this was in striking contrast to the simplicity of Saul, who lived quietly on his own family estates.

Solomon also allied himself by marriage with an Egyptian princess, who received as her marriage dowry the Canaanite town of Gezer, west of Jerusalem on the borders of the Philistine plain. Thus from the first it was evident that Solomon's ambition was to take his place side by side with the other oriental rulers of southwestern Asia and to rival in magnificence the splendor of their courts. Doubtless, he also desired to open wide the doors of commerce to the civilization of that ancient world and to raise his subjects to a level with the surrounding peoples. In striving to accomplish these ends within the narrow limits of a generation he broke rudely with the traditions of the past, and disregarded those democratic instincts which the Hebrews had brought with them from the desert. In the pursuit of material splendor and power, he also neglected the simpler and nobler Hebrew ideals of the kingship. The result was that he who was called to be the servant of the people became their despotic master.

III. Solomon's Wisdom. The magnificence of Solomon's court in part blinded the eyes of his own and succeeding generations. Tradition has preserved the memory of the nobler aspirations of his earlier years. Keenness of observation and insight were regarded as the most desirable qualities that could be possessed by an ancient oriental monarch. A picturesque story has been handed down which illustrates this much-prized gift. To determine who was the actual mother of the child who was brought before him, he appealed to the universal mother instinct. Later oriental tradition has preserved many similar stories regarding Solomon. His reputation for wit and brilliance was in harmony with the magnificence and splendor of his court.

IV. **The Wisdom of the Ancient East.** The ancient Semitic East always paid a high tribute to native shrewdness and insight. Each town and tribe appears to have had its group of wise men or sages who were keen students of human nature and life. They were the repositories of the accumulative experience of their own and preceding generations. They were the counsellors of tribal chieftains and kings, the advisors of the people in deciding the various questions of life, and the teachers of the youths. Certain cities, and especially those like Teman, bordering on the Arabian desert, which appears to have been the native home of wisdom-teaching, were famous for their sages.

The teaching of these ancient sages was ordinarily transmitted in the form of short, picturesque, often epigrammatic, proverbs. Sometimes like the wise woman of Tekoa, they employed the parable or fable. It is probable that they entertained the people at the wedding-feasts and festivals with riddles similar to those found in the thirtieth chapter of Proverbs.

V. **Solomon's Relation to the Hebrew Wisdom Literature.** The book of Proverbs is the characteristic literary product of the wise men. A late Hebrew tradition asserts that Solomon was not only wiser than the wisest sages of Arabia and Egypt, but that he also uttered three thousand proverbs and five thousand songs. It is also stated that, not only did the queen of Sheba come from southern Arabia with rich gifts to admire the magnificence and wit of Solomon, but that representatives of many other nations came to hear his wisdom. Closely related to this late tradition is the statement in the superscription to the book of Proverbs which assigns the entire collection to him. Certain older superscriptions within the book of Proverbs—as, for example, 22^{17} and 24^{23}— plainly indicate that the individual proverbs come from many different sages. The book of Proverbs is in fact a collection of collections. Many of them, such as those which commend monogamy and condemn the tyranny of a ruler, cannot come from Solomon. Most of them are written from the point of view of an ordinary citizen, rather than that of a ruler. It is probable, however, that Solomon did embody certain of the results of his keen observation in the form of proverbs. It is possible that some of these have been preserved to find a place in the Old Testament book of Proverbs. It was also natural that, as Solomon's reputation for wisdom increased in succeeding generations, he should be regarded as the father of wisdom literature, even as Moses was of the law. In the same way the late Jewish book of Ecclesiastes is attributed to him, and a still later work, coming from not earlier than the first century before Christ, bears the title, *Wisdom of Solomon*.

§ LVII. SOLOMON'S TEMPLE

1. Solomon's request of Hiram

And Hiram king of Tyre sent his servants to Solomon because he had heard that they had anointed him king in the place of his father; for Hiram had loved David. And Solomon sent to Hiram, saying, Now I purpose to build a temple for the name of Jehovah my God. Therefore command that they cut for me cedar timber from Lebanon; and my servants will go with your servants, and I will give you wages for your servants just as you shall say; for you know that there is no one among us who knows how to cut timber as the Sidonians.

2. Hiram's reply and conditions

So Hiram sent to Solomon, saying, I have heard your message to me; I, on my part, will fulfil all your wishes in regard to cedar and cypress timber. My servants shall bring them down from Lebanon to the sea, and I will make them into rafts to go by sea to the place that you shall appoint, and will have them broken up there, and you shall receive them. You also shall fulfil my wish by providing food for my household. So Hiram furnished Solomon cypress timber, as much as he wished. And Solomon gave Hiram four hundred thousand bushels of wheat for food for his household, and one hundred and sixty thousand gallons of oil from the beaten olives. This much Solomon gave to Hiram year by year. And there was peace between Hiram and Solomon, and they made an alliance with each other.

3. Solomon's forced levy of workmen

And King Solomon raised a forced levy out of all Israel; and the levy consisted of thirty thousand men. And he sent them to Lebanon, ten thousand a month in relays; a month they were in Lebanon, and two months at home; and Adoniram was in charge of the forced levy. And Solomon had seventy

thousand burden-bearers and eighty thousand hewers of stone
in the mountains; besides Solomon's chief officers who were
in charge of the work, three thousand, three hundred, who
superintended the people who did the work. And the king
commanded that they should hew out great, costly stones, to
lay the foundation of the temple with cut stone. And Solomon's builders and Hiram's builders and especially the Gebal-
ites shaped them and prepared the timber and the stones to
build the temple.

In the fourth year of Solomon's reign over Israel, he built
the temple of Jehovah. And the length of the temple which
King Solomon built for Jehovah was sixty and its breadth
twenty cubits, and its height thirty cubits. And the porch
before the large room of the temple was twenty cubits wide,
corresponding to the breadth of the temple, ten cubits deep
before the temple. And for the temple he made windows
with narrowed frames. 4. Dimensions of the temple

And around against the wall of the temple he built wings,
both around the larger room and the inner room, and made
side-chambers round about. The lower side-chamber was
five cubits broad, and the middle six cubits broad, and the
third seven cubits broad; for on the outside he made offsets
around about the temple in order not to make an inset into
the walls of the temple. The entrance into the lower side-
chambers was on the south side of the temple. And one could
go up by winding stairs into the middle story, and from the
middle into the third. And he built the wings against all
the temple, each story five cubits high; and they rested on the
temple with timbers of cedar. So he built the temple and finished it; and he covered the temple with cedar. 5. The side-chambers

And he built the walls of the temple within with boards of
cedar: from the floor of the temple to the rafters of the ceiling,
overlaying them on the inside with wood; and he covered the
floor of the temple with boards of cypress. And he built off
the back twenty cubits from the innermost part of the temple
with boards of cedar from the floor to the rafters: he built it
within for an inner room, even for the most holy place. And
the temple, that is the large room before the inner room, was
forty cubits long. And there was cedar in the interior of the
temple, carving in the form of gourds and open flowers; all 6. The interior decorations

was cedar, no stone was seen. And he prepared an inner room in the interior of the temple in order to place there the ark of the covenant of Jehovah. And the inner room was twenty cubits long and twenty cubits broad and twenty cubits high. And he overlaid it with pure gold. And he made an altar of cedar wood. And he carved all the walls of the house round about with carved figures of cherubim and palm trees and opening flowers, both in the inner and outer rooms.

7. The cherubim

And in the inner room he made two cherubim of olive wood. The height of the one cherub was ten cubits, and so was that of the other—each ten cubits high. And one wing of the cherub measured five cubits, and the other wing of the cherub also five cubits—ten cubits from the extremity of one wing to the extremity of the other. And the other cherub also measured ten cubits: both the cherubim were of the same measurement and form. And he set up the cherubim in the inner room of the temple, and the wings of the cherubim were stretched forth, so that the wing of the one touched the one wall, while the wing of the other cherub touched the other wall, and their wings touched each other in the middle of the temple; and he overlaid the cherubim with gold.

8. Door of the inner room

And the door of the inner room he made with folding doors of olive wood: the pilasters formed a pentagonal. And on the two doors of olive wood he carved carvings of cherubim and palm trees and opening flowers, and he spread the gold over the cherubim and the palm trees.

9. Door of the large room

So also he made for the door of the large room posts of olive wood, four square, and two folding leaves of cypress wood: the two leaves of the one door were folding, and the two leaves of the other door were folding. And he carved cherubim and palm trees and opening flowers, and overlaid them with gold applied evenly to the carving. And he built the inner court with three courses of hewn stone and a course of cedar beams.

10. Completion of the temple

In the fourth year was the foundation of the temple of Jehovah laid, in the month Ziv [April-May]. And in the eleventh year, in the month Bul [October-November], was the temple completed in all its parts. Thus he was seven years in building it.

11. The pillars at the entrance

Then King Solomon sent and brought Hiram-abi an Aramean worker in brass; and he was gifted with skill, understanding, and knowledge to carry on all kinds of work in brass.

And he came to King Solomon and did all his work. For he cast the two pillars of brass for the porch of the temple. Eighteen cubits was the height of one pillar, and its circumference measured twelve cubits; the thickness of the pillar was four fingers—it was hollow. And the second pillar was similar. And he made two capitals of molten brass, to set upon the tops of the pillars: the height of the one capital was five cubits, and the height of the other capital was five cubits. And he made two nets for the capitals which were on the top of the pillars; a net for the one capital, and a net for the other capital. And he made the pomegranates; and two rows of pomegranates in brass were upon the one network, and there were two hundred pomegranates—two rows round about the one capital. And he did the same to the other capital. And the capitals that were upon the top of the pillars in the porch were of lily-work —four cubits. And there were capitals above also upon the two pillars, in connection with the bowl-shaped part of the pillar which was beside the network. And he set up the pillars at the porch of the temple; and he set up the pillar at the right and called it Jachin; and he set up the pillar at the left and called it Boaz. And upon the top of the pillars was lily-work. So was the work of the pillars finished.

And he made the molten sea ten cubits in diameter from brim to brim, and five cubits high, and its circumference measured thirty cubits. And under its brim on the outside were gourds which encircled it, for thirty cubits, encircling the sea on the outside; the gourds were in two rows, cast when it was cast. And it was a handbreadth thick; and its brim was wrought like the brim of a cup, similar to the flower of a lily. It held about sixteen thousand gallons. It stood upon twelve oxen, three looking toward the north, and three looking toward the west, and three looking toward the south, and three looking toward the east; and the sea was set down upon them, and all were turned inward back to back. *12. Molten sea*

And he made the ten stands of brass: each stand was four cubits long, four cubits broad, and three cubits high. And the stands were made as follows: they had border-frames, and the border-frames were between the upright supports; and on the border-frames that were between the upright supports were lions, oxen and cherubim; and upon the upright supports *13. Movable brazen stands* likewise; and above and beneath the lions and oxen and cheru-bim was bevelled work. And every stand had four wheels of brass and axles of brass. And the four wheels were under-neath the border-frames; and the axles and the wheels were cast as a part of the stand. And the height of each wheel was a cubit and a half. And the construction of the wheels was like that of a chariot wheel: their axles, their felloes, their spokes, and their hubs, were all cast. And at the four corners of each stand were four shoulder-pieces; the shoulder-pieces were cast as part of the stand. And in the top of the stand was a round opening, half a cubit high, and on the top of the stand were its stays and its border-frames. And on the flat surface of the stays and border-frames, he engraved cherubim, lions, and palm trees, according to the space on each, with wreaths round about. And the four corners had shoulder-pieces: be-neath the bowl the shoulder-pieces were cast, with wreaths at the side of each. And its opening within the shoulder-pieces was a cubit and more; and its opening was round after the form of a pedestal (a cubit and a half), and also upon its open-ing were gravings, and its border-frames were square, not round. Thus he made the ten stands: all of them had one casting, and were of the same measure and form.

14. Po-sition of the stands with their lavers

And he made ten lavers of brass: one laver contained three hundred and twenty gallons, and each laver measured four cubits; and on each one of the ten stands was a laver. And he set the stands, five on the right side of the temple and five on the left side of the temple: and he set the sea on the right side of the temple eastward toward the south.

15. Com-pletion of the work

And Hiram made the lavers and the shovels, and the bowls. So Hiram completed all the work that he wrought for King Solomon in the temple of Jehovah: the two pillars and the two bowl-shaped capitals that were on the top of the pillars, and the four hundred pomegranates for the two networks to cover the two bowl-shaped capitals that were on the top of the pillars, and the ten stands and the ten lavers on the stands, and the one sea, with the twelve oxen under the sea.

16. Vast amount of brass re-quired

And the pots, the shovels, and the bowls, and all these vessels which Hiram made for King Solomon in the temple of Jehovah, were of burnished brass. There was no weighing the brass from which he made all these vessels, because it was so very much that the weight of the brass could not be determined. In the plain of the Jordan he cast them, in the clay ground between Succoth and Zarethan.

And Solomon placed all the vessels which he had made in the temple of Jehovah. Thus all the work that King Solomon wrought in the temple of Jehovah was finished. And Solomon brought in the things which David his father had dedicated, even the silver and the gold and the vessels, placing them in the treasuries of the temple of Jehovah. *17. Arrangement of the vessels*

Then Solomon assembled the elders of Israel in Jerusalem to bring up the ark of Jehovah out of the city of David. And all the men of Israel assembled about King Solomon at the feast, in the month of Ethanim, which is the seventh month. And all the elders of Israel came, and the priests took up the ark. And the tent of meeting, and all the holy vessels that were in the tent. Then King Solomon and all Israel were with him before the ark sacrificing so many sheep and oxen, that they could neither be counted nor numbered. So the priests brought in the ark of Jehovah to its place in the inner room of the temple under the wings of the cherubim. For the cherubim spread forth their wings over the place of the ark, so that the cherubim formed a covering above the ark and its staves. And the staves were so long that the ends of the staves were seen from the place before the inner room; but further out they could not be seen. And there they are to this day. There was nothing in the ark except the two tables of stone which Moses put there at Horeb. And when the priests had come from the sanctuary, the cloud filled the temple of Jehovah, so that the priests could not stand to minister because of the cloud, for the glory of Jehovah filled the temple of Jehovah. *18. Dedication of the temple*

Then Solomon said, *19. Solomon's hymn of dedication*

> Jehovah hath set the sun in the heavens,
> But he hath himself determined to dwell in thick darkness.
> So I have built thee a temple as a place of abode,
> A dwelling for thee to abide in forever.

Is it not written in the Book of Jashar?

20. Institution of the regular service of the temple

And three times in the year Solomon used to offer burnt-offerings and peace-offerings upon the altar which he built to Jehovah, and he used to cause the savor of the sacrifice to rise before Jehovah.   So he finished the temple.

I. Solomon's Motive in Building the Temple.   The temple which Solomon built was but one of the many expressions of his ambition as a builder.   The examples of the Egyptians, and especially that of the Phœnicians under the leadership of his contemporary Hiram, were clearly before him.   Originally Solomon's temple was but a royal chapel connected with his palace and court.   There is no evidence that he intended that it should supersede the many other high places scattered throughout his realm.   These long continued to flourish and to receive the homage of their devotees.

The temple at Jerusalem at first performed a double function; it was the court sanctuary, where henceforth the king and the growing army of public officials worshipped Jehovah.   Occupying the highest point on the hill of Ophel, it probably stood on or near the site of an old Jebusite high place.   It quickly became the chief shrine of Jerusalem.   Under the shadow of the throne and supported by the royal bounty, the temple inevitably gained in prestige and importance with each succeeding generation.   Its geographical position and magnificence also from the first exalted it above all the other sanctuaries in the land.   Its preëminence likewise gave added strength and prestige to the house of David.   As it attracted more and more all members of the nation, it silently but powerfully emphasized the fact that one God, Jehovah, ruled supreme in Israel.

II. Preparations for the Temple.   From earliest times the cedars, which grew on the summits of the Lebanons, had been especially prized for building purposes.   The Egyptian kings frequently sent to secure supplies of this precious timber.   Its attractive color and sweet odor made it especially appropriate for interior temple decoration.   It was natural that a close commercial alliance should spring up between the Hebrews, who possessed abundant grain fields, and the Phœnicians, whose productive territory was limited, but whose artisans were skilled in producing those works of art which the Hebrews most needed. Permission, therefore, was readily granted to cut down the needed supply of cedar and cypress timber, and a small army of Hebrew workmen was detailed for the task.   Phœnician artisans directed all the details in the construction of the temple.   Its position facing east, with two great pillars at its entrance, the decorative motives, the palm tree and cherubim, and the general plan are perhaps all traceable to Phœnician influence. The stones for the walls of the temple were probably hewn from the limestone hill on which the sanctuary was reared. Even with the large army of men enlisted, the building of the temple required seven and a half years.

III. Plan and Dimensions. With the aid of a restored text and the later descriptions of Ezekiel (chapters 40–48), it is possible to gain a very definite idea of the general plan and dimensions of Solomon's temple. Compared with many of the public structures of to-day, it was small, but compared with the diminutive houses and hovels in which the Hebrews at this period lived, it seemed huge and magnificent.

The central feature of the temple was the oracle, a perfect cube between thirty and thirty-five feet square, and lighted only through the door which led into the larger audience chamber. This outer room or audience chamber was between ninety and one hundred feet long, and was apparently lighted on both sides by small windows, protected by the overhanging roofs. The outer room was entered through an imposing porch, rising higher than the rest of the temple. The walls of the temple were exceedingly thick; wider on the outside at the bottom, they grew narrower by successive steps toward the top. The interior walls were covered with cedar work, which appears in turn to have been adorned with figures of palm trees and cherubim. Later tradition has also overlaid its walls and floors with gold and elaborate carving. The original temple, however, was stately in its simplicity and adaptation to its purpose.

About the two sides and rear of the temple were built a series of chambers, three stories in height, in which the garments of the priests, the vessels used in the sacrifice, and possibly public and private treasures, were kept. These chambers were entered only from the outside.

From this general plan it is evident that the temple was literally thought of as Jehovah's house in which he dwelt and where he received, like an earthly king, the homage of his subjects.

IV. The Equipment of the Temple. In front of the temple, cut out of the native rock, stood the great altar on which the sacrifices in behalf of the king, the court and the nation were offered. Near by was the great molten sea, about fifty feet in circumference and eight feet in height, holding sixteen thousand gallons of water. This water was for purification in connection with the sacrificial ritual. Ten lavers, on highly decorated, movable, brazen stands, were provided to transport the water.

In the outer room of the temple was found the table of showbread. This ancient form of sacrifice goes back to the beginnings of Hebrew history, and was shared in common with the Babylonians and Egyptians, who placed similar loaves of bread as food before their gods. A seven-branched candlestick also lighted this outer room by night.

Within the inner room or oracle stood two huge cherubim, about sixteen feet in height, with outstretched wings extending about sixteen feet from tip to tip. These probably resembled the great colossi, with the body of a bull and the wings of an eagle, which guarded the old Assyrian palaces. Between the cherubim was placed the ark of Jehovah, the symbol of the abiding presence of the God who had ever led and cared for his people.

V. **Dedication of the Temple.** The completion of the temple was celebrated by the king and the assembled representatives of the nation, first by the formal transfer of the ark to the place prepared for it within the oracle, and second, by elaborate sacrifices. With the aid of the Greek text, it is possible to restore the song of dedication which was sung by Solomon on this occasion. Later prophets have also added an address and a noble dedicatory prayer, which are appropriate to the occasion, but which embody the nobler ethical and religious ideals of a later prophetic period.

In keeping with the earlier usage, Solomon himself, as the religious head of his kingdom, directed the offering of the sacrifices. The king also offered the various offerings in behalf of the nation at the three great annual festivals. In the earliest record, the primary duty of the priests was to care for the ark and doubtless to take charge of the divine oracle. They probably also assisted Solomon in offering the public sacrifices. Because of their close connection with the temple, it was natural that in time the entire charge of the ritual should be turned over to the descendants of Zadok.

Although its importance was not appreciated at the time, it is clear in the light of later history that in many ways the most important event in the period of the united monarchy was the building of the temple. Its priesthood and institutions soon became the most powerful support of the Davidic dynasty. As the prestige of the temple increased, it became the centre about which the thought and religious life of the Hebrew race revolved. The people ceased to look back to Mount Sinai, and came to regard Jerusalem as the special dwelling place of Jehovah. In the sacred precincts of the temple, later prophets, like Jeremiah, proclaimed their immortal messages. Here the ritual slowly developed to meet new con-

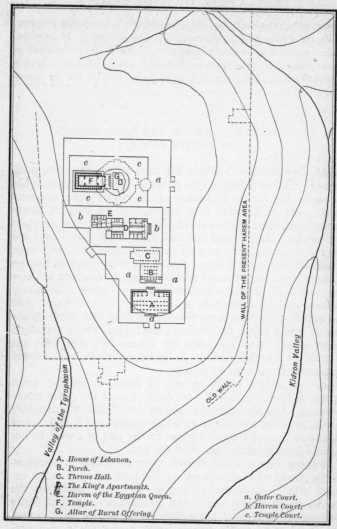

A. House of Lebanon.
B. Porch.
C. Throne Hall.
D. The King's Apartments.
E. Harem of the Egyptian Queen.
F. Temple.
G. Altar of Burnt Offering.

a. Outer Court.
b. Harem Court.
c. Temple Court.

PLAN OF SOLOMON'S PALACE

(ACCORDING TO STADE)

ditions and to incorporate the principles set forth by succeeding prophets. Under the direction of prophets, priests and reformers, the inherited heathen elements in Israel's religion were gradually eliminated, until at last, by Josiah and his supporters, the temple was declared to be the only legitimate temple, and Solomon's royal chapel became the one recognized sanctuary of the Hebrew race.

§ LVIII. THE SPLENDOR AND WEAKNESS OF SOLOMON'S REIGN

And Solomon was building his palace thirteen years, until he had completely finished his palace. There also he built the House of the Forest of Lebanon; its length was a hundred cubits, and its breadth fifty cubits, and its heighth thirty cubits, upon three rows of cedar pillars, with cedar beams upon the pillars. And it was covered with cedar above over the forty-five beams, that were upon the pillars; and there were fifteen pillars in each row. And there were window-frames in three rows, and window was over against window in three tiers. And all the doors and windows were made with square frames; and door was over against door in three tiers. And the hall of pillars he made fifty cubits long and thirty cubits broad; and a porch before them and pillars and a threshold before them. And he made the throne-hall where he was to judge, even the Hall of Judgment; and it was covered with cedar from floor to ceiling.

1. House of Lebanon and Hall of Judgment

And his palace, where he was to dwell, in another court farther in from the hall of Judgment, was of the same workmanship. He also made a palace for Pharaoh's daughter (whom Solomon had taken as wife), similar to his hall. And Pharaoh's daughter came up out of the city of David to her palace which Solomon had built for her.

2. Solomon's private palace

All these were of costly stones, hewn according to measurements, sawed with saws, both on the interior and on the exterior, even from the foundation to the coping, and from the exterior to the great court. And the foundation was of costly great stones—stones of ten cubits and stones of eight cubits. And above were costly stones, hewn according to measurements, and cedar wood. And the great encircling court had

3. Materials used in the palace

three courses of hewn stone and a course of cedar beams; even so it was round about the inner court of the temple of Jehovah and the court of the porch of the palace.

4. Hiram's compensation

King Solomon gave Hiram twenty cities in the land of Galilee. But when Hiram came from Tyre to see the cities which Solomon had given him, he was displeased with them. And he said, What sort of cities are these which you have given me, my brother? So they are called the land of Cabul [Good for nothing] even to the present day. But Hiram sent to the king one hundred and twenty talents of gold.

5. Solomon's additional buildings and forced levies

And this is the way it was with the levy which King Solomon raised to build the temple of Jehovah, his own palace, Millo, the wall of Jerusalem, Hazor, Meggido, Gezer, lower Bethhoron, Baalath, and Tamar in the wilderness in the land of Judah, and all the store-cities that Solomon had, and the cities for his chariots, and the cities for his horsemen, and that which Solomon was pleased to build for his pleasure in Jerusalem, in Lebanon, and in all the land over which he ruled. All the people who were left of the Amorites, the Hittites, the Perizzites, the Hivites, and the Jebusites, who were not of the Israelites, their children who were left after them in the land, whom the Israelites were not able utterly to destroy, of them did Solomon raise a forced levy of bondmen, even to this day. But of the Israelites Solomon made no bondmen, for they were the warriors and his servants, his generals, his captains, his officers over his chariots, and his horsemen.

6. Officers

These were the chief officers who were over Solomon's work, five hundred and fifty, who directed the people who did the work.

7. His Red Sea fleet

And King Solomon made a fleet of ships in Ezion-geber, which is near Elath on the shore of the Red Sea in the land of Edom. And Hiram sent with the fleet his subjects—seamen, who had knowledge of the sea, together with the servants of Solomon. And they went to Ophir, and took from there gold, four hundred and twenty talents, and brought it to King Solomon.

8. Products brought by Hiram's fleet

And Hiram's fleet of ships, that bore gold from Ophir, also brought a great amount of red sandal wood and precious stones. And the king made of the sandal wood from Ophir pilasters for the temple of Jehovah, and for the royal palace, and lyres

and harps for the singers. There came no other such sandal
wood nor has the like been seen to the present day.

Now the weight of gold that came to Solomon in one year
was six hundred and sixty-six talents of gold, besides what came
from the traffic of the merchants and from all the kings of the
Arabians and from the governors of the country. 9. Solomon's income in gold

And King Solomon made two hundred bucklers of beaten
gold—six hundred shekels (about eleven and one-half pounds)
of gold went on one buckler—and three hundred shields of
beaten gold—three minahs (about three and one-half pounds)
of gold went on one shield—and the king put them in the House
of the Forest of Lebanon. 10. His bucklers

The king also made a great throne of ivory, and overlaid
it with the finest gold. The throne had six steps and behind
the throne were heads of calves, and on both sides of the seat
were arms, and beside the arms stood two lions, on the six
steps stood twelve lions on each side. The like was not
made in any kingdom. 11. His throne

And all King Solomon's drinking vessels were of gold: none
were of silver; it was accounted of no value in the days of
Solomon. For the king had at sea a fleet of Tarshish ships
with the fleet of Hiram. Once every three years the fleet of
Tarshish ships came bringing gold, silver, ivory, apes and peacocks. So King Solomon exceeded all the kings of the earth
in riches and in wisdom. And all the earth sought the presence of Solomon, to hear his wisdom, with which God had endowed his mind. And they brought each a present: vessels
of silver and gold, clothing, weapons, spices, horses, and mules,
year by year. 12. His royal income

And Solomon gathered together chariots and horsemen;
and he had one thousand, four hundred chariots and twelve
thousand horsemen that he stationed in the chariot cities and
with the king at Jerusalem. Solomon's import of horses was
from Muçri and Kuë; the king's traders received them from
Kuë at a price, so that a chariot could be imported from Muçri
for six hundred shekels of silver and a horse for a hundred and
fifty. Even so through their agency these were exported to
all the kings of the Hittites and the Arameans. 13. His chariots and trade in horses

Now King Solomon was a lover of women; and he took many
foreign wives—Moabites, Canaanites, Edomites, Sidonians, 14. His foreign wives

Hittites, and Ammonites. And he had seven hundred wives, princesses, and three hundred concubines.

15. His apostasy

Now when Solomon was old, his heart was not perfect with Jehovah his God, as was the heart of David his father. And Solomon built a high place for Chemosh the god of Moab, in the mount that is before Jerusalem, and for Milcom the god of the Ammonites, and also for Ashtarte the goddess of the Sidonians. And so he did for all his foreign wives, burning incense and sacrificing to their gods.

16. Hadad, the Edomite

Then Jehovah raised up against Solomon an adversary, the Edomite Hadad, of the race of Edomite kings; for when David smote the Edomites, he smote every male in Edom. But Hadad being a child, one of his father's servants brought him to Egypt. And he found great favor in the eyes of Pharaoh, so that he gave him to his chief wife, and she brought him up in Pharaoh's palace among the sons of Pharaoh. But when Hadad heard in Egypt that David slept with his fathers, he said to Pharaoh, Let me depart that I may go to my own country. Then Pharaoh said to him, What do you lack with me that you are now seeking to go to your own country? And he said to him, Nevertheless you must let me go. . . . This is the evil that Hadad did; and he abhorred Israel and ruled in Edom.

17. Adad, the Midianite

Also when Joab the commander of the army went up to bury the slain—for Joab and all Israel remained there six months—Adad fled and certain Edomites with him. And they set out from Midian and came to Paran and took men with them out of Paran and came to Egypt to Pharaoh king of Egypt, who gave him a house and land. He also gave him as wife the sister of Tahpenes. And the sister of Tahpenes bore to him Genubath his son, and Genubath lived in Pharaoh's house. *But when he heard that David slept with his fathers, he returned to his land and likewise became an adversary to Solomon.*

18. Rezon the Aramean

God also raised up as an adversary to him, Rezon the son of Eliada, who had fled from his master, Hadadezer king of Zobah. And he gathered men about him and became commander of a marauding band, and they went to Damascus, and dwelt there and reigned in Damascus. And he was an adversary to Israel as long as Solomon lived.

And Jeroboam the son of Nebat, an Ephraimite of Zeredah, an official of Solomon, whose mother's name was Zeruah, a widow, also lifted up his hand against the king. And this was the reason why he lifted up his hand against the king: Solomon built Millo and closed up the exposed place in the city of David his father. And Jeroboam was a man of great ability. And when Solomon saw that the young man was industrious, he placed him over all the forced levy of the house of Joseph. *19. Jeroboam's early history*

Now it came to pass at that time, when Jeroboam went away from Jerusalem, that the prophet Ahijah of Shiloh found him in the way and turned him aside from the way. Now Ahijah had clad himself with a new garment; and they two were alone in the field. Then Ahijah took hold of the new garment that was on him, and rent it in twelve pieces. And he said to Jeroboam, Take for yourself ten pieces; for thus saith Jehovah, the God of Israel, 'Behold, I will rend the kingdom out of the hand of Solomon and will give ten tribes to thee, but he shall have one tribe. *20. Ahijah's prediction*

Solomon sought therefore to kill Jeroboam. Then Jeroboam arose and fled to Egypt, to Shishak [Sheshonk I] king of Egypt, and was in Egypt until the death of Solomon. *21. Jeroboam's flight*

And the length of Solomon's reign over all Israel was forty years. Then he slept with his fathers and was buried in the city of David his father; and Rehoboam his son became king in his stead. *22. Solomon's reign*

I. **Solomon's Palace.** In size and magnificence and in the time taken in their construction, the other buildings of Solomon's palace surpassed even the temple itself. They were placed further down the hill of Ophel, probably on the northern outskirts of the original city of the Jebusites. The largest and southernmost structure was the Forest of Lebanon. It appears to have been so called because it contained forty-five large pillars, made out of the cedars of Lebanon and arranged in three tiers of fifteen pillars each. To the Hebrew peasants, still under the spell of the barren wilderness, this building, about one hundred and sixty feet long and eighty feet wide, must have seemed one of the wonders of the world. It was enclosed, but provided with windows and doors on each side. Here Solomon's famous golden bucklers and shields were stored. From this fact it may be inferred that the building was used as an arsenal, and possibly as the quarters for the royal body-guard.

A little to the north was the Hall of Pillars, about eighty feet long and fifty feet wide. The Hall of Judgment, of which the dimensions are not given, was possibly identical with the Hall of Pillars. As its name suggests, it was probably the place where the king, seated on his throne of gold and ivory ([11]), held court to decide the various questions which were referred to him. Further to the northwest, and under the shadow of the temple, was the private residence of the king and of his Egyptian queen. The palace and the temple were surrounded by a great court, shut in by a high wall of hewn stone surmounted by a course of cedar beams.

II. **His Additional Building Activity.** Solomon's policy and his zeal for building led him to select certain cities outside Jerusalem which he strengthened and made royal arsenals. Hazor in the far north; Megiddo east of Mount Carmel, which guarded the highway along the coast plains and across the plain of Esdraelon; the old Canaanite town of Gezer, which stood sentinel before the passes which led up from the Philistine plain to central Canaan; lower Bethhoron, Baalath and Tamar, which probably guarded the southern approaches to the kingdom, were thus fortified. Solomon's object in building these store cities was to provide garrisons and military equipment at important strategic points. It is probable that they served, not merely to keep out foreign invaders, but also to hold his own subjects in submission.

III. **Solomon's Commercial Enterprises.** In developing the material resources of his empire, Solomon found an able adviser and ally in Hiram, king of Tyre. Already Phœnician sailors had skirted the shores of the Mediterranean, and even defied the waves of the Indian Ocean. From the port of Ezion-geber at the eastern end of the Red Sea, Solomon sent forth a fleet of Phœnician ships manned by Hiram's subjects. The larger craft appear to have been called Tarshish ships, since they were of the type employed by the Phœnicians in making the long journey to distant Tarshish in southern Spain. The combined fleets of Solomon and Hiram came back laden with gold, sandal wood, precious stones, ivory, apes and peacocks. These products point either to eastern Africa or to India as the so-called "land of Ophir" from which they were imported. The fact that some of these articles of commerce bear Indian names favors the conclusion that Ophir was either the Abhira at the mouth of the Indus, or else a seaport of eastern Arabia through which the products of India reached the western world. All these strange and beautiful products of distant lands and civilizations were used to beautify Solomon's palace and court. It is not surprising that later generations regarded the Grand Monarch as a wonder-worker who reared his palaces with the aid of the jinns.

Solomon also added to his royal revenue by importing horses from certain nations in northern Syria and by reselling them to his neighbors on the north and east, and possibly also to the Egyptians. From this time on horsemen and chariots constituted an important part of every Hebrew army. With horsemen at his command, Solomon was also able to control his subjects much more easily and effectively.

IV. The Mistakes of Solomon. Solomon certainly succeeded in introducing his people to the brilliant material civilization then regnant in southwestern Asia. Under task-masters and foreign artisans he taught them how to rear palaces, temples and fortifications. Undoubtedly the common people gloried in the splendors of Solomon's capital and court; but it is clear that they resented the forcing process to which they were subjected. It was impossible in one generation to transform a nation of peasants into a cultured, commercial race. There is no evidence that Solomon sought to improve the material conditions of his individual subjects. Instead, he so completely absorbed their wealth and energies in his own building enterprises that little time was left for the development of their personal and private interests. Jerusalem completely overshadowed the other cities of his realm; and the contrast between his palace and the humble houses of mud and stone in which his subjects continued to live inevitably bred popular discontent.

V. His Many Marriages. Solomon's unworthy ambition to rival in splendor the neighboring kings also led him to make many foreign alliances. In accordance with the custom of his day, these alliances were sealed by marriage between the reigning families. Consequently, he added to his harem princesses from Moab, Ammon, Edom and Sidon. He also intermarried with the older Hittite and Canaanite peoples. These alliances compelled him to recognize the gods of the allied peoples. For diplomatic reasons he reared altars, probably within Jerusalem, and possibly within the temple precincts, to the gods of these allied peoples, and joined with his foreign wives in paying homage to their gods. In the pursuit of his false ambition, Solomon trampled upon the democratic ideals and upon those time-honored and sacred traditions of his race which required absolute loyalty to Jehovah, the God of his nation.

The statement that he had seven hundred wives is perhaps a product of later tradition. In the Song of Songs (6⁷) it is implied that Solomon had but sixty wives and eighty concubines. In any case it is clear, as the biblical writer clearly states, that another fatal source of weakness in Solomon's character was the degrading sensuality which he inherited from his parents and which flourished unchecked in the unnatural atmosphere of the harem. Gifted with great possibilities and the heir of a mighty empire, Solomon, in the light of later events, proved a glittering failure both as a man and as a ruler.

VI. **Consequences of Solomon's Policy.** The biblical writers only suggest the darker side of Solomon's reign. While his rule was peaceful, it was the calm that breeds the coming storm. The peace which he enjoyed was purchased by the loss of a part of his empire. The brief narrative in Kings indicates that in four different parts of his kingdom the standard of rebellion was raised, even before his death. In the southeast, a certain Edomite by the name of Hadad, who had found refuge during the days of David at the court of Egypt, succeeded in throwing off the Hebrew yoke and ruled independently over at least a part of Edom. Another rebel in the south, by the name of Adad, influenced his fellow Midianites to defy Solomon's authority. In the northeast, Rezon, an Aramean, laid the foundations of the important kingdom which later grew up about Damascus as its capital.

The most significant rebellion during the days of Solomon was led by Jeroboam, an Ephraimite. This leader from the ranks had been placed by Solomon in charge of those Israelites from the tribes of Ephraim and Manasseh who had been drafted to build the royal palace at Jerusalem. The uprising was unsuccessful; but the incident is profoundly significant, for it indicates that, even in Jerusalem itself, the growing popular discontent found open expression. It is also noteworthy that Jeroboam was encouraged in his rebellion against the authority and policy of Solomon by Ahijah, the prophet of Shiloh. Evidently the more enlightened prophets, at least of the north, saw in that policy a deadly menace to the liberties of the Hebrews and to the true religion of Jehovah. Confronted by an oriental despotism, which threatened to make the freeborn citizens but the slaves of the king, and which meant to their minds open disloyalty to the God who demanded the entire allegiance of his people, the prophets were ready to preserve Israel's liberties and faith, even at the cost of disunion.

In the light of these facts, it is evident that the disintegration of the Hebrew empire began even before the death of Solomon. By his magnificent but criminally selfish policy, he undid what David and the other patriots of early Israel had accomplished only by great sacrifice and toil. He who was counted by later tradition the wisest proved to be in many respects the most foolish king who ever sat on Israel's throne.

§ LIX. LAW AND SOCIETY IN EARLY ISRAEL

I. If a man buy a Hebrew slave, the slave shall serve six years; but in the seventh he shall go free without having to pay any ransom.

II. If he come in single, he shall go free unmarried.

III. If he be married, then his wife shall go out with him.

IV. If his master give him a wife and she bear him sons or daughters, the wife and her children shall be her master's, but the man shall go out by himself.

V. If, however, the slave shall definitely say, I love my master, my wife, and my children; I will not go free, then his master shall bring him before God, and shall lead him to the door, or the door-post, and his master shall bore through his ear with an awl; and the man shall be his slave as long as he liveth.

VI. If a man sell his daughter to be a slave, she shall not go free as do the male slaves.

VII. If she do not please her master, who hath espoused her to himself, then he may let her be redeemed; only he shall have no power to sell her to a foreign people, seeing he hath dealt deceitfully with her.

VIII. If he espouse her to his son, he shall deal with her as with a daughter.

IX. If he marry another wife, her food, her raiment, and her duty of marriage shall he not diminish.

X. If he do not these three things to her, then she may go out without having to pay any money.

I. If a man strike another so that he die, the manslayer shall be put to death.

II. If a man lie not in wait, but God deliver him into his hand, then I will appoint thee a place to which he may flee.

III. If a man attack another maliciously to slay him by treachery, thou shalt take him from mine altar, that he may be put to death.

IV. He who striketh his father or his mother shall be put to death.

1. The rights of slaves (a) males

(b) Females

2. Assaults (a) capital offences

V. He who stealeth a man, and selleth him, or if he still be found in his hand, shall surely be put to death.

(b) Minor offences

VI. If men contend and one strike the other with a stone or a club, and he die not, but is confined to his bed, then if he rise again, and can walk out supported on his staff, the one who struck him shall be acquitted; only he must pay for the loss of the other man's time until he is thoroughly healed.

VII. If a man strike his male or female slave with a stick so that he die at once, the master must be punished.

VIII. If, however, the slave survive a day or two, the master shall not be punished, for it is his own loss.

IX. If a man smite the eye of his male or female slave, so that it is destroyed, he shall let him go free for his eye's sake.

X. If he knock out a tooth of his male or female slave, he shall let him go free for his tooth's sake.

3. Domestic animals (a) injuries by them

I. If an ox fatally gore a man or a woman, the ox shall be stoned, and its flesh shall not be eaten, but the owner of the ox shall be acquitted.

II. But if the ox was already in the habit of goring, and it hath been reported to its owner, and he hath not kept it in, with the result that it hath killed a man or a woman, the ox shall be stoned, and its owner shall also be put to death.

III. If a ransom is fixed for him, he shall give for the redemption of his life whatever amount is determined.

IV. Whether the ox hath gored a boy or a girl, this law shall be executed.

V. If an ox gore a male or female slave, thirty shekels of silver shall be given to their master, and the ox shall be stoned.

(b) Injuries to them

VI. If a man open a cistern or dig a cistern but doth not cover it, and an ox or an ass fall into it, the owner of the cistern shall make it good; he shall give money to its owner and the carcass shall be his.

VII. If one man's ox hurt another's, so that it dieth, then they shall sell the live ox, and divide the money received from it; they shall also divide the carcass between them.

VIII. If it be known that the ox was already in the habit of goring and its owner hath not kept it in, he must pay ox for ox, and the carcass shall belong to him.

IX. If a man steal an ox, or a sheep, and kill it, or sell it, he shall restore five oxen for one ox, and four sheep for a sheep. If he have nothing, then he shall be sold to pay for what he hath stolen.

X. If the theft be found in his hand alive, whether it be ox, or ass, or sheep, he must pay twice its value.

I. If a man burn over a field or vineyard and let the fire spread so that it devoureth a neighbor's field, out of the best of his own field, and the best of his own vineyard shall he make restitution. **4. Responsibility for property (a) in general**

II. If fire break out, and catch in thorns, so that the shocks of grain, or the standing grain, or the field are consumed, he that kindled the fire must make restitution.

III. If a man deliver to his neighbor money or personal property to keep, and if it be stolen out of the man's house, if the thief be found, the man shall make double restitution.

IV. If the thief be not found, then the master of the house shall come before God to prove whether or not he hath taken his neighbor's goods.

V. In every case of breach of trust, whether it concern an ox, or ass, or sheep, or clothing, or any kind of lost thing of which one saith, This is it, the case of both parties shall come before God; he whom God shall condemn shall make double restitution to his neighbor.

VI. If a man deliver to his neighbor an ass, or an ox, or a sheep, or any beast, to keep; and it die or be hurt or be driven away without any one's having seen it, an oath sworn by Jehovah shall be between both of them to decide whether or not the one hath taken his neighbor's property; the owner shall accept it, and the other need not make restitution. **(b) In cattle**

VII. If it be stolen from him, he shall make restitution to its owner.

VIII. If the animal be torn in pieces, let him bring it as evidence; he need not make good that which was torn.

IX. If a man borrow an animal from his neighbor and

it be hurt or die, while its owner is not with it, the man must make restitution.

X. If its owner be with it, the man need not make it good: being a hired animal, it came for its hire.

5. So-
cial im-
purity
(a)
adul-
tery

I. If, after a man hath married a wife and entered into marital relations with her, he turn against her, and frame against her shameful charges, . . . then the father of the young woman and her mother shall take and bring evidences of the young woman's virginity to the elders of the city at the gate; . . . And the elders of that city shall take the man and punish him; and they shall fine him a hundred shekels of silver, and give them to the young woman's father because the man hath given an evil name to a virgin of Israel; and she shall be his wife; he may not divorce her as long as he liveth.

II. But if it prove to be true that the evidences that the young woman was a virgin were not found, then they shall bring out the young woman to the door of her father's house, and the men of her city shall stone her to death because she hath committed a shameful act in Israel, in that she hath been a harlot in her father's house.

III. If a man be found lying with a married woman, they shall both of them die, the man who lay with the woman and the woman.

IV. If a man find in the city a young woman who is a virgin betrothed to a husband, and lie with her, then ye shall bring them both out to the gate of that city and stone them to death, the damsel because she did not cry out, although she was in the city, and the man because he hath seduced his neighbor's wife.

V. If the man find a young woman, who is betrothed in the field, and force her and lie with her, then simply the man who lay with her shall die; but thou shalt do nothing to the young woman; she hath committed no sin worthy of death.

(b)
Forni-
cation
and
apos-
tasy

VI. If a man entice a young girl who is not betrothed, and lie with her, he must make her his wife by paying a dowry for her.

VII. If her father utterly refuse to give her to him, he shall pay money equivalent to the dowry of young girls.

VIII. A sorceress shall not be allowed to live.

IX. Whoever lieth with a beast shall surely be put to death.

X. He who sacrificeth to other gods, except to Jehovah, shall be placed under the ban.

I. Form and Date of the Primitive Decalogues in Exodus 21^1–23^{19}.

In Exodus 21^1–23^{1a} is found a group of decalogues which throws remarkably clear light upon social and economic conditions in early Israel. The setting and literary form of these decalogues indicate that they were incorporated in the historical record by the Northern Israelite prophetic historian who wrote about 750 B.C. Their carefully developed decalogue and pentad form suggests, however, that they had been handed down orally for generations before they were committed to writing and given their present setting. Most of the customs assumed in these laws, and many of the principles which underlie them, are found in the old Babylonian code of Hammurabi (about 1900 B.C.). Many of the laws in the primitive decalogues of Exodus reflect the early nomadic and agricultural life of the Hebrews. Some, as for example, those which refer to fields and houses, indicate that, when the laws were formulated, the Israelites were firmly established in Canaan. There are no references, however, to the temple of Solomon, or to the institutions which characterize the united kingdom. It is highly probable that most, if not all, of these early Hebrew laws were in existence in their present or slightly different form in the days of David and Solomon. They may, therefore, be studied as a faithful contemporary record of the social, moral and religious standards and customs of the Hebrews in the days of the united kingdom.

II. The Rights and Position of Slaves in Early Israel.

The old Semitic institution of slavery existed in Israel from the earliest times. The man who was unable to pay his debts, or support himself or his family, was forced either to become a slave to his creditor, or else to give his own son or daughter to meet the obligation. The aim of the early Hebrew lawgiver was primarily to protect the rights of slaves, to guard against possible abuses and to provide for the ultimate liberation of the native-born Hebrews.

There is no evidence that other Semitic peoples made any similar provision for the manumission of slaves. The Hebrew law, therefore, marks a great advance over existing oriental usage. It recognizes the fact that slavery was usually incurred through debt, and that, when the debt was discharged, the slave was entitled to his freedom. The narrative in Jeremiah 34 indicates that, in the later days at least, this law was enforced only under the pressure of a great national danger, and that when the danger was passed the masters shamelessly compelled their slaves to resume the old relation. Even though the law of release at the end of six years was not accepted by the people as a whole, it is significant that it finds a place in these early decalogues.

The fact that definite provision is made for cases in which the slaves voluntarily assumed permanent slavery suggests that the institution was very different from what it became in the later days of Rome or in more recent times. For those who were poverty-stricken, or lacking in physical or mental vigor, slavery offered a welcome refuge. It gave them the assurance of a permanent home, food and protection. Their treatment in most cases appears to have been considerate. It is easy, therefore, to understand why many Hebrew slaves preferred to remain in the homes of their masters, especially when freedom meant parting with their wives and children. The rite of piercing the ear was probably performed at the door post, originally in the presence of the household god, or else at the local sanctuary.

The laws regarding a female slave were necessarily different, for she appears in almost every case to have intermarried into the family of her master. After she had become a member of the household, she could be divorced at the pleasure of the master, but not sold, as other slaves, to foreigners. Her rights as wife or daughter were also carefully guarded by the Hebrew law.

III. **Punishment of Crimes.** The laws regarding assaults further reveal the noble purpose of the early Hebrew lawgivers to correct the abuses inherent in existing customs and to protect the innocent as well as to punish the guilty. In contrast to the earlier Semitic laws, as for example, those of Hammurabi, they reveal a remarkably high regard for the sanctity of human life. The ancient law of blood revenge was still in force. To save the innocent manslayer Hebrew law and custom provided that, if he succeeded in escaping and found refuge at an altar, he should be under Jehovah's protection. There the hand of the avenger could not touch him; but, if the man were guilty of murder, the community was under obligation to drag him from the altar and put him to death.

The strong emphasis which the Hebrews placed upon the duty of children to parents is illustrated by the fact that they inflicted the death penalty upon the son who struck either his father or his mother. The law of Hammurabi is rigorous but not quite so severe; "If a man has struck his father, his hand shall be cut off" (§ 195). In punishing by death the heinous crime of kidnapping, the Hebrew lawgivers simply reiterated the ancient law of Hammurabi, "If a man has stolen a child, he shall be put to death" (§ 14).

Hammurabi's enactment in the case of personal injury incurred in a quarrel anticipates, in principle at least, the corresponding Hebrew law. It directs that, "If a man has struck another in a quarrel and cause him a permanent injury, that man shall swear, 'I struck him without malice,' and shall pay the physician" (§ 206). In providing that the master should be punished for killing his slave, the Hebrew law is far in advance of the standards maintained by other Semitic peoples, and even more modern codes. The nature of the penalty, however, is left to the decision of the judges. In case the blow was not immediately fatal, the early Hebrew lawgivers accepted the prevailing standards and freed the master, in view of the loss of his slave, from all personal responsibility. Their eagerness to correct possible wrongs is again shown by the regulation that for minor injuries, such as the loss of an eye or a tooth at the hand of the master, the slave should in every case have his freedom.

IV. **Laws Regarding Domestic Animals.** The regulations regarding injuries to and by animals also illustrate the aim of the Hebrew lawgivers to guard against the loss of human life, and to place the responsibility for the injury where it belonged. A corresponding law of Hammurabi enacts, "If a man's ox be a gorer and has revealed its evil propensity as a gorer, and the man has not blunted its horns or shut up the ox, and then that ox has gored a free man and caused his death, the owner shall pay half a mina of silver. If it has been a slave that has been killed, he shall pay one-third of a mina of silver" (§§ 251, 252). The comparatively small fine thus imposed for criminal carelessness is in striking contrast to the corresponding Hebrew law which makes the punishment death. Possibly under the influence of the older custom, the Hebrew code also allows for the substitution of a ransom in case the judges shall so decide.

The moderation of the Hebrew laws in punishing theft is in favorable contrast to the rigorous regulations of even such a benign ruler as Hammurabi, who decreed that, "If a patrician has stolen ox, sheep, ass, pig or ship, whether from a temple or a house, he shall pay thirty-fold. If he be a plebeian he shall return tenfold. If the thief cannot pay, he shall be put to death" (§ 8). While the Hebrew law is very similar in form to the older enactment, the later lawgivers have in each case reduced the penalty. Apparently they also aimed to punish the thief in proportion to the value of the stolen animal. In case the thief had nothing, slavery was substituted for the death penalty. If the animal stolen was alive and could be returned, the penalty was still further reduced.

V. **Responsibility for Property.** The Hebrew laws were clearly intended to place the responsibility for injury or loss of property where it rightly belonged. In case of doubt as to the guilt of the parties involved, the matter was referred to the priest, who probably decided it on the basis of a personal investigation, or else by the use of the sacred lot. If property held in trust was lost through death or injury or theft, and no witnesses could be produced, the owner was obliged to accept the solemn oath of the trustee. Otherwise the trustee was responsible for the loss.

The code of Hammurabi is much more explicit. It enacts: "If a man has hired an ox or an ass, and a lion has killed it in an open field, the loss falls on its owner. If a man has hired an ox and has caused its death by carelessness or blows, he shall restore ox for ox to the owner. If a man has hired an ox and God has struck it and it has died, the man who hired the ox shall make affidavit and go free" (§§ 244, 245, 249).

VI. **Personal Responsibility to Society.** The Hebrew lawgivers regarded social immorality and all forms of apostasy as crimes against society and therefore against the state. The zeal with which they guarded the sacred rights of the community is shown by the fact that the penalty imposed for these crimes was in almost every case death. This punishment was inflicted by the injured community itself. The code of Hammurabi was equally strenuous: adultery was punished by strangling or burning. In contrast with the laxness of public opinion and of modern laws in dealing with this most hideous of crimes, the strenuousness of the ancient lawgivers is profoundly significant. They endeavored at any cost to preserve the purity of the family and community, and to save the innocent and tempted from lives of unspeakable pain and ignominy.

In general these Hebrew laws reflect a very simple social and economic organization. They anticipate only the more common and typical cases, and establish precedents for the guidance of the judges in deciding the more difficult and complicated questions which might be referred to them. The influences of existing Semitic customs and institutions are always apparent; but the dominant motives are those of justice, mercy, and humanity. In their present form many of these laws have long since become obsolete; but the divine principles which they illustrate, are eternal, and therefore equally applicable to the changing conditions of every age.

§ LX. MORAL AND RELIGIOUS STANDARDS IN EARLY ISRAEL

I. Thou shalt not wrong nor oppress a resident alien, for ye were resident aliens in the land of Egypt.

II. Ye shall not afflict any widow or fatherless child.

III. If thou lend money to any one of my people with thee who is poor, thou shalt not be to him as a creditor.

IV. Neither shall ye demand interest of him.

V. If thou at all take thy neighbor's garment for a pledge, thou shalt restore it to him before the sun goeth down; for that is his only covering, it is his garment for his skin.

VI. If thou meet thine enemy's ox or ass going astray, thou shalt surely bring it back to him again.

VIII. And if he do not live near thee, then thou shalt bring it home to thine house and it shall be with thee until he seek after it; then thou shalt restore it to him again.

VIII. Thus shalt thou do with his ass, and with his garment, and with every lost thing which belongeth to him, which he hath lost and thou hast found; thou mayest not withhold thy help.

IX. If thou see the ass of him who hateth thee lying prostrate under its burden, thou shalt in no case leave it in its plight, rather thou shalt, together with him, help it out.

X. If a bird's nest chance to be before thee in the way, in any tree or on the ground, with young ones or eggs, and with the mother sitting upon the young or upon the eggs, thou shalt not take the mother with the young; thou shalt surely let the mother go (but the young thou mayest take for thyself), that it may be well with thee, and that thou mayest live long.

I. Thou shalt not spread abroad a false report.

II. Do not enter into a conspiracy with a wicked man to be an unrighteous witness.

III. Thou shalt not follow the majority in doing what is wrong.

IV. Thou shalt not bear testimony in a case so as to pervert justice.

[marginal notes:]
1. The duty of kindness (a) toward men

(b) Toward animals

2. The duty of justice (a) as a witness

217

V. Thou shalt not show partiality to a poor man in his case.

(b) As a judge

VI. Thou shalt not prevent justice being done to thy poor in his cause.

VII. Keep aloof from every false matter.

VIII. Do not condemn the innocent nor him who hath a just cause.

IX. Do not vindicate the wicked.

X. Thou shalt take no bribe, for a bribe blindeth the eyes of those who see and perverteth the cause of the righteous.

3. Duties to God: *(a)* worship

I. Thou shalt not make other gods with me.

II. Gods of silver and gods of gold thou shalt not make for thyself.

III. An altar of earth thou shalt make to me, and shalt sacrifice on it thy burnt-offerings and thy peace-offerings, thy sheep and thine oxen; in every place where I record my name I will come to thee and will bless thee.

IV. But if thou make me an altar of stone, thou shalt not build it of hewn stones; for if thou swing an iron tool over it, thou hast polluted it.

V. Thou shalt not ascend by steps to mine altar, that thy nakedness may not be uncovered before it.

(b) Loyalty

VI. Thou shalt not revile God, nor shalt thou curse the ruler of thy people.

VII. Thou shalt not delay to offer of thy harvest and of the out-flow of thy presses.

VIII. The first-born of thy sons shalt thou give to me.

IX. Thou shalt give to me the first-born of thine oxen and thy sheep; seven days shall it be with its dam; on the eighth day thou shalt give it me.

X. Holy men shall ye be to me; therefore ye shall not eat any flesh that is torn by beasts in the field; ye shall cast it to the dogs.

4. Ceremonial duties: *(a)* observing the sacred seasons

I. Six years thou shalt sow thy land, and shalt gather in its increase. The seventh year thou shalt let the land rest and lie fallow, that the poor of thy people may eat; and what they leave the wild beasts shall eat. In like manner thou shalt do with thy vineyard and thine oliveyard.

II. Six days thou shalt do thy work, but on the seventh thou shalt rest, that thine ox and thine ass may have rest, and that the son of thy female slave and the resident alien may be refreshed.

III. The feast of unleavened bread shalt thou keep: seven days thou shalt eat unleavened bread, as I commanded thee.

IV. Thou shalt observe the feast of harvest, [the feast of] the firstfruits of thy labors, which thou hast sown in the field.

V. Thou shalt observe the feast of ingathering at the end of the year.

VI. Three times in the year all thy males shall appear before Jehovah.

VII. Thou shalt not offer the blood of my sacrifice with leavened bread.

(b) Method of observing them

VIII. The fat of my feasts shall not remain all night until the morning.

IX. The first of the firstfruits of thy ground thou shalt bring into the house of Jehovah thy God.

X. Thou shalt not boil a kid in its mother's milk.

I. Obligations to Dependent Classes. These remarkable regulations stand almost alone among the many laws which have come from the early Semitic past, and in striking contrast to the cruelty and brutality of their age. They reveal the spirit of God working in the life of the Hebrew nation. They are the fore-gleams of that unique ethical religion proclaimed by the great prophets of the later period.

In the epilogue to his remarkable code, Hammurabi first voices the motives which are here formulated in definite laws. He declares that his object in publishing his code was to succor the injured, to counsel the widow and orphan, to prevent the great from oppressing the weak, and to enable the oppressed, who had a suit to prosecute, to read his inscription and thus be aided in elucidating their case. This same lofty spirit may be recognized in many of Hammurabi's detailed enactments; but nowhere in earlier or contemporary literature can be found such a noble, humane and philanthropic spirit as breathes through many of these early Hebrew decalogues. As a rule no penalties are imposed, but the appeal is simply to the individual conscience or to the national sense of gratitude to Jehovah for his services to his people and especially for the great deliverance from Egypt.

MORAL AND RELIGIOUS STANDARDS

In the early days many sojourners or resident aliens were found in Israel. These were foreigners who had taken up their permanent abode in Canaan, and who had therefore severed their connection with their native tribe or people. Ancient Semitic custom accorded them no legal rights. The Hebrews, however, in the early days welcomed all additions to their number, and treated these resident aliens as wards of the community. That they were often wronged and oppressed is implied by the laws which aim to correct these evils. With the resident aliens were also classed the widows and fatherless children, who had no protector to plead their cause.

In the simple days of the united kingdom, loans were probably rarely solicited for commercial purposes, but simply to save a poor man or his family from starvation or slavery. The third command, therefore, appeals to the sympathy and mercy of the creditor, who, according to existing Semitic usage, could legally force the debtor or members of his family into slavery. To demand interest was equally cruel, especially in view of the exorbitant rates of interest which prevailed in the East. In Assyria it was often as high as 25 per cent. per annum, and in Egypt the legal rate was 30, or, in case the loan was in grain, 33 1/3 per cent.

In the East to-day, as in the past, a poor man's outer garment is also his bed. To retain it as a pledge over night was therefore an act of cruelty against which the Hebrew lawgivers sought to guard.

II. **Kindness toward Animals.** Most primitive people are brutal in their treatment of animals. The early Hebrew lawgivers, however, protested strongly against the prevailing tendency, and in so doing laid the foundation for the similar philanthropic movements of to-day.

The fuller version of the pentad regarding duties to animals is found in Deuteronomy 22[1-4]. Strangely enough, 'fellow Israelites' has been substituted for 'enemy,' which is found in the older version of Exodus 23[4-5]. This older and stronger form of the law has been restored in the text adopted above. In its original form the command requires that each man shall overcome his revengeful impulses and restore or relieve from its distress any animal which he shall chance to find, even though it belong to his sworn foe.

III. **Justice in the Law Courts.** Among the early Semitic peoples there was no distinct class of judges, but judicial duties were performed by the civil and religious heads of the community and state. Even during the days of the united kingdom, Israel's judicial system remained exceedingly simple. In the villages and smaller towns, cases of dispute were referred to the village elders, or else were laid before the priests at the local sanctuary. More important and difficult cases were carried before some royal official or the king himself. In many cases the contending parties probably decided between themselves the tribunal before which their case should be laid.

The court was usually held in the broad place beside the city gate, which was the common gathering place of the people and the public officials. Probably, as in Babylonia, each disputant pleaded his own case and summoned his own witnesses. One of the laws of Hammurabi enacts that, "If a man has not his witnesses at hand the judge shall set him a fixed time not exceeding six months, and if within six months he has not produced his witnesses, the man has lied. He shall bear the penalty of the suit" (§ 13). The decision, therefore, turned largely upon the testimony of the witnesses. With judges drawn directly from the community, public opinion must also have carried great weight. In view of these conditions the purport and object of the brief, practical commands in the decalogue regarding the duties of witnesses can be fully appreciated. To spread abroad a false report was to exert a malign, yet powerful influence. A later law, which was probably in vogue at this time, enacted that the death penalty should be pronounced only on the basis of the united testimony of two witnesses. By collusion, two false witnesses were thus capable of doing a great injustice. To guard against this evil the later law in Deuteronomy 19[16-21] provides that such false witnesses, when detected, should themselves suffer the penalty which they had sought to bring upon an innocent man.

The law: "Thou shalt not follow the majority in doing what is wrong," like most of the laws in these decalogues has a wide and universal application. The impartial justice of the ancient lawgivers is forcibly illustrated by the surprising command: "Thou shalt not show partiality to a poor man in his case." Their object is evidently to guard against injustice in cases where the sympathy of the witnesses would naturally be with the poorer members of the community. With marvellous brevity and simplicity these five laws define the duties and moral responsibilities of witnesses, and furnish a fitting basis for any and every judicial system.

The next five commands define with equal brevity and comprehensiveness the duties of judges. Inasmuch as the judges were drawn from the ruling classes, their sympathies were naturally with the rich. Hence the need of the command not to prevent justice being done to the poor. The judges are also urged not to be influenced by misleading public opinion to join in a conspiracy to thwart justice. Above all they are commanded to have nothing to do with that most treacherous and insinuating foe of justice—the bribe, "which blindeth the eyes of those who see and perverteth the cause of the righteous."

IV. **Israel's Obligations to Jehovah.** The foundation of Israel's religion, as laid down by Moses, was undivided loyalty to Jehovah. After the Hebrews entered Canaan, the temptation to worship local gods became so strong that each succeeding generation of lawgivers found it necessary to repeat the command to worship no other gods beside Jehovah, and to bow down before none of the molten gods which were found at the old Canaanite sanctuaries.

The old earthen altars, however, scattered throughout the land of Israel, were regarded as legitimate. Thither the people brought their offerings of sheep and oxen. Some of these were presented to Jehovah as "whole burnt-offerings," and were therefore entirely consumed by fire. Some were presented as "peace-offerings"; the victims were slain by the offerers themselves, and the flesh was eaten by them and by the members of their families. In the sacrificial meal which they thus shared with their divine king, Jehovah's part, the fat and the blood, was poured out and burnt upon the altar. The sense of Jehovah's presence, the renewal of the covenant with their God, the feasting and song made these sacrificial meals at the local shrines memorable and joyous occasions in the life of the early Hebrews.

The command not to hew or pollute the rock altar by a blow with an iron tool reflects unconsciously the old belief that the spirit of the deity resided in the sacred rock on which the sacrifice was offered.

It is significant that the Hebrew lawgivers combined in the same command the warning not to revile the Divine King or curse a human ruler. The commands that follow, define the offerings which Jehovah's subjects were to bring to him, even as they brought tribute to their human king. The first-born—which was believed to be the best—of every family and herd and flock belonged to Jehovah. The first-born was thus set aside not merely because he was believed to be the best, but also that Jehovah might never fail to receive his due. In the pentad which defines loyalty to Jehovah, the idea of a holy nation, especially consecrated to Jehovah and therefore under obligations to abstain from eating anything unclean or defiling, is formulated for the first time. It is an idea which was later developed by the priests into the elaborate ceremonial law, and by prophets, like Isaiah, into the noble doctrine of ethical righteousness.

Obligations of the Israelites to Jehovah also involved the observation of certain sacred days and feasts. From the first, these sacred seasons occupied a prominent place in Semitic religion. Practically all of these laws had already been included in the ceremonial decalogue which was the basis of the covenant at Sinai (§ XXIV), but in the later version the seventh year of rest is introduced for the first time. This sabbatical year represented an ideal which the Hebrews probably never realized in practice. It is noteworthy, however, that the sabbatical year is here brought into close connection with the institution of the sabbath, and that both are interpreted in their social and humane rather than their ceremonial aspects. The seventh year of rest was established that the poor of the land and even the wild beasts might enjoy abundant food, for then all classes in the community shared in common the natural products of the soil. The sabbath was intended to give the laboring ox and ass and slave, and even the resident alien, their needed rest.

V. Israel's Conception of Jehovah. In the light of these laws and the earliest historical records of the period, it is evident that the popular conception of Jehovah underwent a fundamental transformation during the days of the united kingdom. Instead of conceiving of him as a storm god who dwelt at Mount Sinai, and who, like a warrior, fought in behalf of his people and was pleased with the wholesale slaughter of innocent captives, as well as hostile foes, the Hebrews came to think of Jehovah as a majestic King, who dwelt in the midst of his people and ruled, in accordance with the principles of justice, both the Israelites and the people subject to them.

After the Hebrews had conquered Canaan, Jehovah naturally became the supreme baal or lord of the land. This change in popular belief is illustrated by the fact that the divine name, Baal, appears frequently during this period in the names of members of the Hebrew royal family. Thus one of Saul's sons is called Ishbaal, and the son of Jonathan is called Meribaal. One of David's sons is also called Baaliada. No attempt appears to have been made to represent Jehovah by an image. In the thought of his followers, the God whom they had enthroned in the royal temple at Jerusalem dwelt in thick darkness, invisible except to the eye of faith.

VI. The Victory of the Jehovah Religion over the Canaanite Cults. When the Hebrews conquered the Canaanites, they entered into possession of the native sanctuaries. At these high places the old rites and ceremonies and traditions and, in many cases doubtless, the original priestly families continued to exercise their potent sway. Many of the old institutions and especially the sacred festivals were also bound up with that agricultural civilization of Canaan which the Hebrews adopted when they became masters of the land.

. In the great conflict which raged through the centuries between the religion of Jehovah and the Canaanite cults, the latter possessed many advantages. In contrast with the attractive, highly developed ceremonial institutions of the Canaanites, the simple worship of the desert must have seemed crude and unattractive. The alluring, seductive cults of Canaan also appealed powerfully to elemental human passions; while the austere religion of Jehovah demanded self-restraint and the entire loyalty of the worshipper. The marvelous and significant fact of this early period of Hebrew history is that the religion of Jehovah survived in the face of all these odds.

It was inevitable, however, that the prolonged and close contact with the highly developed religions of Canaan should make a profound impression upon Israel's faith and forms of worship. Just as the Hebrews, in conquering the Canaanites, assimilated them, together with their arts and civilization, so also the religion of Jehovah to a great extent adopted the rites and institutions already firmly established in Palestine. Although this process was not without its grave dangers, it greatly enriched Israel's religion, especially in its ceremonial forms.

In the victorious conflict with the Canaanite cults, two powerful forces may be distinguished: the one was the influence of the prophets, those valiant champions of Jehovah who jealously guarded the faith imparted by Moses, and held the people loyal to the God of their fathers. The other was the strong tendency toward racial and political unity, which characterized the age. The trend was from the old tribal divisions toward a united monarchy, and from polytheism toward the worship of one national god, and then toward the recognition of but one supreme God in all the universe. "One kingdom, one king, one race, and one God," was the watchword of the patriots and prophets of Israel. Having once caught the vision of a united Hebrew kingdom, ruling over Israelite and foreigner alike, the later Hebrews, especially in the hours of their greatest distress, never ceased to dream of a greater Messianic kingdom and one Divine King, ruling not only over his people, but over all the races of mankind.

APPENDIX

I

A PRACTICAL BIBLICAL REFERENCE LIBRARY

Books for Constant Reference. The biblical sources for the days of the united kingdom are so complete and the extra-biblical contemporary records are so few that the need for books of reference is not as great as in other periods of Israel's history. The first volume of the *Student's Old Testament*, entitled, *The Beginnings of Hebrew History*, gives a detailed introduction to the books of Joshua and Judges, and the reasons which have led to the separation of the older from the later narratives. The second volume, entitled, *Israel's Historical and Biographical Narratives*, furnishes the corresponding data regarding the reigns of Saul, David and Solomon, and an introduction to the books of Samuel and Kings. Variant versions of the important events of this period are printed in parallel columns, and interpretative and textual notes are found at the foot of each page.

At many different points the valuable articles in Hastings' *Dictionary of the Bible* throw clear light upon the events and characters of this period of Israel's history. In addition, the student should have at hand a standard history of the Hebrew people, such as Smith's *Old Testament History*, or else a more compact and popular history, such as Wade, *Old Testament History*, or Kent, *A History of the Hebrew People: United Kingdom*. George Adam Smith's *Historical Geography of the Holy Land* is also especially useful for the study of this age, in which a clear knowledge of the geographical background is essential for the understanding of its stirring events.

Additional Books of Reference: Introductions. In addition to the books for constant reference, the teacher and student should be able to refer readily to certain of the most important books in English which throw light upon the background of the period. The Old

APPENDIX

Testament introductions by Professors McFadyen and Cornill are clear and useful for the general reader. Driver, *Introduction to the Literature of the Old Testament*, is more technical and detailed. The articles on *Joshua, Judges, Samuel* and *Kings* in the Bible dictionaries are concise and illuminating.

Contemporary History and Religion. Breasted, *History of the Ancient Egyptians*, and Goodspeed, *History of the Babylonians and Assyrians*, give clear pictures of events in the contemporary life of the two great nations of the ancient Semitic world. Maspero's *Struggle of the Nations* furnishes much valuable data regarding the broad historical background of Israel's history. Regarding the heritage of religious institutions which the Hebrews received from their Semitic ancestors, Smith's *Religion of the Semites* remains a great mine of information. Briefer and more popular are the little handbooks by Marti on the *Religion of the Old Testament*, and Budde, *Religion of Israel to the Exile*. The latest and in many ways the most satisfactory treatment of the subject is found in the article by Kautzsch on *The Religion of Israel* in the extra volume of Hastings' *Dictionary of the Bible*.

Hebrew History. In addition to the volumes on Hebrew History already mentioned, many students will find the brief, popular histories of Cornill and Ottley useful in gaining a clear view of Israel's history as a whole. Kittel's *History of the Hebrews*, in two volumes, contains a detailed discussion of the sources from a moderately progressive point of view, and presents an attractive reconstruction of the history. Volumes I and II of McCurdy's *History, Prophecy and the Monuments*, deal especially with the political and social life of the Hebrews during the periods of settlement and empire building.

Commentaries. There is no good commentary in English on the book of Joshua. The admirable commentaries on Judges by Professor Moore and on the books of Samuel by Professor Smith in the *International Critical Commentary* leave little to be desired. Kirkpatrick's more popular commentary on Samuel in the *Cambridge Bible* is also useful. Critical students will find Driver's *Notes on the Hebrew Text of the Books of Samuel* and Burney's *Notes on the Hebrew Text of the Books of Kings* both thorough and suggestive.

APPENDIX

II

GENERAL QUESTIONS AND SUBJECTS FOR SPECIAL RESEARCH

The GENERAL QUESTIONS, as in Volume I, follow the main divisions of the book and are intended to guide the student in collecting and co-ordinating the more important facts contained in the biblical text of each section or in the accompanying notes.

The SUBJECTS FOR SPECIAL RESEARCH are intended to point the way to further study in related lines, and, by means of detailed references, to introduce the reader to the most helpful passages in the best books of reference. In classroom work many of these topics may be profitably assigned for personal research and report. The references are to pages, unless otherwise indicated. Ordinarily, several parallel references are given that the student may be able to utilize the book at hand. More detailed classified bibliographies will be found in the appendices of volumes I and II of the *Student's Old Testament*.

§ XXXI. **The Crossing of the Jordan.** GENERAL QUESTIONS: 1. Describe the contents of (1) the book of Joshua and (2) Judges. 2. The Canaanite civilization of Palestine. 3. Effects of Egyptian rule. 4. Historical significance of the visit of the spies to Jericho. 5. The oldest account of the crossing of the Jordan. 6. Later parallels. 8. What did the crossing of the Jordan mean to the Hebrews?

SUBJECTS FOR SPECIAL RESEARCH: 1. The lower Jordan valley. Hastings, *D. B.*, II, 759-60, 764-5; *Encyc. Bib.*, II, 2578-80; Smith, *H. G. H. L.*, 482-96. Libbey and Hoskins, *Jordan Valley and Petra*, II, 137-56. 2. The Northern Israelite and late priestly accounts of the crossing of the Jordan. *St. O. T.*, I, 258-62. 3. Political conditions in Canaan according to the el-Amarna letters. Winckler, *Tell-el-Amarna Letters;* Marti, *Relig. of the O. T.*, 72-6. 4. The religion of the Canaanites. Marti, *Relig. of the O. T.*, 78-96; Wade, *O. T. Hist.*, 84-90.

§ XXXII. **Capture of Jericho and Ai.** GENERAL QUESTIONS: 1. Describe the situation of Jericho. 2. The Canaanite city revealed by recent excavations. 3. Compare the two accounts of the capture of Jericho. 4. Why did the Hebrews slay its inhabitants? 5. Describe the crime and punishment of Achan. 6. The strategy by which Ai was captured. 7. The basis and terms of the treaty with the Gibeon-

APPENDIX

ites. 8. Formulate the testimony of the oldest records regarding the character and work of Joshua.

SUBJECTS FOR SPECIAL RESEARCH: 1. History of the city of Jericho. Hastings, *D. B.*, II, 579–82; *Encyc. Bib.*, II, 2396–2403; Smith, *H. G. H. L.*, 266–8. 2. Ancient Semitic methods of warfare. Hastings, *D. B.*, IV, 893–5; *Encyc. Bib.*, IV, 5264–9. 3. The Semitic custom of devoting captured cities and peoples to the gods. Smith, *Relig. of the Semites*, 453. Hastings, *D. B.*, extra vol., 619–20. 4. Joshua's rôle in the later Hebrew traditions. Hastings, *D. B.*, II, 786; Kittel, *Hist. of the Hebs.*, Vol. I, 293–7; Smith, *O. T. Hist.*, 82–3. 5. The two traditional versions of Joshua's farewell address. *St. O. T.*, I, 297–300.

§ XXXIII. **Conditions and Conquests in Canaan.** GENERAL QUESTIONS: 1. Describe the process by which the Hebrews became masters of Canaan. 2. The friendly Arab tribes in the south (*cf.* map, op. p. 19). 3. The decisive battles in the south, and the cities captured by the Hebrews. 4. The zone of Canaanite cities which separated the Hebrew tribes in the south from those in the north. 5. The important cities in central and northern Palestine retained by the Canaanites. 6. Ehud's act of deliverance, and its significance.

SUBJECTS FOR SPECIAL RESEARCH: 1. The hill country of Judah. *Encyc. Bib.*, II, 2622; Smith, *H. G. H. L.*, 305–20. 2. The central plateau of Palestine. Hastings, *D. B.*, IV, 375; Smith, *H. G. H. L.*, 247–56, 323–64. 3. Excavations at the ruins of the Canaanite cities on the plain of Esdraelon. Marti, *Relig. of the O. T.*, 75–8; Sellin, *Tell Ta'annek*, and *Der Ertrag der Ausgrabungen im Orient*.

§ XXXIV. **The Establishment of the Danite Tribe and Sanctuary.** GENERAL QUESTIONS: 1. Give the history of Micah's sanctuary. 2. Describe the expedition of the Danite spies. 3. The situation of Laish (later Dan). 4. The plunder of Micah's sanctuary. 5. Later history of the Danite sanctuary. 6. The popular ideas of right and wrong in the days of the settlement. 7. The religious symbols and customs. 8. The prevailing ideas of Jehovah.

SUBJECTS FOR SPECIAL RESEARCH: 1. The upper Jordan valley. Hastings, *D. B.*, II, 757–8; *Encyc. Bib.*, II, 2577–8; Smith, *H. G. H. L.*, 471–81; Libbey and Hoskins, *Jordan Valley and Petra*, I, 86–104. 2. The moral standards revealed by the story of the Gibeathites, *St. O. T.*, I, 303–10. 3. The story of Ruth: date, contents, light which it sheds on this period, and its literary, historical, archæological and

APPENDIX

religious value. *St. O. T.*, I, 310–5; Hastings, *D. B.*, IV, 316; *Encyc. Bib.*, IV, 4166–72; Driver, *Introd. to the Lit. of the O. T.*, 453–6; McFadyen, *Introd. to the O. T.*, 290–3.

§ XXXV. Experiences of the Different Tribes. General Questions: 1. Describe the literary form and real character of the "Blessings of Jacob." 2. The early history of the Reubenites. 3. Of the tribes of Simeon and Levi. 4. Probable reasons why the Levites became the custodians of the sanctuaries. 5. Meaning of the oracles regarding Judah and Benjamin. 6. The characteristics and early experiences of the northern tribes. 7. The tribes of Ephraim and Manasseh. 8. Light which these ancient songs throw upon the life of the Hebrews during the period of settlement.

Subjects for Special Research: 1. Ancient Hebrew poetry. Hastings, *D. B.*, IV, 10–12; *Encyc. Bib.*, III, 3795–99. 2. A comparison of the Jacob oracles with the variant version attributed to Moses (Dt. 33). 3. The tradition in Genesis 34. *St. O. T.*, I, 120–3. 4. A map showing the final homes of each of the Hebrew tribes. *Cf.* map, op. p. 19. Kent and Madsen, *Hist. and Topog. Maps for Bible Students*, II. 5. Picture the conditions in Canaan during the period of settlement.

§ XXXVI. The Great Victory Over the Canaanites. General Questions: 1. Describe the two different accounts of the victory. 2. The literary character of the poetic version. 3. Conditions in Canaan before the battle. 4. Deborah's work as a prophetess. 5. The motives which influenced the Hebrew tribes to rise against the Canaanites. 6. Tribes which failed to respond. 7. The battle beside the Kishon. 8. The death of Sisera at the hand of Jail. 9. The political, social and religious significance of the victory.

Subjects for Special Research: 1. The plain of Esdraelon. Hastings, *D. B.*, I, 757–8; *Encyc. Bib.*, II, 1391; Smith, *H. G. H. L.*, 379–409. 2. The position of women among the early Hebrews. Hastings, *D. B.*, IV, 933–4; *Encyc. Bib.*, II, 1499–1501, III, 2946–48. 3. The assimilation of the old Canaanite population, civilization and religious customs. Marti, *Relig. of the O. T.*, 95–111; Smith, *O. T. Hist.*, 172; Hastings, *D. B.*, extra vol., 634–48.

§ XXXVII. Gideon's Victory and Kingdom. General Questions: 1. Describe the points of difference and agreement in the two accounts of Gideon's victory and kingdom. 2. Conditions in central Canaan. 3. The tradition of Gideon's call and its meaning. 4. The successful attack upon the Midianite robbers. 5. The founding of

APPENDIX

Gideon's kingdom. 6. The conspiracy and reign of Abimelech. 7. The significance of Gideon's kingdom.

SUBJECTS FOR SPECIAL RESEARCH: 1. The character of the Midianites. Hastings, *D. B.*, III, 365–6; *Encyc. Bib.*, III, 3079–81. 2. The primitive ideas of sacrifice reflected in the account of Gideon's call. Hastings, *D. B.*, IV, 329–30; *Encyc. Bib.*, IV, 4217–9; Smith, *Relig. of the Semites*, 218–24; 252–65. 3. The Semitic law of blood revenge. Smith, *Relig. of the Semites*, 72, 420; Gordon, *Early Trads. of Gen.*, 201–6; Hastings, *D. B.*, extra vol., 623. 4. Northern Israelite version of Gideon's victory. *St. O. T.*, I, 324–30; Moore, *Judges*, 173–7. 5. The city of Shechem. Hastings, *D. B.*, IV, 484–6; *Encyc. Bib.*, IV, 4437–39; Smith, *H. G. H. L.*, 332–4, 345–6. 6. Jotham's fable. *St. O. T.*, I, 331–2; Moore, *Judges*, 244–52.

§ XXXVIII. **Jephthah's Victory Over the Ammonites.** GENERAL QUESTIONS: 1. Describe the situation and problems of the east-Jordan tribes. 2. Jephthah's early history. 3. The peril of the Gileadites. 4. Jephthah's vow. 5. The rivalry between the Hebrew tribes on the east and the west of the Jordan. 6. The characters and achievements of the deliverers who figure in the period of settlement.

SUBJECTS FOR SPECIAL RESEARCH: 1. The physical characteristics of the territory of Gilead. Hastings, *D. B.*, II, 174–5; *Encyc. Bib.*, II, 1725–8; Smith, *H. G. H. L.*, 548, 575–90. 2. The early history of the Ammonites. Hastings, *D. B.*, I, 82–3; *Encyc. Bib.*, I, 142–4. 3. The vow in early Hebrew religion. Hastings, *D. B.*, I, 479, IV, 872–3; *Encyc. Bib.*, IV, 5252–4; Curtiss, *Primitive Semitic Religion To-day*, 156–69. 4. The analogies between the age of settlement and the colonial period in American history.

§ XXXIX. **Samson's Birth and Marriage.** GENERAL QUESTIONS: 1. Describe the literary characteristics of the Samson stories. 2. Samson's history. 3. The Nazirite vow. 4. Samson's strength and weakness. 5. The relations between the Hebrews and the Philistines. 6. The popular beliefs and standards of the age. 7. In what respects did the period of settlement represent progress?

SUBJECTS FOR SPECIAL RESEARCH: 1. Meaning of the Nazirite vow. Hastings, *D. B.*, III, 497–500; *Encyc. Bib.*, III, 3362–3; Smith, *Relig. of the Semites*, 332, 482. 2. Popular poetry and riddles in antiquity. Hastings, *D. B.*, IV, 270–1; extra vol., 160; *Encyc. Bib.*, IV, 4101. 3. A psychological study of the revengeful spirit. *Cf.* standard psychologies, especially chapters on *Fear* and *Anger*. 4. The chronology of the period of settlement. Wade, *O. T. Hist.*, 195–6; Hastings, *D.B.*, I, 399; *Encyc. Bib.*, I, 773–8. 5. The religious life of the Hebrews during the period of settlement. Smith, *O. T. Hist.*, 104–5; Wade, *O. T. Hist.*, 278–80; Kittel, *Hist. of the Hebs.*, II, 93–102; Kent, *Hist of the Heb. People*, U. K., 92–8.

THE FOUNDING OF THE HEBREW KINGDOM

§ XL. **The Philistine Victories and the Fortunes of the Ark.** GENERAL QUESTIONS: 1. Describe the general divisions of the books of Samuel. 2. The older and later traditions regarding the founding of the kingdom. 3. The origin, characteristics and early history of the Philistines. 4. Reasons why the Hebrews were defeated. 5. History and significance of the ark. 6. Experiences of the Philistines in connection with the ark. 7. Light which the story throws upon conditions in Palestine.

SUBJECTS FOR SPECIAL RESEARCH. 1. The sources of the books of Samuel. *St. O. T.*, II, 10–4; McFadyen, *Introd. to the O. T.*, 84–90; Smith, *Samuel*, xii–xxvi. 2. Traditions regarding the birth and childhood of Samuel. *St. O. T.*, II, 12–13, 51–56. 3. The land of the Philistines. Hastings, *D. B.*, III, 844; *Encyc. Bib.*, III, 3714; Smith, *H. G. H. L.*, 169–97. 4. The references to the Philistines in the Egyptian monuments. Breasted, *Hist. of Egypt*, 477, 512; Maspero, *Struggle of the Nats.*, 697–702; *Encyc. Bib.*, III, 3714–8. 5. Arks among other peoples. *St. O. T.*, IV, 149; *Encyc. Bib.*, I, 306–8; Jastrow, *Relig. of Babs. and Assyrs.*, 653–5.

§ XLI. **Saul's Call and Election to the Kingship.** GENERAL QUESTIONS: 1. Describe the crisis in Israel's history which called forth a king. 2. The origin and character of the sons of the prophets. 3. Real character and work of Samuel. 4. Saul's qualifications for the kingship. 5. Saul's meeting with Samuel. 6. The victory over the Ammonites. 7. Saul's election as king, and its significance.

SUBJECTS FOR SPECIAL RESEARCH: 1. The sons of the prophets in Hebrew history. Hastings, *D. B.*, extra vol., 656; Smith, *O. T. Hist.*, 109–10; Kent, *Hist. of the Heb. People*, U. K., 114–5; Kittel, *Hist. of the Hebs.*, II, 109–11. 2. The later prophetic tradition of Samuel's attitude toward the kingship. *St. O. T.*, II, 65–70. 3. The meaning of anointing. Hastings, *D. B.*, I, 100–1; *Encyc. Bib.*, I, 172–5. 4. The Hebrew ideal of the kingship. Hastings, *D. B.*, II, 840–3; *St. O. T.*, IV, 80. 5. An estimate of the importance of Samuel's work. Smith,

APPENDIX

O. T. Hist., 108, 110–11; Wade, *O. T. Hist.*, 233–4; Hastings, *D. B.*, IV, 381–2; *Encyc. Bib.*, IV, 4272–3.

§ XLII. **The Great Victory Over the Philistines.** GENERAL QUESTIONS: 1. Describe the situation in Israel immediately after Saul's selection as king. 2. Jonathan's bold attack on the Philistine stronghold. 3. Extent and significance of the Hebrew victory. 4. Nature and consequences of Saul's vow. 5. Saul's foreign wars. 6. The organization of his kingdom.

SUBJECTS FOR SPECIAL RESEARCH: 1. The pass of Michmash. Hastings, *D. B.*, III, 363–4; *Encyc. Bib.*, III, 3077–8; Maspero, *Struggle of the Nats.*, 710-2. 2. The priestly oracle. Hastings, *D. B.*, I, 725–6, IV, 838–41; *Encyc. Bib.*, II, 1307, IV, 5235–7. 3. A sketch of the character of Jonathan. Hastings, *D. B.*, II, 753–4. 4. The different traditions of Saul's rejection by Samuel. *St. O. T.*, II, 76–9; Wade, *O. T. Hist.*, 220–2.

THE DECLINE OF SAUL AND THE RISE OF DAVID

§ XLIII. **David's Introduction to Public Life.** GENERAL QUESTIONS: 1. Describe Saul's malady. 2. The oldest account of David's introduction to Saul's camp and court. 3. David's personality and reputation. 4. The two accounts of David's slaying Goliath. 5. The causes of Saul's jealousy of David. 6. Saul's attempts to kill David. 7. The initial stages in David's training.

SUBJECTS FOR SPECIAL RESEARCH: 1. Shepherd-life in Palestine. Smith, *H. G. H. L.*, 310–2; Knight, *Song of the Syrian Guest;* Browning, *Saul.* 2. The late prophetic tradition of the anointing of David by Samuel. *St. O. T.*, II, 80–2. 3. The valley of Elah. Hastings, *D. B.*, I, 674; Smith, *H. G. H. L.*, 226–8. 4. The late tradition of David's slaying Goliath. *St. O. T.*, II, 82–5. 5. Compare David's victory over Goliath with similar deeds of the knights of the middle ages, *cf. e.g.*, the battle of Hastings, 1066.

§ XLIV. **David as a Fugitive.** GENERAL QUESTIONS: 1. Describe Jonathan's services to David. 2. The basis and character of their friendship. 3. The covenant between them. 4. The hospitality of the priests of Nob, and David's deception. 5. David's provision for his parents. 6. His followers in his outlaw life. 7. Saul's slaughter of the priests of Nob.

SUBJECTS FOR SPECIAL RESEARCH: 1. Covenants between individuals in the Semitic world. Hastings, *D. B.*, I, 510; Trumbull, *The Blood Covenant;* Smith, *Relig. of the Semites*, 269–72, 312–7. 2. The use of

APPENDIX

showbread in Semitic religions. Hastings, *D. B.*, IV, 495–7; *Encyc. Bib.*, IV, 4211–2; Smith, *Relig. of the Semites*, 225–6. 3. The position and duties of the priest in early Hebrew life. Hastings, *D. B.*, IV, 67–72; *Encyc. Bib.*, III, 3839–41; *St. O. T.*, IV, 172–4.

§ XLV. **David's Life as an Outlaw.** GENERAL QUESTIONS: 1. Describe the means by which David ascertained the divine will. 2. The dangers of his outlaw life. 3. His magnanimity in sparing the life of Saul. 4. The effect upon Saul. 5. David's services to Nabal. 6. The wisdom of Abigail's action and counsel. 7. The significance of David's marriage with Abigail. 8. David's ambition, as revealed by his marriages.

SUBJECTS FOR SPECIAL RESEARCH: 1. The scene of David's outlaw life. Smith, *H. G. H. L.*, 278–86, 312–6; *Encyc. Bib.*, II, 2618, 2622. 2. Relations between the Arabs and peasants on the borders of southern Palestine. Thomson, *The Land and the Book;* Conder, *Tent. Life in Palestine.* 3. Articles of diet among the Hebrews. Hastings, *D. B.*, II, 27–43; *Encyc. Bib.*, II, 1538–48.

§ XLVI. **David Among the Philistines.** GENERAL QUESTIONS: 1. Describe David's reasons for going over to the Philistines. 2. His reception by the king of Gath. 3. His manner of life at Ziklag. 4. His dilemma when the Philistines set out to invade Israel. 5. The pursuit of the Amalekites. 6. The division of the spoil. 7. Significance of the presents to the southern tribes and cities.

SUBJECTS FOR SPECIAL RESEARCH: 1. Probable site of Gath. Hastings, *D. B.*, II, 113–4; *Encyc. Bib.*, II, 1646–7; Smith, *H. G. H. L.*, 194–7. 2. The Hebrew laws regarding the distribution of the spoils of war. *St. O. T.*, IV, 83–6, 237. 3. A map showing the tribes and important cities of southern Palestine during this period, *cf.* maps, op. pp. 19, 121.

§ XLVII. **Saul's Defeat and Death.** GENERAL QUESTIONS: 1. Describe the tragedy of the closing years of Saul's reign. 2. Saul's visit to the medium of Endor. 3. Details of the battle on Mount Gilboa. 4. Saul's burial. 5. David's song of lamentation over Saul and Jonathan: its literary style, contents and significance. 6. Saul's character. 7. What did Saul do for Israel?

SUBJECTS FOR SPECIAL RESEARCH: 1. The later Hebrew laws regarding mediums, sorcerers and augurs. *St. O. T.*, IV, 102, 103; Driver, *Deuteronomy*, 223–6. 2. Situation of Endor. Hastings, *D. B.*, I, 702; *Encyc. Bib.*, II, 1291. 3. Mount Gilboa. Hastings, *D. B.*, II, 174; *Encyc. Bib.*, 1722–4. 4. The character and work of

APPENDIX

Saul. Hastings, *D. B.*, IV, 415; *Encyc. Bib.*, IV, 4313–4; Wade, *O. T. Hist.*, 236–8; Kent, *Hist. of the Heb. People*, U. K., 133–5; Fleming, *Israel's Golden Age*, 75–7.

THE POLITICAL EVENTS OF DAVID'S REIGN

§ XLVIII. **The Two Hebrew Kingdoms Under David and Ish-baal.** GENERAL QUESTIONS: 1. Describe David's election as king by the southern tribes. 2. The remnant of Saul's kingdom. 3. Reasons and nature of the hostilities between the two Hebrew kingdoms. 4. Abner's character and record. 5. His death. 6. Events which led to the choice of David as king of all Israel. 7. Significance of the act.

SUBJECTS FOR SPECIAL RESEARCH: 1. The chronology of the period of the united Hebrew kingdom. Hastings, *D. B.*, I, 399, 401; *Encyc. Bib.*, I, 788–9. 2. Conditions in the Tigris-Euphrates valley during this period. Goodspeed, *Hist. of the Babs. and Assyrs.*, 155–84; Winckler, *Hist. of Bab. and Assyr.*, 93–9, 198–208; Maspero, *Struggle of the Nats.*, 642–65. 3. In Egypt. Breasted, *Hist. of the Anc. Egyptians*, 357–61; *Hist. of Egypt*, 522–6. 4. Reasons why Palestine enjoyed immunity from foreign attack.

§ XLIX. **The Liberation and Consolidation of all Israel.** GENERAL QUESTIONS: 1. Describe the war of liberation. 2. Subsequent relations between the Hebrews and Philistines. 3. Early history of Jerusalem. 4. Its capture by David. 5. Strategic importance as the capital of united Israel. 6. History and significance of the transfer of the ark to Jerusalem. 7. Compare David's court and policy with that of Saul.

SUBJECTS FOR SPECIAL RESEARCH: 1. The topography of Jerusalem. Hastings, *D. B.*, II, 584–6, 591–3; *Encyc. Bib.*, II, 2410–9. 2. Recent excavations at Jerusalem. Hilprecht, *Exploration in Bible Lands*, 596–606; *Encyc. Bib.*, II, 2409–10; Warren, *Underground Jerusalem;* Bliss and Dickie, *Excavations at Jerusalem;* Baedeker, *Palestine.* 3. Later predictions regarding the house of David. *St. O. T.*, II, 124–30.

§ L. **The Internal Events of David's Reign.** GENERAL QUESTIONS: 1. Describe the ancient belief regarding the meaning of calamity. 2. The popular explanation of the cause of the famine in the days of David. 3. The sacrifice of the sons of Saul. 4. David's treatment of Meribaal. 5. Purpose and result of the national census. 6. The popular interpretation of the census and of the way in which its evil consequences were averted. 7. The prevailing ideas regarding God in the days of David.

SUBJECTS FOR SPECIAL RESEARCH: 1. Heathen, churchly and modern doctrines of vicarious atonement. Hastings, *D. B.*, I, 197–9; Smith, *Relig. of the Semites*, 421–30; *cf.* modern theologies, especially Clarke, *Outlines of Christian Theology*, and Campbell, *The New Theology*. 2. The temple site. Hastings, *D. B.*, IV, 696; *Encyc. Bib.*, IV, 4927–8. 3. Evidence that the Hebrews still thought of Jevovah as simply ruling over the land of Canaan. Judges 11²¹⁻²⁴, I Sam. 26¹⁹; *St. O. T.*, I, 337.

§ LI. **David's Foreign Wars and Conquests.** GENERAL QUESTIONS: 1. Describe the achievements of David's most famous warriors. 2. The organization of David's army. 3. Cause of the Ammonite war. 4. The first and second campaigns. 5. The victories over the Arameans and Ammonites. 6. The conquest of Moab and Edom. 7. Indicate by a map the extent of David's empire.

SUBJECTS FOR SPECIAL RESEARCH: 1. Hebrew military organization. *St. O. T.*, IV, 80–6; Hastings, *D. B.*, IV, 892–5; *Encyc. Bib.*, IV, 5264–9. 2. The Ammonite capital. Hastings, *D. B.*, IV, 189–90; *Encyc. Bib.*, IV, 3998–9. 3. The Arameans in northern Syria. Maspero, *Struggle of the Nations*, 668–70; *Encyc. Bib.*, I, 278–80.

§ LII. **David's Crimes and their Punishment.** GENERAL QUESTIONS: 1. Describe the character of the early records of David's family history. 2. David's wives and children. 3. The Hebrew law regarding adultery. 4. David's double crime. 5. Nathan's fable, and its application. 6. Nature of David's repentance. 7. The effect of David's crimes upon his character.

SUBJECTS FOR SPECIAL RESEARCH: 1. General character, aims and variations of the parallel history in Chronicles. *St. O. T.*, II, 7, 22–8; Hastings, *D. B.*, I, 389–97; *Encyc. Bib.*, I, 763–72. 2. The oriental harem. Erman, *Life in Ancient Egypt*, 74–7; Lane, *Manners and Customs of the Modern Egyptians*, 185–98. 3. Parables in Semitic literature. Hastings, *D. B.*, III, 660–2; *Encyc. Bib.*, III, 3563–7.

§ LIII. **The Crimes of David's Sons.** GENERAL QUESTIONS: 1. Describe the character of Amnon. 2. Absalom's motives in slaying his brother. 3. David's attitude toward his sons. 4. The story of the wise woman of Tekoa. 5. Absalom's appearance. 6. His full restoration to favor. 7. Effect of David's crimes upon his family and court.

APPENDIX

Subjects for Special Research: 1. The land of Geshur. Hastings, *D. B.*, II, 162; *Encyc. Bib.*, II, 1710–2. 2. The wise in Israel's history. *Encyc. Bib.*, IV, 5325–6; Kent, *Wise Men of Ancient Israel and their Proverbs*, 17–25. 3. The character of Joab. Hastings, *D. B.*, II, 658–9; *Encyc. Bib.*, II, 2460–2.

§ LIV. **Absalom's Rebellion.** General Questions: 1. Describe Absalom's method of winning popular favor. 2. The launching of his conspiracy. 3. David's supporters. 4. The curses of Shimei. 5. The counsel of Ahithophel and Hushai. 6. Rally of David's followers east of the Jordan. 7. The battle and the death of Absalom. 8. David's sorrow. 9. His return to Jerusalem. 10. The rebellion in the north; its significance.

Subjects for Special Research: 1. The history of the Benjamites. Hastings, *D. B.*, I, 272–3; *Encyc. Bib.*, I, 534–40. 2. The oaks of Palestine. Hastings, *D. B.*, III, 575, IV, 719; *Encyc. Bib.*, IV, 4975–6. 3. The character of Absalom. Hastings, *D. B.*, I, 18–20; *Encyc. Bib.*, I, 29–31.

§ LV. **Solomon's Election as King.** General Questions: 1. Describe Adonijah's plot to secure the kingship. 2. The action of Nathan and Bathsheba. 3. The public proclamation of Solomon's succession. 4. Concessions to the conspirators. 5. David's weakness and strength. 6. The significance of David's services to his race.

Subjects for Special Research: 1. The law of primogeniture in Semitic life. *St. O. T.*, IV, 72; *Encyc. Bib.*, III, 2728–9; Hastings, *D. B.*, II, 341–2. 2. The tradition regarding David's dying commands. *St. O. T.*, II, 167–71; Hastings, *D. B.*, I, 571. 3. The character of David. Hastings, *D. B.*, I, 571–3; *Encyc. Bib.*, I, 1033–4; Wade, *O. T. Hist.*, 273–6; Smith, *Mod. Crit. and the Preaching of the O. T.*, 155–7. 4. David's relation to the Psalter. Hastings, *D. B.*, I, 571; *Encyc. Bib.*, III, 3930–4; McFadyen, *Introd. to the O. T.*, 244–8.

§ LVI. **Solomon's Policy and Fame.** General Questions: 1. Describe the steps by which Solomon established his absolute authority. 2. Solomon's officials. 3. His ambitions and his measures to realize them. 4. The nature of Solomon's wisdom. 5. The wisdom of the East. 6. Solomon's reputation as the author of later wisdom books.

Subjects for Special Research: 1. The relation between subjects and rulers in the ancient oriental empires. Hastings, *D. B.*, II, 250–3; *Encyc. Bib.*, II, 1907–10; McCurdy, *Hist. Proph. and the Monuments*, I, Ch. III. 2. Conditions in Egypt during this period. Breasted, *Hist. of Anc. Egyptians*, 358–61; *Hist. of Egypt*, 522–8. 3. The

APPENDIX

authorship of the book of Proverbs. Hastings, *D. B.*, IV, 140–1; *Encyc. Bib.*, III, 3911–2; Kent, *The Wise Men of Ancient Israel and their Proverbs*, 58–62.

§ LVII. **Solomon's Temple.** GENERAL QUESTIONS: 1. Describe the origin and purpose of Solomon's temple. 2. Its site. 3. Preparations for its building. 4. Its general plan and dimensions. 5. Its decorations. 6. Objects within the temple. 7. Character and purpose of the side-chambers. 8. The great altar and the vessels used in the sacrifice. 9. The dedication of the temple. 10. Later significance of the temple.

SUBJECTS FOR SPECIAL RESEARCH: 1. Egyptian temples. Erman, *Life in Anc. Egypt.*, 279–88; Maspero, *Struggle of the Nats.*, 300–8; Breasted *Hist. of Egypt*, 341–4. 2. Babylonian temples. Peters, *Nippur;* Maspero, *Dawn of Civil.*, 674–5; Hilprecht, *Explorats. in Bible Lands*, 467–79. 3. Sources from which the different elements in the temple plan were derived. *Encyc. Bib.*, IV, 4923–40. 4. The later prophetic traditions regarding the dedication of the temple. *St. O. T.*, II, 188–92.

§ LVIII. **The Splendor and Weakness of Solomon's Reign.** GENERAL QUESTIONS: 1. Describe Solomon's public buildings and the purpose of each. 2. The fortresses outside Jerusalem. 3. Solomon's foreign commerce. 4. The effect of his foreign marriages. 5. The different rebellions in his empire. 6. The weakness and fatal consequences of Solomon's policy.

SUBJECTS FOR SPECIAL RESEARCH: 1. Phœnician merchant ships. Hastings, *D. B.*, IV, 823–4; Wade, *O. T. History*, 298–300; Maspero, *Struggle of the Nations*, 193–200. 2. Hiram king of Tyre. Hastings, *D. B.*, II, 389; *Encyc. Bib.*, II, 2073–4; IV, 4682–3; Maspero, *Struggle of the Nations*, 741–3. 3. An estimate of Solomon's character. Hastings, *D. B.*, IV, 563–9; *Encyc. Bib.*, IV, 4686–9; Wade, *O. T. Hist.*, 309–11; Fleming, *Israel's Golden Age*, 142–3.

§ LIX. **Law and Society in Early Israel.** GENERAL QUESTIONS: 1. When were the principal decalogues in Exodus 21–23 committed to writing? 2. From which period do they come? 3. Describe the position of slaves in ancient Israel. 4. The laws protecting them. 5. The Babylonian and Hebrew methods of punishing murder and kindred crimes. 6. Responsibility for property under the early Babylonian and Hebrew codes. 7. Punishment of crimes against society.

SUBJECTS FOR SPECIAL RESEARCH: 1. Slavery among the Babylonians. Hastings, *D. B.*, extra vol., 589–90; Johns, *Bab. and Assyr. Laws, Contracts and Letters*, 168–83; Sayce, *Babs. and Assyrs.*, 67–84.

APPENDIX

2. The later Hebrew criminal laws. *St. O. T.*, IV, 109–18. 3. Hammurabi's laws regarding property. Johns, *Bab. aud Assyr. Laws, Contracts and Letters*, 64–7, 250–70.

§ LX. **Moral and Religious Standards in Early Israel.** GENERAL QUESTIONS: 1. Describe Hammurabi's attitude toward the dependent classes. 2. Reasons why the Hebrews were especially considerate in their treatment of resident aliens. 3. Content and purpose of the Hebrew laws regarding interest. 4. The laws enjoining kindness to animals. 5. The Hebrew judicial system. 6. The early laws regarding altars and sacrifice. 7. The sacred festivals. 8. Progress in the popular conception of Jehovah. 9. Causes and nature of the victory of the religion of Jehovah over the local cults of Canaan.

SUBJECTS FOR SPECIAL RESEARCH: 1. Later Hebrew laws regarding dependent classes. *St. O. T.*, IV, 124–32. 2. The Babylonian and Hebrew judicial system. Johns, *Bab. and Assyr. Laws, Contracts and Letters*, 80–99; Sayce, *Babs. and Assyrs.*, 198–207; *St. O. T.*, IV, 86–90. 3. The development of Israel's religion during the period of the united monarchy. Wade, *O. T. Hist.*, 277–293; Marti, *Relig. of the O. T.*, 72–123; Hastings, *D. B.*, extra vol., 645–8.